71 029 3356 1

£4.95

A75

A Manual of Classification

Sayers' Manual of Classification for Librarians

FIFTH EDITION

Arthur Maltby MA FLA FRSA

*Department of Library and Information Studies,
Queen's University, Belfast*

 André Deutsch/A Grafton Book

This edition first published 1975 by
André Deutsch Limited
105 Great Russell Street London WC1

Originally published 1926 under the title
A Manual of Classification by W. C. Berwick Sayers

Second edition 1944
Third edition 1955
Reprinted with corrections 1959
Reprinted 1962
Fourth edition 1967
Copyright © 1959 by W. C. Berwick Sayers
Copyright © 1967, 1970 by Arthur Maltby and W. C. Berwick Sayers
Copyright © 1975 by Arthur Maltby

Printed in Great Britain by
Ebenezer Baylis and Son Limited
The Trinity Press, Worcester, and London

ISBN 0 233 96603 X

'A successful man is usually a classifier and a chartmaker. This applies as much to modern business as to science or libraries . . . A large business or work unclassified or uncharted is not a worthy organization but mere material from which a clever brain may construct one. It differs in efficiency from the ideal as a mob of men differs from a well disciplined army. Piles of bricks and mortar are not a temple any more than heaps of type are Shakespeare's works, though if "classified" and set, each in right relation to the rest, the transformation is brought about.'

MELVIL DEWEY

'As I pondered thus upon the unified nature of library service, I discovered that classification could be thought of only in relation to the part it contributed to a final goal. Again it resumed a kind of central position; but this time, instead of resuming also to separate entity, it seemed to radiate throughout the structure shafts of illumination, lighting up and strengthening all library service. It seemed to me that classification could be made to reinforce the framework of our service and prevent the whole from collapsing into a formless and undirected tangle.'

GRACE O. KELLEY

'A classification does not bring all the resources on a subject together on the shelves of a library, nor does any subject catalogue bring them all together on a table; nor does a subject bibliography. But a classification, a classified subject catalogue, or a classified subject bibliography may have a structural efficiency on which such maximal functional efficiency will largely depend.'

HENRY EVELYN BLISS

Contents

Preface

When Berwick Sayers first produced this *Manual*, he provided librarianship with a textbook that attempted to survey and explain a subject which many had found extremely complex. The *Manual* justly became renowned for the breadth of its author's knowledge, his wise judgement on classification problems and procedures, and his discernible sympathy for younger librarians with regard to difficulties encountered in their studies. Sayers was not only a great librarian and teacher; he was himself a pioneer in the development of the theory of library classification – its first 'grammarian', as the great Indian librarian, Dr S. R. Ranganathan, described him in the Sayers Memorial Volume. But most significant developments in theory and the growing pressure for greater efficiency and sophistication in retrieval systems dated much of his writings; the fourth edition of the *Manual*, revised by the present author, therefore incorporated many new details while retaining, where possible, the ideas and character of the original work.

This fifth edition has taken the revision process much further and is virtually a new work, although a little 'Sayers material' remains, notably in Chapter One and Chapter Seven. I have sought to provide a clear and basic, but very wide-ranging, account of classification theory and policy within the present-day library context and to offer a textbook which can be used as the basis for a course on classification extending over either a semester or a full academic year, thus helping to free more teaching time for discussion and practical work. I am convinced that, despite the essential links between the various ways of organizing knowledge, there is still a place for a text which views all things classificatory as a unity and can complement a work like Horner's *Cataloguing* or Bakewell's *Manual of cataloguing practice*.

'Sayers', a student once said to me, 'was reluctant to criticize any system vigorously. He was generous towards them all.' If that remark has any truth, it probably illustrates a rare difference between WCBS and the present author, who has not hesitated to criticize where he thinks it necessary. In most other respects, I think the *Manual* represents the kind of book Sayers would write today, although – despite my frequent quotations and occasional attempts at humour – I know his splendid and characteristic literary style has not been equalled since the third edition. Several of his expressions find a ready response or echo in my own mind; to take one of many possible instances, there is the statement from an earlier preface – 'I believe that experience proves that workers in almost every sphere in which the organization of materials or time is involved would derive some benefit from a study of the subject; for, in the examples which the use of classification in libraries offers, we have organizing method severely applied to severely practical ends.'

The sections of the new *Manual* attempt between them to cover all aspects of classification – principles, evaluation, a telescoped history of the subject, schemes, policy and application, and classification within an information science context. There is no one ideal sequence for the presentation of these ideas, but I have tried to practice what I preach and select an order which should be as helpful as possible to the majority. I have striven to bring in each important recent idea while looking to shorten rather than increase the total length of the book, and to incorporate useful, but relatively concise, bibliographies at the end of each section. Examples have been drawn from many disciplines and I have endeavoured to maintain a balance in this respect; most are based on actual literature, although a few are, I confess, imaginary and stem from personal experience or sentiment. I have also sought to strike some kind of balance between principles, policy and practice in classification. Some may think there is too much emphasis on the first of these categories, but this is perhaps inevitable in a manual of this kind. There is certainly some imbalance in the attention given to British writers as opposed to those from other countries, for there is clearly a distinct and very active 'British School' of classification thinking now. Yet I have tried to take a wide and international view whenever possible and I hope that, by sometimes emphasizing what I might call the American and British philosophies, I might help to narrow rather than to widen whatever gap exists between them.

The *Manual* retains its original function as a survey of the work of others more than as a vehicle for original thought: this means one must try to gather together and interweave a number of diverse, stimulating, and sometimes conflicting ideas. That I owe a great deal to many writers whose names appear frequently in my pages or to whose work and experience I refer in a bibliography, should be as obvious to my reader as it is to me. I am also indebted to my wife for her patience and continual help, to Mrs M. Ruddy and Miss S. Moore for their secretarial assistance, and to my students – past and present – whose enthusiasm and questions act as a most effective antidote to the tendency (which I suspect attacks many lecturers from time to time) to become too complacent and dogmatic about one's subject.

December 1973   A. MALTBY

Principles of Library Classification

CHAPTER ONE

The Value of Systematic Arrangement in Libraries

From the day when a man first assembled documents and records of any kind or form, men have been interested in ways of arranging them. It is merely a part of the divine instinct that 'order is Heaven's first law': for systematic grouping, that is to say classification, lies at the base of every well-managed life and occupation. In the record of libraries throughout the ages, wherever we have any details of them, we have also evidences of the preoccupation of their librarians with this question. It is one that is of much interest and which has, in the course of very many years, assumed a complexity which may be attributed in part to the tendency of men to seek scientific or philosophic reasons for the processes which they employ, but which is also due to the very rapid increase in the number of documents published annually and the propensity of more and more books and documents to deal with highly specific themes or with the over-lapping of conventional subject disciplines. The act of classification in libraries and information bureaux may be briefly defined as: *The systematic arrangement by subject of books and other material on shelves or of catalogue and index entries in the manner which is most useful to those who read or who seek a definite piece of information.* Library classification, then, is a tool for very simple but infinitely important purposes. Its whole object is to secure an order which will be useful to readers and to those who seek information with the smallest complication of search or other effort. It is a technique designed to expedite the full use of the knowledge stored in books and other material housed in the collection.

Classification in the widest sense of the word has many functions in everyday activities. Every classical reader knows that the word 'class' in our sense has the same meaning given it in Ancient Rome, when the effective nobility were arranged in six orders or ranks according to their real or supposed qualities of blood or wealth.

So, in our studies, a class consists of a number of things which are alike in some particular or have some quality in common by which they may be usefully separated from other things and which at the same time makes their own unity. It may safely be assumed that everything in the universe is a member of some class, but on first appearance the universe appears so great and complex that it is chaos – a tangle of things to which man has no clue unless he provides himself with some sort of map. This map of things is a convenient expression for a classification scheme, for we cannot reason, even in the simplest manner unless we can identify and relate – that is classify – things. So, in varying degrees, we all exercise daily various acts of classification; we sort and arrange mentally the ideas and impressions we receive from our contact with others and we likewise sort and associate, or dissociate, in our minds the objects that we see. There is a little more in this than may appear on the surface. Our definition of classification means not only the grouping of things which resemble one another and the separation of those which do not, but the arrangement within each group of its components according to their degrees of resemblance. To take a simple example, a group of dogs will contain perhaps many kinds of dog – greyhounds, foxhounds, wolfhounds, terriers, Irish terriers and Scotch terriers. All these have the general resemblance which is implied by their common name – dogs. Yet all hounds are more like other hounds than they are like terriers; all terriers more like other terriers than they are like hounds. So these would form sub-classes within the class, dogs; but, again, a bull terrier is more like a mastiff than it is like a hound; and this relationship too must be shown, if possible, in the arranging of our class. Classification, then, is not only the general grouping of things for location or identification purposes; it is also their arrangement in some sort of rational order so that the *chief relationships of the things in question may be ascertained*. This is a vital point in classification theory and must be constantly borne in mind.

Classification is a key to knowledge: because it is clear that if we arrange things in a definite order and we know what that order is, we have a very good map of, or key to, these things. What is the purpose of this and what does this mean in relation to modern libraries? *Merely that classification and classificatory principles are the basis of all order in handling literature and other media.* This is a bold statement, but one capable of conclusive demonstration. Books and other related documents represent a class of things, when we take into our view all the objects in the universe; and when we separate books from all other things, merely as an assembly of books we have performed an act of classification. It is, however, a very elementary one. A huge room or building full of books and pamphlets is, in fact, having regard to the variety of subjects represented in them and the many forms and sizes they take, about the nearest representation to chaos that we can imagine. That is to say, if they are not classified in some way apart from their mere separation from things which are not books. Unless they are well classified, we cannot discover without immense loss of time what books there are on chemistry, history, theology, fluid mechanics, or transport, for example. Some libraries (fortunately few) are still of this kind and are arranged by some accidental feature. When the purpose of the books is simply that they shall be seen and not read, this is an excellent arrangement. Otherwise it has nothing to commend it. A library in which books and pamphlets are arranged by size may look very neat, but it means that we have to search in numerous locations to collect material on Milton's poetry, on plant ecology, on existentialism, or on any other topic on which information may be sought. Examples could be multiplied to demonstrate arrangements which only suffice if the books and other material are viewed as 'museum specimens' and not as having any other significance. In a rather similar manner, if we arrange items by the language in which they are written, we get a very wide separation of subjects; only if the potential user is interested in language alone could this arrangement be justified. Chronological order by date of accession or date of publication could also be considered. Indeed, our older libraries frequently employ a fixed chronological order of books within very broad subject areas. Again, it is usually an order without real utility for reader or librarian, as we shall see.

Yet another possible arrangement, which appeals to some people and is certainly superior to arrangement by date or by factors such as mere size or colour of binding, is to group books alphabetically by the names of their authors. This will almost certainly suffice for fiction. It also has a definite value for the private collection owned or used by students and research workers who know their authors and they often prefer such arrangement. If we know, for example, that Charles Darwin was a great naturalist, we know that under his name we shall find works on natural science. But the author order tells us nothing about naturalists of whose names we are ignorant and it is no disparagement of the ordinary user of most libraries to say that he is usually unacquainted with authors. It is true that the author approach for non-fiction tends to be a dominant one in many academic libraries where students determine their reading chiefly by the details provided on supplied lists of recommended works, but even here the advantages of subject arrangement on the shelves for saving the time of the person wanting to consult books on a subject, drawing attention to other useful works, and perhaps stimulating thought, are inestimable. We must therefore rely on the library catalogue to cater for the author and title approach to knowledge and adopt a *subject* order on the shelves. An alphabetical sequence of some kind might, of course, be employed for the latter task. This does have the merit of locating books and other material on a particular subject for us and would be superior to the alphabetical author order in grouping items conveniently for use and thus saving time. Unfortunately, the alphabetical subject order also has its limitations.

Firstly, it is extremely difficult to decide how specific our terms should be for such an arrangement; secondly, the problem of synonyms must somehow be solved; thirdly, and this is the most important factor of all, the alphabetical sequence results in the scattering of related subject material. (Indeed, although precision in arrangement is usually needed, the more specific an A–Z subject order the more scattering we find!) We may, for instance, have such an arrangement as:

Abbeys	Battles
Accidents	Bible
Adhesives	Bombing
Agriculture	Bowls
Angling	Buildings
Animals	Bulldogs
Architecture	Cabbages, etc.

The order is not altogether without use, but is obviously most imperfect, as the random selection of examples suggests. Abbeys have no apparent relation to Accidents, but they have to Architecture. Items dealing with Angling or Bowling would be more usefully placed near to other material, including general works, on sports and recreations. Even the 'classified' sections of telephone directories succumb to this type of sequence, for they group such diverse headings as Entertainments; Envelope manufacturers; Estate agents; and Excavating equipment suppliers. Subjects are not *systematically related* to each other in such arrangements; they are not classifications in the truest sense of the word, for each topic is separated from kindred ones unless, by sheer chance, the alphabet juxtaposes a few related themes. If we are only concerned with locating material (as in telephone directories we are) then this may not matter. In libraries and information centres, there is often a further important purpose; it is that of *relating* subject material as far as is possible, in addition to locating each specific theme.

This point is deserving of a little elaboration since it is basic to good classificatory practice in the library world. An American librarian at the turn of the century, E. C. Richardson, once wisely remarked that 'use is the watchword of arrangement' and it is thus essential that the organization on the shelves of a library should reflect the use made of recorded knowledge, not only enabling books on a specific theme to be *located* together, but also *subordinating each specific subject to the appropriate general one and demonstrating the most important relationships between subjects.* At the risk of over-simplifying the situation it is fair to say that several librarians in the United States since Richardson's day have often tended to stress solely the location value of classification and to see it as a 'marking and parking' device for book order on the shelves. In Britain and many other European countries, however, there has been an emphasis too on the fuller meaning of classification, that is on its role in systematically displaying relationships. As we shall see, the latter viewpoint can be especially helpful in subject analysis and indexing in addition to its value in enabling a search for documents or information to be broadened or narrowed down with relative ease and convenience. Thus the library classification systems do, for the most part, strive both to locate subject information and to display major subject relationships in a gradually unfolding general to specific order. We begin with the broad classes, then we have their chief divisions, then the major sections of each of these. Such systematic progression has many advantages over the casual subject order of the alphabet in a library of any size which receives many subject enquiries or has readers wishing to browse intelligently and easily in particular subject areas.

The great need to relate systematically, in addition to locating subject material within a classification, has resulted in nearly all libraries adopting a system which depends upon *relative location* rather than *fixed location*. In a fixed location system, such as is found in very old and primitive attempts at classification schemes, every volume is allocated to a particular and permanent position on a particular shelf of the library; each new book, whatever its subject, takes the next vacant shelf place. Under relative location, as exhibited in all the classifications now employed, books are not 'fixed' to any one position in the library, but are moved to and fro as required, so that new material can be inserted in the correct place, according to its specific subject, in the sequence. Fixed location is implied by chronological order of accession and by other artificial and superseded systems, but it is the negation of true classification. It is only by means of relative location that new additions to a growing library can take up a place in the sequence where they will lend most support to the existing stock. Volumes must be moved as required to provide the necessary flexibility demanded by an efficient system seeking to organize the collection with maximum advantage. Fixed location saves some space and has a place in stackrooms and stores, although even here it can result in some loss of time in getting together the books that are used together. In the open-access library, however, relative location, as found in classification, is imperative and is a tremendous time-saver for reader and librarian alike.

The acknowledgement that a classified subject arrangement, displaying major subject relationships and relying upon the idea of relative location, is essential in most libraries leads on to the natural question – what is the subject of a book or other item of recorded knowledge? We shall find that the classifier needs to observe rules for dealing with multi-subject works and must beware of confusing the true subject of a book with some emphasis or bias which may be evident in a particular book's treatment of that subject. Yet a point that can and should be grasped from the outset is that, to classify accurately and precisely, we must place each book under its *specific* subject, for it is only in this way that we can adequately arrange material, or entries in a classified catalogue, in a helpful sequence and can maintain that arrangement. Within each major subject field, the sequence should begin with general material and proceed slowly to more and more specialized branches of the subject, the exact order of progression being determined by an accurate analysis of the subject of books and by observing the needs of the majority of specialist readers in each field of activity. Thus a history of the town of Leeds, for example, should be classified as such and not hidden away with more general material under British history or even the history of Yorkshire. The helpful sequence of the history class should then enable a reader or enquirer to see first material on 'the History of Britain' as a whole, then to survey works on the 'History of Yorkshire' (or of any other county) and finally to encounter specific works dealing with the history of individual towns, or even areas within towns. Each town will be subordinated to its parent county, each county to the country as a whole. Thus it is that the widening or restriction of a search becomes more easy in a well-classified library and both general (or generic) and specific searches can be made. The same procedure is followed in other subject fields, with classification being carried out precisely, or as precisely as the system in use allows, unless it is known that the library in question has deliberately opted for a policy of broad, that is less detailed classification. The normal procedure is to assume that classification means exact classification and S. R. Ranganathan defined the phrase *specific subject* as being 'that division of knowledge whose extension and intension are equal to those of its [the document's] thought content'. That is to say, we must constantly beware, when classifying, of selecting a theme more general than that of the book with which we may be dealing. If we classify books on Calculus under Mathematics without sub-division, we shall mix up the specific works with the more general ones and the person searching for books and other documents on the subject of calculus may have to look through the whole of the maths section to find them all. The correct procedure is to keep all works on calculus together as a distinct group within the broader subject area of mathematics.

We find that, where a rightly designed classification exists, the librarian or reader may go to a definite set of shelves and see at their beginning the works which are preliminary to or are the foundation of the sought subject; find, following these, the books on the subject itself; and following them in turn, the books on themes which develop from that subject. If classification is applied to a subject catalogue or bibliography the entries will be in an equivalent systematic order. In later chapters, the methods for achieving an order of the optimum helpfulness are considered, but it must be stressed at once that such an order is the way to avoid the colossal waste of time that would be involved in continually bringing together wanted items from a collection arranged in haphazard manner. The time and money spent on the selection of library material demand efficient methods for its storage and display, so that the full use of the stock may be promoted.

It must be recognized nevertheless that alphabetical order is not to be entirely rejected and a short digression from the main theme of this chapter will serve to show its utility. Bliss has said that 'alphabetic arrangements . . . are illogical and unsystematic, everywhere dispersing related subject matter; they are the very antithesis of classification'. This statement is a little too harsh and was made with the intention of refuting the claim that alphabetical order was superior to the classified subject arrangements. Yet there is no reason why A–Z order should not be used, to a certain extent, within a classification scheme whenever it is the most sensible method of sub-arrangement or whenever it can bring about a more useful grouping than can a classified sequence. These occasions, it must be confessed, are (with the outstanding exception of alphabetical author order for fiction) destined to be comparatively rare. But many libraries introduce alphabetical order into the biography class to produce a helpful 'quick-location' sequence of great lives and most libraries have some material – current periodicals, street directories, publishers' catalogues, ephemeral pamphlets, for example – which may lend itself to an alphabetical arrangement. Within the classification, alphabetical order by *author* is used as a final method of sub-arrangement for a group of books classified at the same location and there may be occasions when, because no logical alternative order commends itself, alphabetical arrangement by *topic* within a class can prove superior to further sub-division on systematic lines. This last point is well illustrated in the Library of Congress Classification scheme, although perhaps sometimes over-employed there. Special libraries and information services make use of different and more fluid alphabetical systems for organizing knowledge and this usually involves the technique known as post-co-ordinate indexing, in which concepts are not assembled, or pre-combined as in classification systems or traditional alphabetical headings in subject catalogues, but are kept uncombined and separate until an actual search for information is made. More will be said of these indexing methods later; here it is enough to accept that librarians do make use of A–Z order by subject, by author, or even by title if necessary and that every classification needs an alphabetical index as a key to its helpful, but unfamiliar, arrangement. This does not detract one iota from the claims that have been made for the value and overall efficiency of subject arrangement via classification in our libraries. For the bulk of the material the best arrangement is the classified one, especially if serious reading is being done or a reference and information service is being provided.

A subject classification of this kind has the obvious value of economizing time and effort, always provided that it is constructed in a way which closely reflects the use made of literature. It is an economy in the mere finding of books; for it is clear that if all the books and other materials on a subject are assembled as nearly as is physically possible in one place there will be an important saving of time in obtaining a general view of the literature. By relating subjects in a rational way, it ensures that, if we have few items immediately available on a particular specific subject, we will find near to these volumes on the shelves other material on closely related themes which will assist the reader. A chapter in a general work nearby may prove of great value in providing the enquirer with the facts he seeks. Likewise classification aids the librarian in recording issues, in deciding what special subject displays need to be created and, by showing the strength and weakness of his collection in each subject area, in book selection and stock revision. Nor is classification limited to the shelves; it has an analysing use in that a classified card catalogue may contain a card under every subject with which a document is in any important way connected. That catalogue then becomes a more or less complete record of all important subjects dealt with by a document (and these may not all be indicated by its title or by the shelf sequence). The economy value of this is clear; it is evident that classification has an immense part to play in both the arrangement of books and the context of information retrieval. How many a research worker, inventor, thinker, writer has wasted an immense time in finding out and solving for himself facts and problems with which other workers have already dealt! Were only the results of former labours recorded in classified catalogues and bibliographies, many such men would be saved from the effort of duplicating work that has already been done and from the vexation of discovering their waste of energy. Life is too short to allow the neglect of classification.

The foundation of the library is the book; the foundation of librarianship is classification. Tremendous difficulties face the readers and staff in an unclassed or badly arranged library, for books must be assembled from all parts of the collection in response to a request, only to be scattered again when the request has been dealt with. It may well be that an enquiry will call on items from several parts of a classified sequence, but this is very different from the position where, if a hundred books are available on a subject, they may virtually be in a hundred different places in the collection. We fear that much inefficient library work has resulted from the want of good classification. It is valuable in small libraries and especially so in larger ones. Those in charge of major libraries have sometimes advocated the close classification of entries in catalogues, but have favoured broad or simplified classing for their shelf arrangement. The reasoning upon which this advocacy is based is rarely convincing. At any rate, general libraries arranged upon the open-access system are impossible to work without adequate and reasonably specific shelf classification and special libraries with large book stocks have found that they need a very detailed scheme. The vital character of our subject is thus easily revealed and the growth in the quantity of literature in modern times demands increasingly careful selection and specialization on the part of the user; this demand is also, in effect, a silent plea for sound and thorough classification of that literature by librarians.

Despite the clearly demonstrable advantages of the systematic subject arrangement, bibliographical classification has never been without its critics. The famous nineteenth-century economist and logician, W. S. Jevons, considered the subject classification of libraries to be impossible because of the complex way in which knowledge is presented in books while a twentieth-century librarian-critic, Grace Osgood Kelley suggested that detailed classification actually defeated its own ends by separating like material and resulting in complex symbols being used to represent subject. Jevons's objection can largely be countered by pointing to the development, in modern classification theory, of a body of sound and coherent principles aimed at the subject analysis of knowledge as it is presented in books and other media. The late L. S. Jast said, 'This statement of Jevons reminds me of the keeper who went up to the trespassing angler with the remark, "My man, you can't fish here", and who received the reply, "But I am fishing".' Librarians, in their wisdom or unwisdom, have trespassed on Jevons's precious waters and have shown that they can classify. (Shades of the cod war!) Dr Kelley's objections are considered further in a later chapter devoted to the limitations of classification theory and practice, but it can be mentioned that the solution she proposed to her colleagues in the United States – broad classification with detailed alphabetical subject cataloguing to carry out the further subject analysis of the stock – has its own problems, for the complexity involved in selecting and relating subject headings in alphabetical subject catalogues has caused increasing concern in the thirty or more years that have elapsed since her findings were published.

There are many factors that can adversely affect classification or pose serious problems for it. Multi-topical documents can only go in one place in a classified sequence, although they can have two or more subject entries in a classified catalogue or information file; the various forms which media now take – books, pamphlets, periodicals, tapes, films, reports and so forth – means that some items seem to defy reliable classification, or at least that we need several 'parallel' classified sequences in the library. In addition to these problems, there is the fact that we need to use symbols to represent subjects in the classified order and this notation, as it is usually called by librarians, can become long and unwieldy if we strive for specific classification in all instances. The longer and more complicated it is, the more difficulty there is in following the helpful classified order intelligently. Then, again, there is the fact to be faced that the field of knowledge is constantly changing. New subjects emerge; old ones grow or diminish in status; new subject relationships are formed and some previous ones are dropped. A good bibliographical classification endeavours to take account of this constant change and development (which can be discerned in most subject areas, but is especially noticeable in some of the sciences), although too rapid change on the part of the classification system results in heavy reclassification problems for the libraries committed to that scheme. The restrictions of any system which assembles concepts into a definite order that is only one of several possible orders is yet another point that merits attention in appreciating the problems and imperfections of bibliographical classification systems.

These points serve to remind us of the weakness as well as the strength of classification and are worthy of some attention, however cursory, at the outset of the student's course. There is one other factor, even more basic than some of the above, which affects classification and which needs to be carefully understood from the very beginning. This is that, although classification locates and relates material, no classification can show every feasible subject grouping. The process of division, means that the maker of any classification system – called by Ranganathan a *classificationist* as distinct from a *classifier*, the person who applies a system – must decide at the outset what is to be collected and what is to be scattered. A scheme of library classification may be a general one covering the whole field of recorded knowledge or it may be a special one which is restricted to a single subject area or to a group of allied subject areas. In either case, the classificationist must decide which relationships are major and are to be stressed in the scheme and which are minor relationships, from the point of view of users and potential users, and therefore can be relatively neglected. Simple examples may serve to illustrate this point. If we have a document on 'Employment problems in the motor industry' and one on 'Employment problems in the textile industry', we could find that the former goes under motor industry and the latter under textile manufacture. This means that information on 'employment problems' has been scattered by our classification. Alternatively we may, with much justice, keep these documents together under 'employment'. In this instance, we have separated the first document from material on other aspects of the motor industry and the second from other material on textiles! This apparent dilemma reappears with uncompromising insistence in all subject areas. By classifying French drama under French literature and English drama under English literature, for example, we separate material on the subject 'drama'. Yet the problem is not as serious as it may at first appear; a wise scrutiny of the structure of each subject area enables the modern classificationist, whether he be assisting in the construction of a scheme for widespread use or building a classification for a single library, to decide which relationships deserve prominence. A–Z subject indexing – a vital adjunct to any classification system – can also be used, as we shall see, to at least partially atone for the inevitable scattering that does take place. Although a classification cannot show *all* subject relationships, we must never assume that it should therefore show none! A good scheme can bring out the most helpful groupings and leave allied tools to stress those subject affinities which it has been forced to ignore.

Thus it must be reiterated that classification, wisely designed and applied, can have a transforming influence in most libraries. It brings order and method to what might otherwise be a mere jungle of books and other material and has, or ought to have, a profound influence in reference and information work in particular – for the way in which a classification rationally displays the structure of a subject field can be of great assistance in clarifying and dealing with requests for information. In addition, the study of classification can be of great personal benefit to the young librarian; his own powers of organization are sharpened by a growing appreciation of the principles involved, while the perusal of the systematic plans of the whole field of learning, as found in the major general classifications, gives an unrivalled opportunity to improve his store of general knowledge and to see the pattern and framework which exists in any serious subject discipline. He is also, through his scanning of classification schedules, able to comprehend to some degree the major links that have been forged between various subject areas.

There are many classification systems. The *Dewey Decimal Classification* (sometimes abbreviated to DDC or just DC), the *Library of Congress Classification* (LC), and the *Universal Decimal Classification* (UDC) are widely used. Lesser used classifications which also embrace the whole field of knowledge are the *Colon Classification* (CC) of Ranganathan and the *Bibliographic Classification* (BC), originally complied by H. E. Bliss. They are assessed later, but while they differ in details and probably in effectiveness also, they largely share the basic aims of a classification that have been outlined. There also exists an increasing number of systems which classify a restricted area of knowledge and a few of these specializing schemes should also be selected for scrutiny and study.

A classification cannot and does not stand alone in catering for the organization of knowledge by subject. It needs to be supported by library catalogues, and indexes, by good indexing and arrangement in the publications themselves, and by published bibliographical aids, some of which themselves utilize classification or principles of a classificatory kind. Nevertheless, the well-structured classification, relying, as all modern schemes do, upon relative location and based upon carefully thought out decisions as to which subject relationships need to be brought to the fore, can bring a high degree of system and benefit to the librarians which it serves. A general-to-special order of optimum helpfulness within each distinct subject area does a great deal to display fully the library's resources and to save time and effort both in purposive and defined browsing and searches for information, although the type and size of library has an understandable influence upon the nature of classification practice. Yet much remains to be achieved. If the student is inclined to think (especially if he comes from a small library) that far too much stress is placed upon theory and upon specialized terminology in the chapters which follow, he must consider that precision in language is customary in technical subjects and realize how a faulty and inadequate arrangement hinders the effective organization of material, particularly in large and specialized collections, impeding the discovery of relevant subject material by or for readers. To abandon the search for better principles and new or improved classifications would be to evade in part the challenge of efficiently housing and helping library users to exploit the world's expanding supply of literature – which is in fact the essence of the practical librarian's work. Although no classification can eliminate the need for a good staff with a thorough knowledge of the stock and an appreciation of readers' requirements, a sound scheme will speed up the work of the service and will facilitate the confident handling of enquiries; thus, to a large extent, staff time and labour are saved through classification also.

CHAPTER TWO

The Task of Subject Analysis-I: Facets of a Single Subject Field

Having decided that the absolute necessity for systematic subject classification in the vast majority of libraries is recognized, how can a bibliographical scheme best be constructed? It is no disparagement of the pioneers – Dewey, Cutter, Brown and others – to say that, in the early years of open-access libraries, classificatory practice forged ahead of theory. Despite the fact that three of the important general schemes were available, or in course of preparation, by the end of the nineteenth century, the first systematic attempt to set down the theory of library classification did not come until 1901. This was Ernest Cushing Richardson's book entitled *Classification*. The views of this American writer were to be supported, broadly speaking, by his fellow-countryman, Henry Evelyn Bliss and also by the early editions of this *Manual*. They rely chiefly on the idea that classification of knowledge, or parts of it, similar to those constructed in the past by scientists and philosophers such as Linnaeus, Bacon, Coleridge, Comte and Spencer, provide us with the essential basis for the making of a book classification. The latter, it is suggested, is fundamentally a classification of knowledge or ideas, with the addition of certain auxiliaries necessitated by the complexity of knowledge as found in book form.

The older ideas on book classification also owe much to the principles of classification as taught by logicians. The major principle originally expounded in logic was that classification should start with knowledge in its totality and divide it up into classes. The process would continue until division was exhausted, but two classes only would appear at each stage of division and one of these would be merely the negation of the other. Some dichotomous division is still occasionally found in part when any categorization is attempted – witness the following simple key:

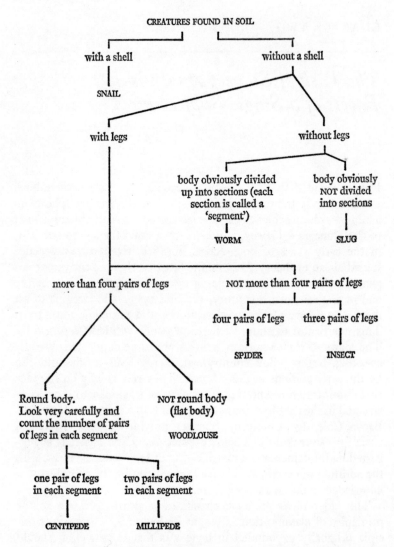

But the strict Aristotelian kind of dichotomy, with its pairs of positives and balancing negatives, was applied more rigorously than our diagram suggests and is futile for practical library purposes.[1] The

---

[1] The intricacy and yet inefficiency of dichotomy in any practical situation is well illustrated by an amusing anecdote in R. A. Fairthorne's, *Towards Information Retrieval* (Butterworth, 1961, p. 4). Here, an enquirer entering a building is faced with successive pairs (one 'positive' and one 'negative') of doors. Selection of the appropriate door from each pair eventually brings him back on to the street.

older book classifications that are still in use today rejected the notion of dichotomous division, but leaned heavily nevertheless on the idea of starting with large subject fields and dividing them up, using one characteristic at a time, so that eventually they had attempted to list all departments of knowledge in a systematic sequence moving from the very general to the highly specialized in a series of regulated steps. The ideas borrowed from the rules of formal logic assume that in a general classification designed to cover all departments of knowledge we will break down a collection of books into organized subject groups, using one *characteristic* at a time. The characteristics used in division will enable us to assemble things according to their degree of likeness to make a specific class. To use a formal phrase, a classification proceeds from terms of great *extension* and small *intension* to terms of great *intension* and small *extension*. Or, more simply, it proceeds by taking class terms which connote great areas of subject matter and divides them by gradual steps into terms less and less extensive until division is no longer possible or necessary. In strictly logical terms, each class is said to be a *species* of the one immediately above it in the hierarchical chain and a *genus* in relation to the one below. This process, in which one characteristic only is used as the dividing principle at each stage, will eventually enable us to enumerate all branches of knowledge in the form of an organized 'family tree'. (It is an inverted tree, in that the upper part of the hierarchy forms the 'trunk'.) For example, in the class Commerce, we might have:

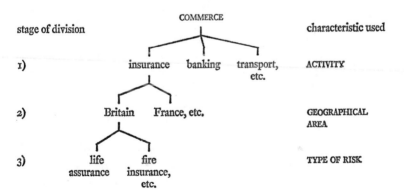

stage of division	COMMERCE			characteristic used
1)	insurance	banking	transport, etc.	ACTIVITY
2)	Britain	France, etc.		GEOGRAPHICAL AREA
3)	life assurance	fire insurance, etc.		TYPE OF RISK

A classification schedule, then, is a series of terms arranged in orderly rows or columns and our diagram shows how certain characteristics of division might be used to split the Commerce class into organized groups. Division has been pursued here under the topic Insurance; the classes Banking, Transport and other divisions of Commerce could, of course, be also further sub-divided and in this way we could itemize any specific theme, showing it in a vast 'tree' containing all branches of knowledge, as a part of the more general class to which it belongs. Division is, in one sense, the exact opposite of classification or grouping. Yet, paradoxical though it may seem, we must divide our larger classes in order to obtain more specific groupings, each consisting of closely allied material. The same methods can be used when making a special classification but, in this instance the 'tree' will be confined to the departments of the specialized area of activity. Thus our classification, based on the rules of logical division, moves in systematic stages from general subjects, like Commerce, to specific ones, such as (and we can visualize this if we imagine our diagram in extended form) 'the value of a fire insurance policy in 1966 for business firms in Britain'.

The undoubted links which this older approach has with the Greek logicians and references to the 'Tree of Porphyry' and the 'Five Predicables' are no longer of real significance in the study of bibliographical classification. But the characteristics, or principles of division, examples of which are given in the diagram, are important for at least two good reasons. First of all, the characteristics employed must be essential to the purpose in view. Thus, in each subject field, the classificationist selects relevant characteristics and strives to apply them in the order which will result in the most useful final arrangement that is possible. There are, of course, several useful arrangements in some fields, but the object is to offer the best of these; a good classification must emphasize the most important subject relationships and restrict scattering to comparatively minor associations. This makes it imperative that characteristics of division are applied in a suitable order. With this in mind, the order of application of characteristics in the above diagram can and should be challenged – it is obviously wrong as it stands, if the most helpful arrangement is sought.

A second point which arises is that each characteristic should be exhausted before the next is used. For if we apply two or more characteristics at the same stage of division, we have a muddled state of affairs which is known as cross-division, or cross-classification. Thus in our diagram, if we used the characteristics of insurance risk and geographical area at the same step of division a confused arrangement would result and we should not know, for example, whether to place an item on 'Life assurance in the United States' under hierarchy A or B:

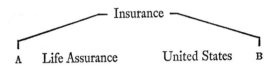

However, our diagram avoids this problem by using only one characteristic at a time and it would apply this exhaustively before the next was used. Thus the hierarchy for the above example would be (assuming the order of characteristics is rectified):

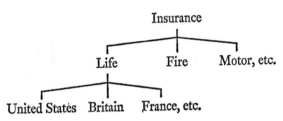

According to the strict rules of formal logic, cross-classification is a state of affairs to be avoided at all costs, for it may well result in doubt in the classifier's mind and consequently in the scattering of a number of items on the same theme. However, it will be found that it does occur at times in the established bibliographical schemes. This is often unfortunate in practice, but is not necessarily *always* a fault; the way in which knowledge is presented in documents brings about some overlapping of categories. No theoretical canon or standard is so sacred that it cannot occasionally be ignored in the interests of a more helpful arrangement. If cross-division *is* adopted, it is up to the classificationist to justify it: it cannot be condoned if it leads to indecision by the classifier or books on a specific subject being separated because of inattention to fundamental principles.

The early explorations into the theory of bibliographical classification showed that, on one point at least, classificationists and other librarians were more or less unanimous. They accepted that fact that a general book classification should start with knowledge in its entirety and break it gradually down into classes and sub-classes by the application of a series of characteristics, thus eventually listing all topics in systematic fashion. This approach is inevitable if we view our classification as a 'family tree' following, at least in part, the rules of division accepted by logicians. Thus the older general bibliographical schemes tended to enumerate all subjects in this way and to provide symbols as a ready-made class-mark for each subject identified and listed. A different approach is now favoured by many classificationists, but widely used schemes – particularly LC and to a somewhat lesser extent DC – adhere strongly to the idea of the systematic listing or enumeration of subjects in a gigantic classificatory map. They are thus sometimes referred to as *enumerative classifications*.

The newer method relies on *synthesis* – the fitting together of various components to specify a subject – rather than an enumeration. It is often associated with the eminent Indian librarian, S. R. Ranganathan, and was put forward, somewhat tentatively, in 1933 in the *Colon Classification*. It would indeed be difficult to overestimate the importance of this extraordinarily prolific writer in our studies. Ranganathan had been a student of classification in England under Sayers, but many of the ideas expressed in the Colon scheme and in his other writings are essentially the product of his own fertile and ingenious mind. The main principle to be considered is one which can be seen slowly evolving in the listing once and for all of certain recurring divisions, notably for forms of presentation and geographical areas, in many of the older schemes and most particularly in the *Universal Decimal Classification* (predating CC by some thirty years), but which first emerges in a full and clear form in the original edition of the Colon scheme and has been developed considerably since then. It is argued that, instead of attempting to list all subjects, a classification should identify main classes or distinct disciplines. Then, within each discipline, it need only enumerate basic concepts or elements, arranging these in appropriate categories or *facets*. Most subjects are compounds made up of two or more elements drawn from the various facets of a subject field. To classify a document, we first of all analyse its compound subject and recognize the facets represented and, within each of these, the component elements or concepts concerned. We then employ the method known as synthesis by linking together, in a specified manner, the symbols representing these elements – thus gradually building up an appropriate class-mark.

The distinction between the two approaches may be clarified by means of examples. Consider the specific subject: '*The doctrine of Grace in Methodism in Britain during the eighteenth century*.' A *completely enumerative* classification would try to provide the *classifier* with a complete class-mark for this, as for all other subjects. (It may be noted that the older schemes are rarely enumerative to this degree, but the method of listing all topics is essentially the major principle which they try to follow.) A *completely synthetic*, or *faceted*, scheme on the other hand would instruct the classifier to break down the subject into its component parts and then to build the required class-mark by linking together the part representing Methodism (as a branch of Christianity in the Religion class), the part representing Grace (from the Doctrines facet of that class), the part representing Britain (from the geographical facet common to all classes), and the part representing the eighteenth century (from the Chronological facet applicable to each class). Ranganathan has likened the synthetic method of book classification to a child's Meccano set. Perhaps a Lego kit is a more acceptable modern analogy: both the kit and the synthetic classification provide for the fitting together of standard unit elements in order to construct compounds.

Elements or concepts defined and isolated, but left in an unorganized state, are sometimes called *isolates*. When a fully synthetic classification is constructed, facets are formed within each discipline, each facet being the total sum of elements produced by the application of any one single characteristic of division. Each element is then called a *focus*. If we turn to our example again, the organized elements might be set out thus:

CLASS OR DISCIPLINE: RELIGION   Common to all classes

Religions facet	*Doctrines facet*	*Geographical facet*	*Time facet*
Buddhism	Faith	France	18th century
Hinduism	Repentance	Germany	19th century
Judaism	Grace	Britain, etc.	20th century, etc.
Christianity	Regeneration, etc.		
Protestant			
denominations			
Methodism			

Islam, etc. (indentation above shows hierarchy)

We use the analytico-synthetic approach by first of all analysing the subject (after the basic discipline to which it belongs is identified) into its facets. We then synthesize by focusing our attention on the appropriate element in each facet and joining together these elements, or rather by joining the symbols that will be assigned to represent them. From the use of the verb 'to focus' in this context, Ranganathan has used the word 'focus' as a noun to describe an element within its appropriate facet.

In any classification, general or special, we can look for the facets of a subject field and our recognition of them and the way in which they have been combined is the clue to the way in which that classification has organized the subject concerned. In Literature, for example, the facets are Language, Literary form, and Literary period or movement. The element 'drama' is a focus in the Literary form facet, the focus 'English' belongs to the Language facet, and so on. Among general schemes, CC and (to a slightly lesser extent) UDC typify the synthetic approach and many special schemes, including Coates's classification for the British Catalogue of Music, the English Electric scheme for Engineering (now published in expanded form as a *Thesaurofacet*), D. J. Foskett's *London Education Classification*, and the *Classification of Business Studies* compiled by K. D. C. Vernon and V. Lang at the London Graduate School of Business Studies, are fully faceted. But a scheme may be primarily enumerative and yet have *some* provision for synthesis. The DC originated at a time when subject analysis had not been fully worked out and thus it relies largely on the enumeration of compound themes. It does, however, give a certain amount of scope for synthetic classification or, as Dewey called it, 'number building'. Let us illustrate this by means of some straightforward examples. Consider the journal: *European training: a professional review of theory and practice*. Now, a periodical or serial publication may be regarded as a recurring aspect or form of presentation and it is one of a host of such aspects, viewpoints or forms which are listed once and for all in the table of *standard sub-divisions* in DC. The number in that table for serials or periodicals is 05 and so, by adding this to our basic class-mark for *Industrial training and education*, enumerated in the main schedules we have our final 'synthetic' number – 658.312405. Geographical divisions are also viewed, quite rightly, as being applicable to all subject areas. We can have economics in France, scientific research in France, French philosophy and so forth; any geographical area is a potential addition to a subject as such. Thus in DC there is a common geographical facet called the *Area Table*. We can add its regional numbers to a subject number from the main schedules when so instructed. Thus, if we take the case of the subject *Magnetic surveys in the United States* we begin with the basic number for magnetic surveys, which is

538.78, and by adding area-table notation, as instructed, our final class-mark becomes 538.7873 (73 being the number which denotes United States in the area table).

In the UDC, the idea of arriving at any compound by the logical joining of elements has been carried much further, despite the fact that the International Federation of Documentation adopted the enumerative structure of DC as the basis of their classification. UDC recognizes that time, race, language and point of view must be regarded as common facets as well as space, or geographical region. This emphasis on the synthetic approach in a scheme which originated at the turn of the century is undoubtedly due to the fact that, from its inception, UDC was concerned with the detailed and specific subjects that are the themes of articles and report literature rather than with the arrangement of books on shelves. Thus in UDC, if we had as a specific subject – *The cost of living in the West Indies in the wintertime* – how do we classify it (assuming precise classification is required)? The basic theme (cost of living) is enumerated in the main schedules at 338.585.3, but we turn to synthesis for the rest of the class-mark and we look at the common space and time facets which are common to all subject areas. Space is indicated by parentheses and the number for West Indies is (729). Time, introduced by inverted commas, has the number "324" to denote winter. So our full class-mark would be 338.585.3 (729) "324". This is admittedly complicated, but is precise and unmistakable. There can be no ambiguity since each facet is introduced in a distinctive manner. Thus (729) can only mean 'West Indies' and is, as it were, reserved for this concept. It is stressed that UDC is intended for reports, pamphlets, periodical articles or for the organization of vast classified catalogues rather than for book arrangement. Here are some other examples from it, based (unlike the earlier example) on recent literature:

The sources of words: a polyglot guide to learning languages in schools 418 (075) = 00.
Sex education in the United States: a report (stressing social implications) 613.88.009 (73).

The first of these shows a basic enumerated class-mark extended by a concept from the form of presentation facet, represented by numbers in parentheses introduced by a zero (the use of the zero prevents confusion between this facet and the space or geographical numbers) and the language facet, represented by an equals sign. Polyglot works are shown by = oo and school textbooks by (075). The second example takes the listed basic class-mark from the main schedules of UDC and adds the appropriate number for the social and ethical viewpoint from another facet – that representing viewpoints. This is introduced by .oo (reserved for this purpose). The concept United States involves the space facet once again.

It is clear that there is a good deal more potential for synthesis in UDC than in DC, but nowadays even schemes primarily concerned with book arrangement need to consider the faceted approach. Several books now have subjects which possess two or three distinct facets. Yet the other member of the three great classifications (in terms of use), LC, offers little or no synthesis and relies on the enumeration of specific topics on a massive scale. The synthesis which it does have is restricted to certain classes and there is no attempt to equip the scheme with common facets of space or time, or to have a set of standard subdivisions of universal application like those of DC. So at one end of the scale we have CC and UDC with their extensive reliance on synthesis – CC indeed is fully synthetic, for it consciously employs the technique of facet analysis. At the other extreme, as far as general classifications are concerned, is the highly enumerative LC. In between we have general schemes which are basically enumerative but offer reasonable prospects for number-building or synthesis – DC, the original edition of BC and J. D. Brown's *Subject Classification*, which is now moribund. The latter, developed chiefly between 1904–13, is interesting to students who want to see the growth of the idea of synthesis in historical perspective. It indicates, more clearly than do its contemporary editions of DC, the embryonic beginnings of modern faceted schemes of classification.

Synthesis in classification and its logical culmination in the fully-faceted approach has been described but not, so far, evaluated. It has been implied that the fact of assembling units to form compound subjects is generally superior to the attempt to enumerate all compounds. Some advantages of synthesis and in particular of fully faceted classification are as follows:

1) The arranging of elements into facets, each facet consisting of all the elements or isolates produced by a single characteristic of division, provides valuable clarification of the issues in the quest for the most helpful order – clearly the order of the classification

will, to a very large extent, depend upon the order of facet citation or combination. (Clear facet analysis is also a sure way to remove unwanted cross-classification.) The librarian as well as the classificationist benefits here. As we see, within each subject field, an indication of the order of facet combination, so we can see and appraise the sequence of the classification. This is much harder to do in a mainly enumerative scheme where the mode of division within each class is not revealed, as a rule, to the classifier and the latter has, if he wishes, to search for it. (An effort to ascertain the mode of division in such cases is usually only made if the classifier is perturbed by the end product, the resulting order of compound topics.)

2) A faceted classification is the best way to provide detail and accuracy in classification. If detail is not wanted it can of course be ignored by an individual library, but it should be there for those who do need it. We cannot possibly enumerate or list *all* compound topics. It is simpler and wiser to cater for them by means of synthesis. It is, in fact, noteworthy that the LC classification fails, despite its great bulk, to cater accurately for several feasible compound subjects.

3) Allied to the above point is the fact that a fully synthetic or faceted system can keep pace with the growth of knowledge much more readily than one which is mainly enumerative in structure and which thus has virtually a built-in obsolescence. Many allegedly 'new' subjects are in reality merely a new compound arising from a combination of elements that have been already recognized and listed within their appropriate facets. It can be said, indeed, that an enumerative classification, with its strict attempt at a 'genus to species' type of progression, is very like a photograph, or portrait, of a person. As a photograph shows an individual at a particular time and from a particular angle, so the enumerative classification arrests knowledge at a given stage of its development and organizes it rigidly in a selected form. Thus only certain basic concepts are combined; many topics cannot be accurately specified. Likewise, as a photograph is inanimate and unchanging, so the enumerative classification has great difficulty in keeping up with a world in which knowledge is in a constant state of flux. It may be that no classification can be fully self-perpetuating or can be completely abreast with modern thought in every subject field, but the

entirely synthetic system is much more flexible in this respect than its older rivals.

4) The more synthetic a classification, the shorter its schedules are likely to be and their compact character should make them easier to handle and consult. If recurring isolates like 'France' or '18th century' are listed every time they are needed, the schedules are bulked out enormously. To provide for the element 'France' once and for all within a common geographical facet is much more economical than to enumerate it constantly thus –

> Education in France
> Customs in France
> France and her architecture
> Technology in Modern France
> France's political parties, etc.

Yet much of this kind of repetitive listing of recurring concepts on each occasion that they are required does take place in largely enumerative classifications. There are numerous examples of it in LC and the original edition of BC, despite the presence of a common geographical facet, is sometimes prone to needless enumerated detail also, viz:

> Anglican church
> Anglican church in the United States
> Anglican church in Gibraltar, etc.

It can be argued that sometimes a particular subject area benefits from having a series of sub-divisions, geographical or otherwise, which are unique and specially designed for it. The chosen period divisions for English literature, for example, might not suit the literary movements of France or Italy. Doubtless the Congress classifiers, with some justice, would argue on such lines, but even allowing for this it cannot be denied that there is much needless repetition in the schedules of DC and LC. The slimmer appearance of the abridged UDC is not primarily due to the fact that it is an abridgement but is a direct testimony to the economy of synthesis – for space is saved to an enormous degree by listing once and for all, within their facets, recurring ideas relating to time, language, space and so forth.

5) Faceted classification enables the accurate specification of many

compounds which would be 'locked out' of the schedules in a *purely enumerative* system. For example, if we have a fixed, listed hierarchy such as:

English literature
English drama
20th-century English drama

then we cannot easily specify, unless some form of synthesis – however primitive – is introduced, '20th century English literature'. In a faceted scheme, the classifier can combine the facets Language, Literary form and Chronological period, but can also, when the occasion demands, simply ignore the second of these and thus reject an unwanted intermediary step.

6) The memory-value of a highly synthetic classification is potentially very great. Each basic element or isolate can be represented by a particular symbol (usually a number or a letter) or small group of symbols, so that by constant use and practice the classifier and the librarians who use the scheme come to associate the concept with the symbol or symbols concerned. Thus the UDC "324" always means and can only mean – 'wintertime'. In DC this idea is found too, although it is not so clearly followed; for instance, 44 is the number for France in the area table which serves as a common space facet, but 44 may, in some other contexts, convey a meaning other than France and complications thus arise in the application of the scheme. The problem is that of clear identification and 'labelling' of concepts. (This idea is discussed further under notation.) It may have special value in connection with the unique identification of concepts for machine storage and retrieval.

7) Faceted schemes are almost certainly easier to compile.

8) The 'genus to species' kind of classification, on which the enumerative approach seems to be largely based, is demonstrably unsuitable for bibliographical purposes since the type of relationships which exist there are rarely of this kind.

The extent to which facet analysis is used is, however, by no means the only criterion by which a classification should be assessed. Important and valuable though it is, it leaves unresolved the fundamental issue of order – which relationships the classification should demonstrate. It must be recalled that *no* classification, faceted or otherwise, can display in linear sequence *all* subject groupings. (Thus only the primary facet of a subject has any major say in determining a sequence of books on shelves.) In addition, the faceted approach may be said to have problems as well as advantages. It is sometimes associated only with very detailed classification and is thought of by some as a tool for information science, inapplicable to small libraries. It is often, rightly or wrongly, thought to involve great notational complications – certainly the need to introduce each facet in a distinctive manner as in UDC (= for language, " " for time, etc.) and also, as will be shown, in CC, is a problem for shelving or filing. There are now a number of special classifications connected on fully synthetic lines but, despite much current work and research, the only general classification we have that is truly completely faceted is that of Ranganathan and it is complicated in many ways by its attempt to keep pace with the rapidly developing ideas of its author. Apart from CC, UDC and the new BC, general classifications do not apply facet analysis or its equivalent in anything like a complete or fully predictable manner at all. Most of them practise number building to a certain extent, but the older idea of a vast 'tree of knowledge', which eventually lists all branches of thought and experience and provides ready-made class-marks for each branch, is nearer to the aims of their compilers than are the newer theories. This nineteenth-century approach certainly imposed limitations upon book classification. Nevertheless some of these earlier ideas still have much value for us; as one modern writer puts it, 'it is a mistake to consider that they cannot usefully complement other principles . . . however limited, they are certainly not invalid'.[1] Unless we appreciate them, we shall obtain a rather distorted picture of the *Decimal Classification*, the *Congress Classification*, and other great schemes which were constructed or begun in a period when librarians virtually had only the findings of philosophers and logicians and their own tentative experiments, or those of colleagues, to guide them.

In short, we would do well to remember that it is likely, for years to come and despite the more fluid and 'logical' nature of synthesis, shelf arrangement in public and academic libraries will be dominated by what we choose to call enumerative classifications. They have some practical advantages and are stubbornly resilient, refusing to be cast on the fires of Gehenna. A grasp of faceted classification is

[1] J. R. Sharp. *Some Fundamentals of Information Retrieval*, Deutsch, 1965, p. 33.

nevertheless important for an understanding of new developments in the DC, and for an appreciation of special schemes, the role of classification in information science and the aims of much contemporary research into the subject. A good understanding of synthesis and the theory of facet analysis is also a highly useful and powerful apparatus with which to examine and criticize the order, subject analysis, and potential capacity for detail which must underlie any classification system.

CHAPTER THREE

The Task of Subject Analysis-II: Multi-Topical Documents

The analysis and subsequent notational synthesis for the specification of compound topics is by no means the only problem of subject analysis, although it is the most usual and significant one. Essential in a classification for information retrieval, it is also useful in classified catalogues and for classification on the shelves because – even if, in the latter sphere, notational complexities sometimes deny the specification of all facets within a class-mark – it is an indispensable aid for the clear thinking necessary to 'see' a subject area in its entirety, to map out its compartments without ambiguity, and to proceed to demonstrate its major subject associations. We may briefly digress to say that it is thus important to face up to the definition of and distinction between terms such as *facet, compound subject, synthesis, focus* and *enumerative classification*. A few more such terms are now to be introduced, but it is worthwhile to accept this 'jargon' to achieve accuracy of thought and precision in the 'technical' aspects of classification. Once this is accepted, in addition to viewing compound topics within a single subject area and their facets, we can go on to study techniques designed to cope with those items which are multi-topical. In part, we can only do this by employing cataloguing and/or alphabetical subject indexing as an aid to shelf arrangement, but certainly classification too has a role to play in the organization of multi-topical works. Such works can, for the sake of convenience, be divided into distinct categories.

Generalia Class. A generalia class, or its equivalent, is found in every bibliographical scheme. The need for it arises because several books are polytopical. If we were merely classifying abstract ideas, individual ideas could be isolated and appropriate ones grouped, but when we come to classify physical entities, many of which are composite in that they gather together writings on several subjects, a general works class is an obvious requirement. It has been called the waste-paper basket of a classification scheme, but we must not infer from this that it is chaotic or that its contents are worthless. This is certainly not so: it is rather a class designed to house works that overlap many departments of knowledge or which are so varied in their content that they simply cannot be placed elsewhere. Emphasis must be laid upon the *general* nature of all parts of this class. Publications such as *The Times*, the *Encyclopaedia Britannica* and the *Spectator* rightly go within it; there is no topic which may not properly come within their scope and to class them under History, Sociology, Science or even Current Affairs would be to ignore all other subjects with which these publications deal. But a periodical exclusively on art goes with other items on that topic; the encyclopaedia which is restricted to philosophy is likewise placed in the appropriate subject class. Generalia is thus left to accommodate *general* encyclopaedias, periodicals, or essay collections on a host of subject themes and any other polytopical work which simply cannot be legitimately placed elsewhere. It is also customary for it to accommodate books which are in some way rare or special, and being valued for their special features (for example, fine bindings) rather than for their subject content are best set aside in a special collection. In its basic role as the custodian of works covering all knowledge, or a very large part of it, and in its supplementary task as a home for book rarities or perhaps for a distinct and specialized collection of documents such as manuscripts, the generalia class is an important practical auxiliary feature of any classification scheme which endeavours to contend with the whole field of knowledge; it is fair to assume that Jevons did not contemplate any such provision when he attacked the notion of classifying books.

A glance at the generalia classes of the principal schemes shows that the Congress Classification has a general works class on strictly orthodox lines embracing general newspapers, periodicals and works of reference, multi-topical encyclopaedias and the history of knowledge and learning. It was closely modelled on the equivalent in an earlier scheme – Charles Cutter's *Expansive Classification*. The *Decimal* and *Universal Decimal Classifications* are equipped with basically sound generalia classes too; the only possible surprise here is the inclusion of librarianship, which may be thought of as an interdisciplinary topic concerned with the storage and utilization of the knowledge accumulated by specialists in all areas of human activity. The subject undoubtedly merits more distinctive treatment;

probably it would have received such treatment had an alphabetical notation been used. The *Bibliographic Classification* of Bliss and the *Colon Classification* of Ranganathan both have a relatively orthodox and straightforward generalia class. That of BC was originally designed to accept many special collections which would not be distributed on a subject basis. Now, however, it has been recast and embraces certain basic entities common to many subjects and some interdisciplinary topics. The BC equivalent also uses distinctive terminology, for Bliss speaks of 'Anterior Numeral Classes'. The expression is a simple one when we realize that the 'generalia' divisions are represented by numbers while the main notation of the system is composed chiefly of letters and that these divisions precede or are anterior to the individual subject classes. The latter point serves as a reminder that generalia classes are invariably first in any scheme; as classification seeks to proceed systematically from the general to the particular it is logical and obvious that the most general material of all should come at the very beginning of the whole classified sequence.

It was the *Subject Classification* of the British librarian, J. D. Brown, now virtually obsolete, which had the most unusual generalia class. In addition to the material we would expect, it took in all subjects which Brown considered to be interdisciplinary or pervasive of other classes; that is, areas which are necessary to the study of every subject in greater or lesser degree. These, according to Brown, included subjects such as education, logic, mathematics, general science and a portion of the fine arts. Brown was right, in a sense, in his prophecy that many of the barriers between disciplines would break down and he argued almost persuasively in favour of this and other theories. But the result he offered is a highly subjective and practically unsound arrangement: despite changes in the field of knowledge since the start of the century and the intermingling of disciplines, the 'pervasive' classes really belong elsewhere, with the exception perhaps of general science, which (in its position at the end of the generalia class) heralds the physical sciences that follow in *SC* Brown's argument is largely shattered by his own admission that certain arts subjects went into his generalia class owing to lack of room elsewhere – so the sequence offered can be justly described as unorthodox and inefficient.

Two subject works. Sometimes a document or book does not deal with a host of subjects and cannot qualify for inclusion in generalia, yet is not restricted to a single compound topic. It covers *two or three related yet distinct themes.* At times it is both possible and sensible to place under a general heading a work that deals with three or more specific topics relating to that heading. For example, a book or other document concerning enzymes, vitamins and hormones might be placed under the generic label that contains them all – 'biochemistry'. There are, nevertheless, a number of items which give information on two related subjects which may or may not be juxtaposed in the classification scheme in use. If faced, say, with the classification of books on a pairing such as any of the following:

Billiards and snooker
Arithmetic and accountancy
Electricity and magnetism
Cookery and needlework

what alternatives confront us? It is usually unwise or even absurd to suggest the physical break up of the document so that appropriate parts can be filed in different places within a classified sequence, and may be equally foolish to suggest that two copies of such documents be purchased – one to be filed at each of the two possible class-marks. A few libraries, however, have been known to favour the selective adoption of the latter alternative and one classification system seems to suggest that, within an information retrieval context, both courses merit some consideration.[1] It is far more customary and sensible in practice to employ the simple expedient of classifying these items under the theme which receives the greater degree of prominence within the text or, if the dominant topic cannot be easily ascertained, under the one first mentioned on the title page. The secondary topic of the pair can, if need be, be given some prominence in a classified catalogue or information file where the librarian is dealing with entries rather than documents and each document can receive as many subject entries as is deemed necessary.

Phase analysis. The above may all be regarded as straightforward 'two-subject' books or documents. There are, in addition, a small but increasing number of examples which are more subtle and complex, for they do not cover two subjects as separate themes but deal rather with the impact of one subject upon another or the interaction between subject fields. Some examples of these topics, which we may call *complex* rather than compound, are:

[1] Royal Institute of British Architects. *SfB/UDC Building Filing Manual*, 1966.

1) A comparison between the findings of the social and the natural sciences.
2) Workshop technology for mechanical engineers.
3) The use of electricity in the greenhouse.
4) The effect of company mergers on industrial library services.
5) Job evaluation: implications for the textile industry.
6) The influence of the Puritans on the growth of capitalism.
7) Mathematical analysis for management decisions: the application of calculus and linear algebra in industry.
8) Gardening for the physically handicapped.

It is clearly impossible for any scheme to anticipate and list complex examples of this kind. The *Decimal Classification* at times attempts to do so; a classic example is in fact 215 Science and religion, which is really for works dealing with the impact of scientific discovery on religious belief. The *Library of Congress Classification* yields several examples of enumeration with regard to problems of this sort, or indeed for any two-subject item. For instance, under HX Socialism, we find headings such as:

HX 519 Socialism and co-operation
HX 521 Socialism and art
HX 530 Socialism and the law
HX 536 Socialism and religion
HX 545 Socialism and war
HX 546 Socialism and women
HX 550 Socialism and particular social problems (sub-divide by A–Z order)

Although any scheme *can*, if it is thought desirable, list such complex themes as are already recognized by existing literature, this method greatly bulks the schedules and *cannot anticipate new associations of this kind*. Again, the best answer undoubtedly lies with the employment of synthesis. If we can link together class-marks in some approved and satisfactory way, we can cope with whatever new complex 'two-subject' examples may arise. It is, as might be expected, the *Colon Classification* which, among the general systems, has consciously recognized this problem and gone to the root of it by means of the technique known as *phase analysis*.

A phase is that portion of a complex subject[1] which has been

---

[1] The expression 'complex subject' is used in somewhat different ways in various textbooks. Its meaning is restricted here to the description of works demanding phase analysis.

derived from any one single class. So, to utilize but one of the topics originally cited, we may have a work on job evaluation written with an emphasis on the requirements of a particular industry. The true core subject 'job evaluation' constitutes one phase (the primary one) here and the secondary phase is represented by the industry towards which the work is slanted or biased. Ranganathan and others have identified various types of phase relation. The chief ones are 'influencing', 'bias', 'tool or exposition' and 'comparison'. Thus, examples such as *the impact of civil disturbance on mental health*, or our earlier example of *the effect of the Puritan attitude and temperament on the historical growth of capitalism* give rise to the use of the influencing phase. The primary theme here is the topic influenced, but it is the secondary theme or phase which gives the phase relation its distinctive name. Again, in the case of bias phase, it is customary to class such works under their subject rather than under 'class of reader for whom written'. So a book on *Workshop technology for mechanical engineers* is to be classified under the primary phase (Workshop technology) with the class-mark for the secondary theme indicating bias or emphasis (for mechanical engineers) following on by means of synthesis.[1] Likewise, with tool or exposition phase: the 'tool' used in the study or pursuit of the subject is of secondary consideration to the subject concerned. When we come to comparison phase, it is difficult to tell which part of the subject is primary and which secondary and a somewhat arbitrary decision must be made.

So, if we classify one of the above examples with the aid of the *Colon Classification*, we can prise the two phases apart.

Job evaluation for the textile industry (Example of bias phase. Primary phase: 'Job evaluation'. Secondary phase: 'bias towards needs of textile industry). In CC we get:

x:91&bM7

where x:91 stands for job evaluation, M7 for textile industry, and b denotes the type of phase. The ampersand is reserved, in CC, for a linking device in complex subjects. (In editions prior to the seventh, a zero was used for this function.)

Three observations on the above points must be made. Firstly, it may well be asked why should we classify as specifically as this when (assuming that the 'heretical' practice of purchasing two copies and giving them different locations is rejected) documents can only

---

[1] Bias phase is the most controversial category: even today, some would dispute the ruling cited and argue for placing by 'reader appeal' rather than by true subject in such instances.

go in one place in a classified sequence? The answer is that we normally seek to classify as precisely as possible and we would wish to distinguish *Job evaluation in the textile industry*, for instance, from a work on job evaluation in general; we would wish to indicate, to use one of the other examples, that certain works deal with bookkeeping in general, while others are restricted to some aspect of it or present the subject with the needs of a particular category of reader specially in mind. The second observation is that it is necessary to clearly distinguish between *compound* subjects requiring facet analysis and the much rarer *complex* subject, to which phase analysis may be applied. The former involves the linking of two or more elements from the facets of a single subject field; the latter involves a bond between two separate subjects or disciplines. The third observation is that, although we can classify complex examples, if we wish, with great precision when employing *Colon* or some of the special schemes, it is often impossible to do this with other classifications. The *Congress* system virtually evades the whole problem of dealing with complex subjects by means of synthesis. If a multi-phased theme is not enumerated, we must classify it as best we can under a broader heading. (It may be added that, because of its fidelity to the actual volume and character of published literature, the *Congress* scheme *does* list many of the complex themes that the practical classifier encounters, but they are often presented in an uneconomical and rather unsatisfactory way and if a multi-phased subject is *not* listed there is no way of correctly anticipating the right class-mark.) The *Decimal Classification*, although improving in this respect, also fails to recognize that no system can possibly anticipate and list all complex examples that may come before the classifier and it does not make consistent and satisfactory provision for multi-phased themes. Some are enumerated; others are ignored. A few can be catered for by the DC synthetic apparatus. In Table 1 Standard Sub-divisions, we have the number 024, for instance, which can express bias phase, since it stands for 'works for particular groups of people' and can be used in association with Table 7 Persons. Thus *Operations studies for dairy farmers* can go at 658.542024637. (Here 024 added to a basic subject number introduces the bias – for dairy farmers.) It may be added that there is only moderate likelihood of such a complex theme being inserted in the correct place in a DC detailed classified sequence, but at least it can be specified.

There are also improvements for the treatment of complex subjects in the revised BC and the *Universal Decimal Classification* does cope with complex themes in the right way, through the provision of synthesis; it does not, however, attempt to distinguish clearly between the different types of phase relation. The colon is the chief sign used as a relationship indicator here, but it is loosely employed and might, in different contexts, indicate that one subject influences another, that a work is written with a bias towards the needs of a certain category of reader, or that a document contrasts two different subjects. Thus, 659.4:02 might conceivably convey *the influence of librarianship on public opinion* or *public relations – for librarians*. As might be expected from a scheme aimed at specific classification for information science rather than shelf arrangement, however, the UDC deals with what are now recognized as complex or multi-phased documents more adequately than the two other widely used classifications – the Congress and Dewey Decimal systems.

The *Colon Classification* has even more finesse in this sphere than has been so far indicated, for Ranganathan has distinguished between phase analysis as such – the impact of one subject area upon another – and the interaction of two concepts or themes from one and the same subject field, say Literature or Psychology, which may fall within the scope of either intra-facet or intra-array relationships. Thus topics such as *The influence of Wordsworth's poetry on Edmund Blunden* or *The impact of Freud on modern psychoanalysis* are not viewed, strictly speaking, as examples requiring phase analysis because both parts of the subject are drawn from the same single area of knowledge. The method of subject analysis and subsequent synthesis is, none the less, very similar.

Phase analysis may appear to be an excessively intricate or over-elaborate technique, especially in libraries which are relatively small and think of classification almost exclusively in terms of a shelving device to facilitate browsing. At a deeper level, where exact classification is a *sine qua non* (unless classification in the strictest sense of the word is completely discarded in favour of natural language indexing), it has an important part to play in subject analysis and the proportion of documents which may be categorized as *complex* may well grow rather than diminish. Ranganathan has drawn attention to what he calls the migration of subjects from the 'periodical level' to the 'book level' and the history of classification shows that techniques originally used only in relation to highly specialized 'packages' of knowledge are slowly but surely demanded too in book arrangement, although it must be confessed that there are grave attendant problems of notational complexity to overcome.

A distinction has been made above between three categories – the truly multi-topical work which necessitates a generalia class, the 'straightforward' two-subject work giving information on topic A and on topic B, and the complex example where one subject reacts upon or is interwoven with another discipline. For the theoretician, the latter case is by far the most rewarding intellectually, although the other categories will appear at least as frequently in practice. Phase relations, in fact, represent an interesting area of study for those who wish to consider the structure and character of the field of knowledge as represented in printed and other records. A. C. Foskett has commented, with perception, that examples of phase analysis and tool and bias phase in particular may represent the first sign of the emergence of what, in time, will come to be seen as subjects in their own right. Thus, if we look at modern themes such as *medicinal chemistry, agricultural economics,* or *mathematical sociology,* we see topics which can now, if the classificationist so wishes, be enumerated. They all represent, nevertheless, the fusion of existing disciplines as boundaries have been crossed in a way which more likely than not manifested itself originally as a phase relationship problem. It is interesting to examine examples such as these and ask, have they emerged from bias phase or exposition/tool phase – that is, was medicinal chemistry originally *chemistry for the medical practitioner* or the *use of chemistry in the field of medicine?* Such questions, if rightly answered, help us by providing a check on the rules of phase analysis and they assist us in deciding, for instance, whether a work on one subject with a bias towards readers in a different area is best treated with the subject as such as the primary phase or whether, as a minority believe, 'reader appeal' could possibly prevail. There is certainly a very understandable temptation to put *maths for economists,* for instance, with the rather different topic *mathematical economics* under 'economics'. But if we do this we are not really classifying by subject as such and would certainly have difficulty in applying the same kind of decision to, say, *German for sixth formers, chemistry for the general reader, fossils for amateurs,* or one of our earlier examples – *gardening for the physically handicapped.* To class with the 'bias' rather than the true subject is really at best a concession to what is, later in this book, described as reader interest order. In some cases it is not a concession at all, but rather a practical impossibility.

All these rules and questions have to be squarely faced in libraries whatever classification we employ and whether we use the expression 'phase analysis' and kindred terminology or not. Nowadays, of course, they are often largely resolved for us by centralized classification services. But, notwithstanding the help offered by such services, all classifiers have to look to cataloguing and alphabetical indexing to support classification in the control of multi-topical documents and certainly the provision made for generalia material and for multi-phased topics are two more among the many points which may be considered in the review and evaluation of the potential of any general classification.

CHAPTER FOUR

The Achievement of Helpful Order

Facet analysis for compound subjects and (to a much lesser extent) the understanding and construction of phase relationships for complex ones constitute a large part of modern classification theory. With their aid, we are able to incorporate new subjects into the structure of a scheme so that the minimum of difficulty and of tedious and repetitive enumeration of concepts is involved. They enable us to classify with great detail and accuracy, if we so wish. Although we still only see these ideas 'through a glass darkly' in some accepted general and special schemes, their use – now that they have been recognized and clearly defined – is on the increase, as the growth in the synthetic apparatus of the DC testifies. It is clear, however, that classification has the great potential value of systematically relating subjects, as well as accurately specifying and locating them. Thus synthesis in no way diminishes the problem of seeking out a helpful arrangement; it is rather a complementary task. There is in fact a long-standing hypothetical question – 'which is the most important in classification, helpful order or detail?' Lest hard thought is given to it, let it be said that the real answer is that we should not assume that the two are incompatible! With this in mind, the problem of arriving at and maintaining a helpful sequence in a classification which allows for the specification of compound and complex themes can be considered.

As a would-be classificationist seeks for such a sequence, or as any librarian endeavours to appraise the order of an existing system, he must remind himself of certain basic facts. One is that we normally expect classification to be exact or specific (with individual libraries having the liberty to reduce the detail if they wish). Much of the achievement of synthesis may seem unnecessary in the context of a small library, but the apparatus is, of course, optional and can be used selectively. But detail is needed if we want to specify accurately themes such as *Saw mill residues and lumber as raw material for the wood industries in Europe* – a topic which now has literature in book form. Synthesis is by far the best way to secure such detail. Another fundamental fact is that no classification can show *all* subject relationships. The major groupings must be stressed and relatively minor ones sacrificed; the latter can and should be displayed by the use of tools other than the classification schedules. These include the A–Z index. A third important point, not previously introduced, is that arrangement of documents or entries should take into account not only the basic, 'core' subject of a book, but also *the subject discipline or intellectual environment to which the basic subject belongs.* 'Water', for instance, may be thought of as a basic subject or concept, but there is no *one* place for it in most classification schemes, for it can appear in such diverse contexts as *'water engineering'*, *'water divining'*, *'water gardens'*, and *'the use of water in religious rites and ceremonies'*. Likewise 'The moon' can fall within the contexts of astronomy, astrology, space exploration and comparative religion. It is customary to take into account the context or environment into which a topic falls to distinguish, say, between *'boat building'* on the one hand and *'transport by boat'* on the other. Many themes are unaffected by this matter of discipline or intellectual context, but it is hoped that the above examples suffice to show that there *are* cases where the distinction is valid if some impractical or even ludicrous results are to be avoided. Thus almost all schemes do, where necessary, separate documents on certain basic themes through *classification by correct discipline.* So the works on water are not all together but are under engineering, gardening and so forth. That classification by discipline is generally much wiser than the reverse process, which has been dubbed 'classification by attraction', there is no doubt. Brown's *Subject Classification* ignored the problem of discipline classification, with unfortunate results, in its attempt to provide a simple 'one place per topic' ideal order. The problem must be faced and accepted although, it must be confessed, we do encounter the occasional work which deals with a theme such as those cited in a truly interdisciplinary way. We really need a place too for a *rara avis* such as *'The use of water throughout the ages'* and many systems, while fully accepting and applying classification by discipline when the need arises, are now also trying to cater for such a comprehensive work. Keeping these preliminaries in mind, the quest for the best possible order within a classification can begin. At the outset, it must be pointed out that to decide upon the sequence to use in a classification or in evaluating an existing one, we have certain fundamental hints to guide us. They are:

(*a*) To consider the opinions and wishes of experts in the subject field with a view to providing the arrangement which the majority of specialists accept as the wisest.

(*b*) To observe and – if possible – record the way in which our readers (who may *not* be experts in their subject field) demand and use the literature when making subject requests. There is, alas, all too little objective 'hard' evidence on this point.

(*c*) To study the pattern and character of published literature itself. E. W. Hulme, librarian of the Patent Office early in the century, concentrated in his writings upon this last point because he argued that the classification theorists of the day, with fewer large-scale bibliographies to act as guide-lines, paid too much attention to the idea of classifying knowledge (in the abstract) and insufficient heed to the distinctive problems of classifying knowledge as recorded in literature. Hulme coined the phase 'literary warrant' to mean that the schedules of a classification should be moulded to fit published literature, being dictated by what actual (and if possible potential) literature itself merits or warrants. The idea is a useful and important corrective to an over-theoretical approach: it helps, among other things, to ensure that a classification does not offer enumerated details for which no books or documentation exist or provide a framework of principles which is at variance with reality. It has many important practical implications. Whether we classify broadly or in detail should, for instance, rest largely on a consideration of present and potential literary warrant – the present and likely quantity and character of the material to be classified.

Yet, although these fundamentals may and should pervade all our thinking in seeking helpful arrangement or in evaluating the order of an existing classification system, it is possible to consider the subject in much more detail. There are separate, but related, problems which concern the sequence of the major disciplines (this is the 'main class' or macro order of a scheme); the more specific micro order *within* each distinct discipline; the problem of filing elements so as to make sure that a sequence of compound subjects *does* – through its notation – reflect the order decided upon; and the conscious use of the A–Z index to bring out subject associations which the scheme neglects. In the remainder of this chapter these four topics are considered in turn.

Macro or 'main class' order. The order of the principal disciplines has caused much heart searching among some classificationists and writers on classification, while others have paid less attention to it and have preferred to concentrate on what is called here micro-order, helpful order *within* the individual disciplines or main classes. In the DC, for example, the order of principal classes seems to be somewhat arbitrary and haphazard, with history separated from the social sciences and literature from philology; it is based, at least in part, on the order of an earlier system with dubious philosophical origins. But some of Dewey's contemporaries and successors were much more fastidious on the question of the order of main classes. E. C. Richardson and Charles Cutter, looking back to the work of philosophers and other scholars of earlier times for guidance, were involved principally with order at the broad 'macro' level, for philosophical classification was usually so concerned. Both look for a stable and enduring order in the universe itself, an evolutionary or progressive order of nature which a classification can capture and record. 'Nature itself is classified' Cutter asserted and Richardson spoke of the necessity for a lasting classification to adhere to the true order of the sciences. Whether this quest is a valid or illusory one is a debatable point. What can be said with little fear of contradiction is that, in Cutter's case, the search led to an order of classes which, in utilitarian and not merely in philosophic terms, is superior to that of the DC. Cutter's *Expansive Classification* has, it is true, been long dormant; nevertheless it greatly influenced the sequence of classes in LC so that the latter scheme, in many ways so pragmatic, ironically owes much of its scholarship to Cutter's philosophical explorations. The search for an 'enduring order of nature' is one of perennial interest to classificationists and in recent years it has been apparent in the study of integrative-level theory which is described later in this book.

Those two great American librarians, Ernest Richardson and Charles Cutter, were succeeded by another, Henry E. Bliss, who prefaced the construction of his BC with a long and arduous study of the philosophic systems of the past, and the needs of libraries of the present. Bliss too was in many ways, although not entirely, concerned with what is here called main class or macro order: the relationship between areas such as, for example, biology, sociology and anthropology. He looked hard for signs of a majority viewpoint among experts, a 'consensus of opinion' which could act as a reliable and durable guideline for acceptable groupings or collocations of subjects and the impressive architecture of his own completed system reflects his intensive efforts to find one.

Bliss indeed occupies a transitional place in the development of the principles of library classification. Some of his ideas are rooted in the past, but he has also offered us some suggestions which harmonize well with the findings of Ranganathan and his British disciples. His idea concerning the educational and scientific consensus is important, for it is essential that a book classification should group material effectively according to the established needs of the majority of readers. Bliss's *Bibliographic Classification* has several classes where its creator's regard for this consensus has produced a far more scholarly and helpful grouping than is to be found in the equivalent areas of the *Decimal Classification*. Another contribution from Bliss has been the principle of *alternative location*. This involves the provision of two or more locations for certain subjects in a scheme of classification. A library must select *one* of these – the one corresponding most closely to its needs, and leave the alternative(s) unused. This can be extremely useful in the case of subjects which seem clearly to have two or more possibly justifiable places in a classification. So far, among the general schemes, only Bliss's own classification has applied this interesting idea. Whatever our assessment of his strenuous efforts it is conceded by many that, of the predominantly enumerative classifications, it is BC which offers the most helpful order at main class level.

But it may be objected – is main class order so important? Must we not accept that subject searches are usually much too specific to be concerned with main class order and that, as far as classification for the shelf is concerned, the physical layout of individual libraries tends to distort the best-planned of main class sequences? Many modern themes are interdisciplinary and, in any case, a main class is difficult to define with precision, as Palmer points out in the appropriate part of *Itself an Education*. It would be naive to assume that a scheme with an alphabetical notation, fully employed, has twenty-six main classes, while DC and UDC have a maximum of nine plus generalia! In effect, a main class is simply any area large enough to lend itself to facet analysis and to equate main classes with the breadth of any one notational base is an illusion. Perhaps this is why Ranganathan, striving for helpful order *within each class* in CC, stated 'the order of the main classes in the layout of a scheme of classification is not of much moment as long as it is reasonably tolerable'.[1]

Certainly the order within classes is *more* important than main class order, but the study of the latter and the attempt to criticize and improve upon any existing macro order has its value. Among other things, it sets the student to study the structure of the field of knowledge itself. It is interesting, if perhaps slightly irrelevant, to note that the examination of the pattern, structure and interlocking of subjects, the 'universe of knowledge', is now a recognized study in its own right on some library school courses, as a useful preface to classification and a most valuable part of the budding librarian's education. How Bliss would have relished this development!

Micro-order: sequence within classes: citation order. Whatever our views on the achievement of main class order, we must pay particular attention to the problem of order of specific subjects *within* any single subject area or discipline. This problem lies at the core of the task of classification; if it is evaded, the result is not a classification in the truest sense but solely a locating device which pin-points topics but does not really systematically relate them. No system can display, in a linear order of books or catalogue entries, all sought relationships and the onus of deciding what shall be collected and what must be scattered rests with the classificationist. The primary part of the problem concerns the *sequence* in which we move from general topics to specific ones. To use a similar example to that from an earlier chapter, should a document on 'Employment at the docks' have its elements cited as Employment / Docks or Docks / Employment? The first grouping will collect information on employment at the expense of those who want all data on docks (both technical and economic aspects) together; the second grouping separates, by individual industry, material on employment.

The maker of one special faceted scheme (for the Arts) has, for instance, told of his deliberation between citing facets in the sequence

    Medium – Period – Style   –   Country
or Medium – Period – Country – Style

and of his choice of the latter as more helpful.[2]

Clearly, one arrangement has to be chosen and others sacrificed, but neglected groupings can be brought out, to some extent, in the alphabetical subject index to the classification. In modern classi-

---

[1] *Prolegomena to Library Classification.* Asia Publishing House, 1937, p. 210.
[2] Broxis, P. F. *Faceted classification and the fine arts.* Journal of Documentation, March, 1966, pp. 40–54.

fication theory it is, in fact, axiomatic that the index should display the subject groupings that the systematic sequence has been forced to ignore. Yet the index should be left to display only relatively minor groupings; the classification itself should indicate the principal subject relationships. Its success in doing this depends on the citation order of facets in a subject field. Thus, in considering helpful order, we are not simply interested in a sequence of subjects; we are also interested in the sequence of elements within any single compound subject.

The question of citation order of facets was introduced briefly in the examples above. It needs, however, to be examined in rather more detail. Consider the familiar subject area Literature. We can divide up this area by language, then by literary form, and then by chronological period; *or* we may divide by language, by period, then – if necessary – by form. DC and CC favour the former approach, but the latter, as applied in LC, is better for the serious student of literature in any language. Whichever order we select, however, we make a conscious choice with regard to which subject relationships are to be displayed and which can be ignored. In modern parlance, this boils down to the combination or citation order of facets. Is this to be Language / Form / Literary period or Language / Literary period / Form? The search for an answer takes us back to the points previously raised; we must bear in mind the opinions of specialists, the character of the documents in the subject area and the use made of those documents.

When a citation order has been chosen, we can see which relationships are to receive precedence in the sequence. Thus, to change examples, if we select the subject area *Education* we may have:

Education

Facets → (in order of citation)	(1) *Educand*	(2) *Curriculum*	(3) *Teaching method*
Foci →	Primary Schools Secondary Schools Higher Education, etc.	Maths History Physics, etc.	Lectures Seminars Tutorials, etc.

If the facet citation order is 1–3 as shown above, we know that a subject such as *Teaching history in higher education by means of tutorials* would have as its combination sequence of foci – Higher education / History / Tutorials. The effect of this, in practice, is to keep together all related documents as far as the first facet to be cited is concerned, to provide much collocation but some scattering in the next, and to offer a considerable and unavoidable amount of separation in the facet cited last. Thus, in our hypothetical example, *Tutorials in higher education* would be subordinate to higher education, while *Tutorials in secondary schools* would go under Secondary Schools.

Must each class have an individual and distinct order for citation, or is it possible to provide some worthwhile rule or common pattern for a citation order which will apply to disciplines as diverse in scope and content as chemistry and philosophy, or as sociology and music? The best-known attempt to achieve a pattern is found in CC. Here, within a rapidly evolving scheme of things, Ranganathan tried to relate *all facets* to one or another of five concepts – Personality, Matter, Energy, Space and Time – which he claimed are basic or fundamental to every subject. *Time* and *Space* are self-explanatory; they cover past, present or future time-periods and geographical regions – continents, countries or towns – respectively. As facets, they can be applied to all subject fields and are thus often said to be common facets. *Energy* is used to represent processes, activities or operations which consume physical or mental effort. Every class has an energy facet in CC, but the energy concepts differ from class to class. *Matter*, only rarely used before edition 7, covers all materials. *Personality*, which along with *energy* is most important, is nevertheless remarkably elusive when succinct unambiguous definition is demanded. But it is best expressed as the core part of a subject which imparts meaning and cohesion to the other facets. Its divisions, like those of the *Energy* facet, differ from class to class. The five fundamental concepts said to be the basis of all division are usually simply written as PMEST and this sequence conveys their citation or combination order. Thus we have no scattering in the P facet, some distribution of related ideas in M and E and much scattering under S and T.

Let us illustrate Ranganathan's facet formula by means of an example which uses it to the full. (Most examples do not.) If we want to classify *The administration of manuscript collections in British academic libraries in the 1970s*, we first of all find the main class, which is Library Science. We then recognize that we will not find a ready-made class-mark for this topic, but must assemble one and we thus practise facet analysis:

	Main class	– Library Science
	Personality facet	– focus is *Academic libraries*
	Matter facet	– focus is *Manuscripts*
	Energy facet	– focus is *Administration*
These are common {	Space facet	– focus is *Britain*
to all subject fields {	Time facet	– focus is *1970s*

Drawing our guidance from edition 6 of CC, we see that each facet, apart from Personality, is introduced by a distinctive punctuation mark; originally there was only one and CC was named accordingly. Now *Matter* is introduced by a semi-colon, *Energy* by the colon, *Space* by a full stop and *Time* by an apostrophe. We can thus re-write our citation order as P; M: E. S 'T and when we switch from analysis to notational synthesis and take the appropriate digits from CC we have as our end product:

Class-mark –	2	3	;12	:8	.56	'N7
	/	/	/	/	/	/
Analysis –	Main	(P)	(M)	(E)	(S)	(T)
	Class					

Before this is dismissed as remarkably ingenious but hopelessly complicated, some facts must be listed and considered.

1) This *is* too complex for shelf classification, but the example is imaginary and represents a degree of detail which, even nowadays would never be found at the book level.

2) The system has remarkable structural precision and each facet can be clearly identified. This would be important in a sophisticated information-retrieval context.

3) Although PMEST is the citation order, in most examples only one or two facets would be present. When a facet is absent, the others combine in their usual way. Thus, our example is highly unlikely (and is only offered to show the full formula in use). More probably, actual examples, based on this one, would include:

2'N7   *Libraries in the 1970s*
2.56   *Libraries in Britain*
2:8'N7 *Library administration in the 1970s*
23:8   *Academic library administration*

Although complicated for shelf arrangement, the scheme is clearly not impossible to apply; it has a great deal of logic in its 'Lego kit' approach and philosophy. (The P facet, incidentally, is introduced by a comma in edition 7.)

But problems do exist and a few may also be briefly introduced and listed:

1) Do the categories PMEST really cover *all* concepts? This is doubtful and writers such as Vickery and De Grolier have argued that a full formula would specify other categories, such as substance, organ, property, action, operation, and form. 'There are more things in heaven and earth . . .'

2) Is PMEST *always* the best citation order? The simple answer is 'no'. It is not useful to have works on university library administration separated from those on public library administration or works on cataloguing, for instance, separated by type of library on the grounds that the kind of library is [P] and administration or cataloguing belong to [E]. A faceted classification devised and used in *Library and Information Science Abstracts* has encountered this problem and sought a solution. When we study CC in more detail we shall see that Ranganathan too has needed to seek a way of extending or modifying the scope and effect of the PMEST sequence.

3) There are problems arising out of the definition of [P]. Some concepts (eg, Manuscripts) appear in the [P] facet of one class and the [M] facet of another. Ranganathan's contention is that PMEST gives us a citation pattern for all subjects in that it is an order of decreasing concreteness. [P] is the most concrete or important concept when present in a subject, [S] and [T] are the least important or most nebulous. This is accepted but to many students of classification it seems rather odd that the most 'concrete' fundamental category is the most difficult to define.

What we can say, with confidence, about the PMEST formula is that the scheme, in practice, decides for us what is [P] or [M] or [E] and gives the individual classifier the benefit of a predictable and fairly consistent pattern that can be applied to each subject area. It has flaws and most faceted schemes have not copied it slavishly; they have, nevertheless, found it an interesting and influential factor in grappling with the crucial question of citation order which – within each and every subject field – does so much to determine order and collocation. Ranganathan's own restlessness with the formula is indicated by a change in CC's seventh edition – many properties and some activities are now deemed to be a manifestation not of Energy, but of Matter.

Micro order: sequence within classes: order of co-ordinates inside a single facet. In addition to the problem of citation order within any individual class, we also have the problem of arranging topics which are co-ordinate or equal in rank within a facet. Should *French literature* and *German literature* come before or after *English literature?* Should *lectures* come before or after *tutorials* within the 'Teaching methods' facet of the subject Education? In contrast to the matter of the combination order of facets, this is the question of sequence among equals that exist within each and every facet. Various methods can be used on appropriate occasions; these are enumerated below, but no one method can be said to be advantageous for *all* situations and indeed some methods are not relevant for many of the subject areas for their significance is restricted to certain disciplines or topics. The possible methods include:

1) An order which is traditional or customary.
2) Chronological order.
3) Geographical order.
4) Developmental or evolutionary order.
5) Favoured category order; (ie, English might thus be given precedence over other languages in a scheme designed mainly for English-speaking countries).
6) Alphabetical order (often useful – but can be over-employed).
7) Order of serial dependance. (Known too as gradation by speciality.)

Many of these sequences are self explanatory, but the last is a notion especially associated with Bliss. It argues that, in a series of co-ordinates, some classes or concepts will draw on the findings of others and depend upon those findings. The dependant classes or concepts are, in a sense, more specialized and should follow those on which they depend.

Sometimes the best order within an array of co-ordinates and the selection of a concept or focus to be *primus inter pares* will be obvious; on other occasions it will not. But all the alternatives should be carefully reviewed, for order of co-ordinates within a facet, although not really as vital to a scheme's structure as the question of citation order, undoubtedly has its part to play also in the total achievement of a sequence of the optimum usefulness within a given subject field or discipline.

Filing order. An interesting and important question which concerns any classification with at least an element of synthesis is – how do we file compound themes consistently so as to reconcile detail with helpful order? How does *18th-century English drama* file in relation to *18th-century literature* or *English drama* (in general)? How does *the administration of manuscript collections* stand in relation to, say, *the administration of British academic libraries*, or to *the administration of manuscript collections in British academic libraries*? The key to the question lies in the citation order of the scheme used. Facets are cited so that the most concrete, significant or important facet (we may use what adjective we will) comes first; remaining facets are cited in diminishing order of importance. Thus, it may be repeated, it is in the facets that are cited last that the scattering of related material occurs and is presumably most tolerable. Hence our filing order must ensure that the final linear sequence brings together ideas or concepts from the facets which are deemed to be significant and appear early in the citation order and confines scattering as far as possible to ideas or concepts from the facets which are cited later. How *do* we ensure this? Odd though it may seem at first acquaintance, we ensure it by filing facets in the order which is the exact reverse of that in which they are cited. But this 'principle of inversion' is best demonstrated by examples which are notated. Consider the following notated examples which come from CC, UDC, and a draft of a faceted scheme for literature (which appears as a short appendix to Chapter 5).

1) To take the literature example first of all, it is recognized that the citation order of facets should be one of *decreasing concreteness*, the most important facets being to the fore for combination purposes –

B	ds	I	o4
English literature –	Shakespeare –	Drama –	Essays

But, in a general to special sequence, *English drama* BI would come before *Essays on Shakespearian drama* and *Essays on English literature* BO4 would precede both documents. Thus o4 files before I and I before ds; that is the vertical filing order of elements should be one of increasing concreteness for a sequence of the optimum value to be attained.

3

2) Our UDC example in an earlier chapter is:

338.585.3(729)"324" Cost of living in the West Indies in winter. We may need to file this in relation to other documents in the same subject region and the correct sequence (assuming our citation order is accepted) must be:

338.585.3   Cost of living (in general).
338.585.3"324"   Cost of living in winter (no place specified).
338.585.3(729)   Cost of living in West Indies (no time specified).
338.585.3(729)"324" Cost of living in West Indies in winter.

In an acknowledged general to special arrangement the position of the first and last items in the above example is surely self-evident. Their intermediaries are positioned by arguing that filing order reverses citation order. Thus, since (729) is *cited* before "324" we file 338.585.3"324" before 338.585.3(729). The result is the one we want, for the scattering in the short example relates to time and not to place – the two documents containing 'West Indies' are together.

3) The idea that the (vertical) filing order of elements must be the reverse of the (horizontal) citation order can be demonstrated also by the example from CC which uses no fewer than *five* facets. There are too many possible combinations to justify a complete enumeration below, but – given the validity of the citation order – the following ten may vindicate the principle of inversion – filing TSEMP – as a device for bringing out in a sequence the desired effects of that order.

Main class	2				Library science
2	[T]				Libraries in the 1970s
2	[S]				Libraries in Britain
2	[S]	[T]			Libraries in Britain in the 1970s
2	[E]				Library Administration
2	[E]	[S]			Library Administration in Britain
2	[P]				Academic libraries
2	[P]	[T]			Academic libraries in the 1970s
2	[P]	[S]	[T]		Academic libraries in Britain in the 1970s
2	[P]	[E]	[S]	[T]	Administration of academic libraries in Britain in the 1970s
2	[P]	[M]	[E]	[S]	[T]	Administration of MSS in British academic libraries in the 1970s

The sequence is incomplete, but it reveals a general to special order with collocation under the [P] facet, a little less under [E] ([M] until recently was rarely used in practice) and much scattering under [S] and [T]. Unlike UDC which is slightly flexible in this respect, CC recognizes and consistently applies this inversion principle. Those who claim to disagree with the principle – presumably in the interests of flexibility and individual liberty – should try out examples both with and without the use of the inversion idea and ask themselves if the 'flexibility' is worth the resulting confusion if this rule is abandoned. In short, the inversion rule is infallible; if it does not produce the right results in a full and representative range of examples, then the citation order itself is faulty. The rule is one which, as we shall see, has implications for the allocation of notation within a faceted scheme.

There is also a simple, but not insignificant filing matter relating to complex, or multi-phased, subjects. The rule for these is that they *follow* subjects dealing with the primary phase only, but precede subject sub-divisions of that topic. So we might have a general to special sequence such as:

Workshop technology (in general)
Workshop technology for mechanical engineers (bias phase)
Foundries ⎫
Pattern and die making ⎬ subject divisions of workshop technology

This is eminently sensible and easy enough to achieve, although there are again notational implications, within a scheme which makes a wholehearted attempt to come to terms – via synthesis – with the various complex subjects that now exist.

The A–Z subject index. There remains to be considered only the contribution of the index. A necessity in any sound classification is an alphabetical subject key which lists topics, locates them and includes all necessary synonyms. Classified order is more complex than an A–Z sequence of topics, but it is also far more useful; that is why the alphabetical order is, apart from its occasional use within a few specific classes, reserved for the index. It must be stressed that the alphabetical index is no substitute for a good classification. The suggestion has been made that 'it does not matter where we classify a book so long as it is properly indexed'. This is very specious reasoning; it might be acceptable if the only purpose of classification was to make the finding of particular books an easy process. There the advantage, or merit, of a system which places books in an indifferent manner and relies upon the index, ends. It is only a *small part* of the work of classification to make the finding of particular books easy, although admittedly a most convenient and practical part. The accepted definition of classification not only implies this, it implies a cardinal purpose which this ignores – the arrangement of books so that the likeness in subject matter between them is revealed. Thus a classification cannot justly be called a good one which does not show a true sequence of subjects; demonstrate to the left of a particular document, or group of documents, the documents which lead up to it, and to the right those that lead away from it. The same principle holds, of course, for a classified catalogue or bibliography. It must be reiterated that classification is primarily an arrangement with a definite collocating function and not a mere random filing of books or entries in separate subject compartments with an alphabetical index. Melvil Dewey once rashly claimed that the fine DC index was the most important feature of his scheme. No index can be that; an alphabetical order might be rich in literal mnemonics, but this is more than offset by its utter inability, except occasionally and then by chance, to group related topics. The understandable appeal of alphabetical simplicity and the less understandable cry that a good index can atone for a faulty classification have proved, in certain quarters, to be perennial attractions in the history of our subject. The latter erroneous notion was described by Bliss as the 'subject index illusion'. He stated that 'no index, however convenient or necessary, can convert an arbitrary or disordered arrangement into a systematic classification'.

The index is, nevertheless, an essential tool. Having stressed that it cannot be expected to do the work of the classification, we must see what duties we *do* expect it to perform. A good index should carry out thoroughly two definite functions. It must:

(*a*) locate topics within the systematically arranged classification;
(*b*) show related aspects of a subject which the classification has scattered, for no classification can bring together *all* branches of a complex subject. By collecting these 'distributed relatives' as Savage has so aptly called them, the index reveals subject relationships, albeit usually minor ones, which the classification has been forced to ignore and these are thus rescued from oblivion.

In carrying out these functions the index should strive to complement, rather than duplicate the work of the scheme. It should not, therefore, repeat information which is easily accessible in the main tables. It must also be noted that it is most unwise for the classifier to try to place books in the scheme by using the index alone. Indeed it is essential that the index should be used merely as a check; the classifier must find the appropriate place in the tables and ensure that the specific class-mark chosen is correct, and that the containing general heading is a suitable one. This tends to assume that the classification concerned is of the basically enumerative type; if, in fact, it is entirely synthetic there should be less chance of error once principles are mastered. Nevertheless the index must only be used in practical classification in conjunction with the schedules.

The indexes of nearly all schemes are described as relative, since they *do* seek to show relationships in addition to locating topics. Some relative indexes, however, although reasonably efficient, are bulky and wasteful in the sense that they repeat the display of subject associations shown in the classification schedules. Consider an example from the original BC, part of which is set out below, including entries that are essential, but some others which are superfluous.

Literature in general	YU
Benefits of	YUA
Censorship in	YUM
Genius in	YUH
Pathos in	YUO
Religious	PAW
Teaching literature	JKW
Transcendental	YUI

Is it really necessary to repeat *all* the divisions of YU from the schedules in the index? (Including synonyms, the BC index enumerates 104 divisions of YU under this heading.) To be economical as well as functional, the relative index should merely *support* the classification by locating topics and displaying the scheme's *distributed* relatives. It need not repeat the (presumably major) associations which the scheme itself indicates through its choice of citation order and grouping. A good example of such indexing can be seen in the DC extract on page 70, which is, by and large, both sound and frugal – although some additional terms under this heading are possibly superfluous too.

As a final word on the important question of the index, it should be mentioned that one scheme, Brown's *Subject Classification*, offered a rather different kind of index. To a large extent, this index

Drugs

Control: public administration	350.765
Ethics	178.8
Manufacturing: production economics	338.47615191
Pharmacology	615.1
Social Services	363.45

wrongly presumed that SC had succeeded in locating all material on one subject at one constant, specific and unmistakable place. It thus offered locations, but made little attempt to display distributed relatives – they were claimed to be non-existent. Such an index, called by Berwick Sayers a specific index, is an incomplete tool and in SC it is part and parcel of Brown's total outlook and philosophy. It ignores the problem of classification by discipline and the basic fact that all classification scatters as it collects. No such index can be really effective, since we *do* expect an index to show relationships (presumably comparatively minor ones) not expressed in the scheme; these are, in any given subject field, those concerning the facets which appear late in the citation order or relationships which have, on balance, been wisely sacrificed in the schedules in order to distribute sensibly certain themes according to context or discipline.

We have, after some important preliminaries, considered the achievement of helpful order in a classification at the broad level and at the more important level within subject areas where what is collocated and what is scattered is determined largely by measures such as citation order and the inversion principle in the filing of facets, with the index displaying distributed subject relatives. The question of the importance of helpful order in relation to detail was posed at the outset and answered to the effect that both are possible and may well be necessary. There may be value, however, in concluding with the similar query: just how important *is* order within a classification? Certainly it is not the sole guarantee of success in terms of the use made of a scheme; were it so, we would rightly conclude that the most used schemes have the most satisfactory order. There are obviously several other factors which also help to determine the success or failure of our classifications, but the quest for helpful order still remains significant and the ideas of Bliss and Ranganathan in particular provide an apparatus with which we can appraise the order of any scheme. In some subject fields there are various orders which may seem to have equally good claims and any one preferred order then has grave weaknesses, although it provides consistency and banishes cross-classification. In other subject areas, we may as yet know too little about reader preference and the use made of the literature to regard any one chosen order with confidence. In every subject field the order chosen, however helpful, must be well displayed and supported by guiding which is clear, ample and – on occasion – imaginative. Yet, when all this is said, the search for a helpful sequence within each subject field and the scrutiny and appraisal of sequences within existing classifications remains vital if we regard that part of the technical processes we call classifying as classification in the truest sense of that word and not a mere exercise in pigeon-holing.

CHAPTER FIVE

Notation

Notation has, of necessity, already been used to demonstrate the principles discussed, but it demands separate and more lengthy consideration. As a method for concisely indicating the subject content of books and other documents which have been systematically arranged, its aim is to show the sequence of the chosen arrangement and assist in simplifying the maintenance of the order. Many disciplines have a series of symbols which, like the notations of classification systems, stand in the place of terms. Even punctuation is a notation of a kind – a comma is a symbol indicating that here you take breath; a full stop indicates that the expression of an idea ends here; and so on, throughout the literary symbols: each is a shorthand sign. But probably the most vivid example that we can contrast with notation as used in classifying, is that of the symbols employed by chemists to indicate chemical elements and compounds. Notation is a very necessary auxiliary feature in systematic arrangement, as we cannot put at full-length the names of subjects upon every book and against every entry in our catalogues. Even if we could, the result would not make the sequence readily apparent.

As notation is merely symbols standing in place of terms, it cannot be more important than the terms themselves; it is a piece of apparatus, added after the classification schedule has been planned. This may seem obvious enough, but there have been so many wrangles about notation that one might almost be forgiven for concluding that it is the one thing that really matters in classification. Many other things matter also and notation should in no way pre-determine the structure and arrangement within a scheme. There has been a tendency in some quarters virtually to equate notation with classification; this is very wrong, for many systems which ignore symbols and index documents by means of alphabetical subject terms and phrases inject a degree of classification (often informally and at times quite unconsciously) into the natural language indexing. Bliss once wrote, in a personal communication to a British colleague,[1] 'I regard notation as a subsidiary device, and I hold that classification . . . deals rather with the concepts, or their terms.' This expresses the place of notation very neatly. Nevertheless, as it is essential to the practicability of a formal classification, representing it on the spines of books and on various records and acting as the link between the alphabetical subject index to the scheme and the classification schedules, it is by no means negligible. Its qualities and functions should be carefully considered.

A notation, from which we derive our call-marks, may be made up of figures, Arabic or Roman; of letters; of various arbitrary signs; or of a mixture of several or all of these. A notation which consists of only one type of symbol is said to be *pure*; one consisting of two or more types of symbol is a *mixed* notation. Most notations are, in fact, of the latter variety and mixed notations have been commended by some writers, including Bliss. The outstanding example of a pure notation can be seen in the DC. Such a pure notation of numbers has definite advantages in that it is internationally acceptable, creates no difficulty in conveying order to us clearly, and is relatively simple. It also, alas, has drawbacks, in as much as it imposes a restrictive pattern upon knowledge – a pattern which makes it appear that each topic divides conveniently into nine or ten parts and that no subject has more than ten subdivisions. Fremont Rider, whose *International Classification* (1961) is the latest general scheme to be published, has praised the pure notation of the Dewey scheme and believes that it has made an enormous contribution to the success of that classification throughout the world. But a decimal notation has a narrow base; that is to say, it can only accommodate nine topics (or ten, if the zero is used) at each step of division. It is significant that Rider, in his own classification, decided to use a pure notation of letters, offering twenty-six places at each step of division. The increase in the *capacity* of the notation to house topics, where the alphabet is used, is enormous – although capacity is gained at the expense of some loss in international appeal and significance. However, many schemes do prefer mixed notations, beginning with a base of letters but employing numbers also as more specific topics or concepts are identified.

[1] Letter to C. B. Freeman, University of Hull, Institute of Education Library, September 19, 1950.

The features of a good notation that are most commonly accepted may be summarized as follows:

(*a*) It should be as brief as possible.

(*b*) Notation ought to be simple – easy to say, to read and to write or type.

(*c*) It *must* convey clearly the order of subjects in the scheme.

(*d*) It should, if possible, reveal the hierarchy of the system, indicating by its length and structure which subjects are equal in rank or to which theme a specific topic has been subordinated.

(*e*) Notation *must* be hospitable to new topics and should permit any theme that is new to the system to be inserted into the most appropriate place in the existing system, so that helpful order is preserved.

(*f*) It may have special mnemonic aids to promote and assist the librarian's ability to recollect class-marks. In some schemes these *mnemonics* also assist in correctly forecasting the class-mark for a new topic.

(*g*) Notation should reveal each change of facet and cater for phase relationships.

Each of these features deserves further comment. With regard to brevity, Bliss argued that a notation should be 'as short as is feasible' and the British writer Raymond Moss has, in various papers, shown how long notations are difficult to retain in the mind and may well lead to inefficiency. Long class-marks may possibly be tolerated in bibliographies and catalogues, but they are certainly an impediment to the easy maintenance of the classified order of books. In addition, they may hinder the task of notation in acting as the effective link between the catalogue and the shelves. If we can make two symbols, say, stand for a subject instead of three or four, it is evident that class-marks will be more easily written, typed and remembered. It is sometimes thought that specific classification is the *sole* reason for long notations, but this is not so. There are at least four separate factors which help to determine the brevity or otherwise of a notation.

1) *The amount of detail provided.* Sometimes one can classify precisely and keep notation short, but often this is not possible and a choice between brevity of class-marks and specificity in arrangement must be made.

2) *The allocation or apportionment of notation to subjects.* Some specific topics have long class-marks in a scheme partly because the subject field to which they belong has been given too small a slice of the notational cake. Other subject areas, to which too much of the notational base has been allocated may then have some unused notation.

3) *Notation can be shorter if it gives up the idea of consistently displaying the structure or hierarchy of the classification served.* (This is discussed below.)

4) *An alphabetical notation tends to be shorter than a numerical one.* A notation of decimal numbers, used hierarchically, offers nine places, but an alphabetical base caters for twenty-six co-ordinate topics and even a mixed notation based on letters has a much higher capacity than a purely numerical one. Or, to look at the question from a slightly different viewpoint, let us imagine that a classification is based on traditional ideas and has to accommodate 17,000 topics. A pure notation of letters, if non-hierarchical and fully employed, could cope with these without ever exceeding a three-letter maximum; Rider's scheme illustrates this point very well. A pure notation of numbers, however, would have some class-marks of five-figure length to cope with these subjects. Thus Dewey's choice of the decimal numbers has not promoted notational brevity, although there are, of course, other factors which can be cited in its favour.

Brevity is much more important in manual than in mechanized systems. The four ways of achieving it which have been noted are all used to good effect in BC. The notation here is mainly composed of capital letters and has been allocated with scrupulous care. It does not necessarily lengthen by one symbol at each step of division in order to display hierarchical progression and detail has been sacrificed – in the original BC, at least – if it interferes too much with the aim of short class-marks. Ranganathan and Bliss differed on this last point, the Indian librarian insisting that notation is a tool for librarians which need not hamper readers and pointing out the merits of what he called 'co-extensiveness of subject and class-mark'. Long notations hinder the easy maintenance of the classified sequence on the shelves, but for large libraries specific arrangement is important; otherwise items on specialized topics will be lost among material on a more general theme. One cannot be too dogmatic here for much depends on particular situations, but the detail should be there for the larger libraries; smaller ones can always simplify the system if they wish.

Simplicity of notation is often associated with the ability to convey the chosen sequence of subjects. It is also closely linked with brevity, but the two things are not the same. Simplicity depends on the length of notation, but also on the type of symbol used. A comparatively brief notation using capital and lower-case letters and, say, squares or triangles would not be simple to use. Any employment of points, commas, colons, or other punctuation marks detracts from the simplicity of a notation, although – in a sense – it may help brevity by breaking a lengthy class-mark into manageable groups of digits. It is advantageous also to have a notation that can be quickly placed on various records and can be easily read or pronounced. Brevity and simplicity in the conventional sense will do much to achieve this for us, but a pure notation is probably better, in this respect, than a mixed one of equal length. For instance, 624.58 is easier to say and recollect than AB73K. We may note the interest shown these days in the phonic as well as the graphic length of notations. Research has been carried out with regard to letter notations that are readily pronounceable – is this not the age of pronounceable abbreviations?

The work of Eric De Grolier is significant in this respect and, of the special schemes made, D. J. Foskett's London Education Classification is still the outstanding example of a letter notation where each focus employs three symbols, the second of which is a vowel, to give a syllabic or pronounceable effect. Thus we have elements or foci such as:

Jip   Assessment
Mob   Sciences
Ser   Further education

So that Ser Mob Jip would represent *Assessment of scientific subjects within further education*, and note that the significant fact that the citation order is the reverse of the alphabetical notational sequence greatly facilitates the correct use of the inversion principle. The class-marks are certainly easy to say and recollect here, but the results are somewhat humorous (the school dentist is, for example, elevated to the status of God!) Pronounceable notations may well be an asset for simplicity in certain situations, but they must be applied with great care.

Ability to convey order is of supreme importance. Unless the sequence of the classification is quickly demonstrated by the notation, it will be impossible to locate classes readily on the shelves or in the classified catalogue. The notation must, then, serve as an indication of the place occupied by a topic within the classification and, as such, it is invaluable in referring readers and staff quickly from the catalogue to the classified arrangement on the shelves; it is also necessary that it should demonstrate the sequence in the main part of the classified catalogue. Thus the ordinal value of the notation cannot be over-emphasized. Arbitrary signs which convey no definite order should rarely, if ever, be used; they must be rejected in favour of numbers or letters. Perhaps the former convey order most readily and it may also be thought that any pure notation will reveal the sequence of the classification more readily than a mixed one. It is dangerous to be too dogmatic about the relative merits of letters and figures in this respect and the choice as far as this feature of notation is concerned will depend largely on personal preference; we can nevertheless say with certainty that a notation which failed to reveal the classified order would be quite useless. True, some schemes, especially those designed for documentation purposes, make some use of symbols which have no apparent filing order; in these cases the classificationist must determine an appropriate order for users of the scheme to observe and follow. But all modern systems employ, for the most part, letters and figures. If they did not use one or both of these types of symbol they would prevent the librarian from clearly guiding the sequence and it would be extremely difficult for the reader to find his way easily around the organized arrangement on the shelves; it would be most difficult for staff and readers to use the catalogue freely; and the task of returning a volume to its proper place on the shelves quickly would be a laborious one. Because every practical notation *does* in fact convey order, notation is sometimes said to *mechanize* the classified arrangement – that is to say, it makes the replacement of volumes in the classified sequence a simple and mechanical task.

In addition to its ordinal significance, notation *may* demonstrate the hierarchy or structure of the classification scheme. We use the word 'may' advisedly here. In the past, it was almost automatically assumed by librarians that the notation expressed the relationship between topics. That is to say, that as the classification divides classes into divisions, and these in turn into sub-divisions, so it was expected that the rank of any topic would be discernible from its class-mark. Indeed, most people still do assume this; they think that 824 represents a class which is a division of 820, which is in turn a branch of class 800. Likewise, ABF is taken to be a sub-division of class AB, if an aphabetical notation is employed. It would be assumed also that class-marks such as 821, 822, 823, 824, or ABA, ABB, ABC, ABD, represented topics of equal status from the same array of classes. Earlier editions of this *Manual* would emphatically support the notation which expressed the hierarchy of a scheme; nowadays we are not so sure. Modern classification theory has shown that a non-structural notation also has definite merits. Nor do the established general schemes themselves provide us with a clear guide. They all have notations which convey order (although the schemes of Bliss and Ranganathan and the *Universal Decimal Classification* do include some symbols which cannot convey a sequence automatically to us). When it comes to the question of the notation expressing the hierarchy, however, we find that the *Decimal*, *Universal Decimal* and *Colon Classifications* attempt, for the most part, to do this; the LC and BC notations are often more casual in that they may or may not express the structure or hierarchy of the scheme and indeed there is a considerable departure from the idea of *structural, hierarchical or expressive notation*, as it is variously called, in the new edition of the BC and in some specialized systems, notably the English Electric Company's *Thesaurofacet*. Other special schemes, such as the *London Classification of Business Studies* (1970) retain the idea of a hierarchical notation.

The benefits of a notation which *is* expressive may be summarized as follows:

1) One normally expects the notation to reveal the hierarchy – thus confusion may arise if it does not. It is also easier to broaden or narrow down a subject search if the notation expresses the classification's hierarchy.

2) A hierarchical, or structural notation, facilitates the compilation of the subject index to a classified catalogue by the procedure known as *chain indexing*. (This is described in Chapter 15.)

3) The guiding of the classified shelves or of the classified catalogue may be more easily accomplished if the notation is of the hierarchical type.

4) It is probably easier to remember hierarchical notations than non-hierarchical ones of equal length.

5) The structural notations may have especial merit in mechanized

information retrieval in that the logical expression of the hierarchy through the length of the notation can assist the computer in the broadening or narrowing down of a subject search.

Some disadvantages which should be noted are:

1) It is extremely difficult for any notation to be completely hierarchical and in any case, as Coates once remarked, 'a hierarchical notation implies an unchangeable hierarchy'.
2) A non-structural notation may be much briefer than a hierarchical one.
3) The length of each array may be freely manipulated in a non-structural notation; thus it is far more hospitable than the traditional type of notation to the inclusion of new topics at the most appropriate point of the classification.
4) It is often difficult for mixed notations (and nearly all modern systems rely on these) to reveal the hierarchy of the scheme clearly.
5) A structural notation may waste symbols, as many figures or letters in a particular array may remain unused.

Research has shown that non-hierarchical or merely ordinal notations (that is where the notation shows subject sequence, but not subject status) are worthy of serious consideration and the points made about brevity and hospitality warrant further explanation. The gain in brevity with a non-hierarchical notation can be illustrated, for instance, by means of an example with two imaginary notations – the one is structural, or expressive; the other is merely ordinal:

Hierarchical or expressive notation	*Subject*	*Non-structural notation*
A	Technology	A
AB	Chemical technology	AB
ABR	Metallurgy	AX
ABRG	Non-ferrous metals	AXD
ABRGL	Light metals	AXN
ABRGLP	Magnesium	AXW

It will be seen from this illustration that the completely hierarchical notation lengthens by one symbol at each step of division in the subject chain. The notation which simply concentrates on conveying order without attempting to signify the structure of the scheme, however, may not do this. In our example above with a pure notation of capital letters, the non-structural notation allocates to a sub-division of class AB the notation AX. These classes look co-ordinate, but they are not; likewise AXW represents a sub-division of the class denoted by AXN and this, in turn, is actually a sub-division of the class represented by AXD. Thus, in a non-hierarchical notation, arrays can be lengthened or shortened, depending on the needs of the literature in each class – the notation no longer dictates the pattern in which knowledge must be presented in the classification. The non-expressive notation is also briefer; our class-marks for Magnesium clearly indicate this. Some readers may favour the notation that clearly expresses the hierarchy as being the more logical of the two. Certainly it clearly shows which classes are of equal status and which are branches of larger classes; the benefits of this must be weighed against the need for concise notations and an alphabetical, non-structural notation can certainly achieve brevity by shortening the arrays, while the hierarchy of the classification can still be indicated by suitable indentation in the schedules themselves. Indeed, the non-structural notation of Coates's *British Catalogue of Music Classification* even affords the occasional example of a well-documented sub-division being represented by a shorter class-mark than its parent class.

An attribute, or quality, without which notation would be quite valueless is that of hospitality – the ability to accommodate new topics and concepts. Without this, the maintenance of a helpful order would be impossible. It can be said that a notation is perfectly hospitable when, by the addition of a symbol or symbols, any new subject may be inserted into any place in the classification without dislocating the sequence of either the notation or the classification itself. One rather important point may be noted before the ways of achieving hospitality are considered; most schemes are hospitable in that new subjects can be accommodated, but sometimes the new topic cannot be inserted into the most logical and *useful* place in the existing sequence, as the notation is not completely hospitable.

Methods for obtaining hospitality are:

1) By leaving gaps between numbers or letters. Thus, if we consider the sequence represented by different types of notation –

7273	ABHM	RK 16
7274	ABHO	RK 17
7275	ABHP	RK 18
7277	ABHQ	RK 20

it is clear that, if these class-marks are all in use, new topics may be inserted in the pure notations and the mixed one at 7276, ABHN, and RK 19 respectively. But this idea is crude and most unsatisfactory in practice; the gaps will soon be filled, making further expansion by this method impossible. Also, no classificationist can anticipate all future developments in knowledge and so there is no assurance that the gaps will have been left in the most appropriate places; subjects may have to be forced into the nearest available pigeon-hole.

2) A more useful notion is to recognize from the outset that a notation will be used in the decimal sense. The *Dewey Decimal Classification* has a notation which permits a chain of classes to be indefinitely extended thus:

562.1
562.11
562.111, etc.

Of course, the class numbers for many of the highly specific subjects which librarians have to classify these days will be long; but this is almost inevitable in a general classification, where we must choose between a broad arrangement of knowledge as presented in books or specificity with comparatively long class-marks. Decimal notation is a tremendous improvement on the gap idea in achieving notational hospitality and it is also vastly superior to notations of the integral, or arithmetical, kind. There is more hope for hospitality in thinking of, say, 712 as a division of 71 than in thinking of these numbers as separated – seventy-one and seven hundred and twelve.

3) Notations of faceted systems are in fact extremely flexible, for they can grow in more ways than one. Traditional notations can only be extended by adding symbols at the right-hand end of each class-mark or by the leaving of gaps; the faceted notation, on the other hand, permits the extension of the symbols representing any of the isolates involved.

Thus, in CC (6th edition):

R4.56'N denotes Ethics in Britain in the twentieth century;
(R 4 being ethics, 56 Britain and N representing the Time isolate).
R 42.56'N stands for Family ethics in twentieth-century Britain;
(this reveals an extension of the focus in the Personality facet).
R 42.56124'N denotes Family ethics in twentieth-century London;
(showing further extension, this time involving the Space focus).
R 4217.56124'N denotes Marriage ethics in twentieth-century
London;
(further extension of the focus in the Personality facet).

There are many other possible extensions with the above example;
nevertheless the ones quoted should serve to show the possibilities
of a faceted scheme with regard to notational hospitality. True, the
Colon Classification often has a complicated notation and the filing
order of documents has to be carefully noted when dealing with
examples such as the above; yet, from the point of view of flexibility
in accommodating new topics, it might almost be said that Ranganathan's faceted approach has provided us with a new dimension
in notation. Our earlier CC example can likewise be expanded to
(for instance) 'The administration of manuscript collections in
University libraries in *Wales* in the 1970s'.

4) There is no guarantee of perfect hospitality from the above
measures. Decimal notation allows the extension of a *chain* of classes
and a scheme which is faceted in the notational as well as the con-
ceptual sphere enables any element or focus in a compound number
to be sharpened or intensified (witness how Ethics/Britain/twentieth
century becomes *Family* ethics/Britain/twentieth century or *Family*
ethics/London/twentieth century). There remains the problem of
hospitality in an *array* of classes. If our notation offers room for
9 or 26 co-ordinates at each stage of division and these places are
filled, what happens to additional co-ordinate subjects, if there are
any? Also, how can new co-ordinates – assuming that there is room
for them – be inserted into the *most suitable* place in an array rather
than simply into a gap that happens to be available? The traditional
attitude to these problems was largely to ignore them; a striking
example from the DC is that of Electrical Engineering at 621.3,
which should have been shown as co-ordinate with Mechanical
Engineering at 621, but which has been forced by the notational
structure of the scheme into what appears as a subordinate position.
Ranganathan tried to provide means for the extension of an array

by what he calls the Sector Device (originally termed *Octave Device*). This involves the last symbol in each array being reserved for the special purpose of extending that array. Therefore, in a numerical notation, the 9 would never stand alone; it would serve to introduce more co-ordinate classes and a typical array might be:

581 582 583 584 . . . 588 5891 5892 etc.

The idea certainly has merit and is similar to the notion employed in the 400 and 800 classes of the *Dewey Decimal system* where, in Linguistics for example, 420 430 . . . 480 represent the major languages and minor ones are shown at 491 492, etc. Dewey does not seem to have fully worked out this idea and it does not, in any case, solve the problem of inserting new topics at the most suitable point in existing arrays for, while it encourages the addition of new subjects at the end of an array (*extrapolation*), it does not permit the *interpolation* of topics at any point. A similar inherent weakness exists in the UDC idea of *centesimal notation*. This means that instead of using .1 to .9 as decimal sub-divisions, we extend the base and employ .11 to .99 for an array. The practice has merit, for the capacity of the array can, if needed, be increased enormously in this way, but there is still no assurance that a new topic can be successfully interpolated at any point. The centesimal and sectorizing devices may be considered together as an interesting venture, but not a completely successful one, for coping with the problem of hospitality in array.

5) Remaining with the problem of interpolating new co-ordinates into an existing array, it can be admitted that this can and is sometimes achieved by the relocation of topics. Indeed, although extensive relocations are always distasteful to libraries employing the scheme concerned, some transfer is often necessary; 'new' subjects often do not appear overnight but are older topics which have grown in stature and demand a fresh place in the hierarchy. Leaving aside the sector and centesimal devices and the possibility of achieving hospitality by the judicious transfer of subjects and disturbance of the existing order, it may still be asked – is there a way to produce a notation which is truly hospitable in array as well as in chain? The affirmative answer takes us back to the idea that a notation need not be hierarchical or expressive. If we accept that the notation is non-expressive and we see a sequence –

A   AK   AN   AT   B   BG   BL   BV

we know the *order* of the eight subjects represented, but we do not know from the symbols alone if AK, for example, is subordinate to A or whether the two class-marks represent co-ordinate topics. Thus, in making a new scheme, it is possible to have completely hospitable arrays with infinite possibilities for interpolation provided that a non-structural notation, with its problems as well as its strengths, is accepted and provided that the notation is suitably planned and allocated. The sub-divisions of a class, say K, must begin at KB rather than KA, for instance, to allow for further possible interpolation between K and KB. This in turn might be at KAL to allow further scope for insertion between the new subject and K. A numerical notation would be subject to the same kind of planning if used in purely an ordinal and not in a hierarchical sense and with maximum hospitality as a primary goal.

We now leave the topic of notational expansibility, important though it undoubtedly is, and consider some other features which a notation may possess. One of these is memory value, or mnemonic qualities. By mnemonic notation we usually mean that whenever a topic appears in the classification it is represented by the same symbols. It is quite impossible to do this for all topics or concepts, but many recurring forms of presentation, for example, can be constantly represented by particular letters or figures. Thus, in the *Decimal Classification*, we tend to associate the symbol 05 with periodicals and 09 is linked with the standard sub-division which can be added to any subject number to indicate that the subject is treated from a historical viewpoint. Likewise, the *Decimal Classification* has an area table in which each country is represented by a distinctive number. These numbers can be added to subject class-marks at various parts of the classification to indicate that a subject is confined to a particular geographical region. The continual representation of certain ideas by the same digits is useful to the librarian as it enables him to remember many class-numbers and to deduce others from the mnemonic features supplied. There are many more examples of such mnemonics in the *Decimal Classification* and in the majority of other schemes; examples are given in Section Three of this *Manual* and many more can be gleaned from an examination of the classifications themselves. Here it will be enough for us to recognize that mnemonics are not a vital feature of notation – they may help the librarian, but are rarely if ever of direct assistance to readers – and to note that there are distinctive ways in which mnemonics can be used in notation.

Systematic mnemonics are the main type and relate to the definition of mnemonics we have already given. They occur whenever a topic or form of presentation is continually represented by the same symbols, as in the periodicals and history examples given from Dewey's scheme above. Their value lies in the fact that the classifier quickly becomes familiar with the scheme because of the repetitive pattern within much of the notation. A synthetic scheme is particularly rich in mnemonic possibilities, as each basic concept listed within a class will be continually represented by the same letters or digits. If there are exceptions to these systematic mnemonics, they are said to be variable rather than constant; most schemes, however, tend to use such systematic mnemonics as they choose to employ in a consistent manner. Sometimes, if the notation consists purely or partly of letters, we find that another type of mnemonic can be introduced; this second way of providing memory value in the notation is known as the use of *literal mnemonics*. These arise whenever a topic is represented by its initial letter or letters. Thus, to use a few examples from Bliss's scheme, U stands for Useful Arts, UE for Engineering, and in Class US – Mechanic Arts and Trades – USC denotes Carpentry. Of these two varieties of mnemonic notation, the literal mnemonics are certainly the least valuable. They can of course occur only in notations which employ letters, and in addition to this there is the danger that if the classificationist places too much value on them they may be over-employed and the preferred order may be distorted merely to gain mnemonic effect. This would inevitably lead us back eventually to alphabetical subject arrangement, with its scattering of kindred topics. But the literal mnemonics may be used whenever it is possible to have them *without* disturbing the carefully worked out helpful order of subjects. The examples cited from the *Bibliographic Classification* illustrate just such an occasion. Bliss was far too convinced of the need for a scholarly and practical arrangement to fall into the trap of allowing the notation or its mnemonic features to detract from the carefully worked out systematic order; thus his literal mnemonics appear only when the accepted order permits and some of the mnemonic possibilities of this idea have been ignored in the interests of the sequence of topics in the classification.

Yet another form of memory aid, albeit a specialized and possibly subjective one, can be seen in the *seminal mnemonics* of CC. Here it is claimed that, if related basic concepts are continually associated with each other and if each group of concepts so related is continually associated with a particular digit, then we will have not only a memory aid but also a powerful apparatus which enables the individual classifier to anticipate new class-marks. It is this latter feature which distinguishes seminal mnemonics from the more customary (systematic) mnemonic aids of faceted classifications. Thus, in CC the digit 1, for example, is used as a mnemonic for a cluster of ideas deemed to be related. These include – wholeness, unity, God, the world. They are all to be associated with the number 1. So, if we are classifying a subject and one concept is new, in the sense that it is not explicitly stated in the schedules, we can safely assume that 1 is the digit for it, provided it is associated with one of the above ideas or a correlated one from this group. The idea behind seminal mnemonics was to provide classifiers with the power to anticipate revision correctly and arrive at a new class-mark without awaiting revised schedules. The attempt to make CC almost self-perpetuating along these lines has not succeeded, although the mnemonics associated with these numbers are infectious, for some of us and have, on occasions, proved their worth in practice.

Systematic mnemonics are, in most situations, certainly much more prevalent and probably more useful than either literal mnemonics, which *can* confuse rather than assist us (eg, in LC the symbol AM stands for Museums; in BC the M in AM represents Mathematics) or the experimental seminal mnemonics into which, we are told, classifiers can have special insight. Memory aids anyway are very much a tool for the librarian and the reader is likely to benefit much more from guiding and staff help in finding his way about a classified library. Aids for librarians, who themselves are striving to aid readers, cannot be lightly dismissed, but all mnemonics are inevitably affected by psychology and personal idiosyncracies – what is a mnemonic to one person may not be to another.[1] The most used of the systematic mnemonics that are directly the result of synthesis are certainly a memory aid, but there are limits to the mnemonic power of notation.

Finally, what of the role of notation as a tool for revealing each change of facet or phase? It is clear that in employing synthesis we need to indicate each facet or distinct mode of division. In CC, for example, G.5 means something quite different from G:5 – but punctuation signs are a cumbersome way of revealing the facets of a subject embodied in a class-mark. Nor is the use of the ampersand,

[1] They are also sometimes unintentional, e.g. IC for Perception in the *Bibliographic Classification*.

&, now adopted for the introduction of the secondary phase within a complex subject commendable. UDC, too, employs parentheses, inverted commas and equals signs to introduce the form and geographical divisions and the time and language facets; these are only some of the symbols used and they do not make for simplicity of notation even if we concede that UDC and often CC are aimed at intricate work in the realm of documentation and information retrieval rather than in the helpful order of books on library shelves. Some of these symbols are perhaps inevitable in dealing with multi-faceted subjects and complex topics, but if they can be avoided, so much the better. Perhaps there are alternative ways for librarians to avoid ambiguity in synthetic notation by clearly distinguishing between facets and to show the individual components of each compound or complex theme. Consider the following examples:

Bck8o6
EpmFmWse

The first of these assumes a special subject field with four facets. A citation order having been determined, the facets are represented by capital letters, lower-case letters, numbers and numbers preceded by a zero. We see the class-mark then, in this instance, as one involving all four of the facets:

B/ ck/ 8/ o6

This method was used, for instance, by the author during the 1960s in the construction of a faceted scheme for literature, designed merely to display the principles of faceted classification to students. It is simple enough (accepting that numbers file before letters, so that B8 files before Bck and the principle of inversion applies) but has the problem that it is hardly suitable for a subject area with many facets. The second example uses only letters, but adopts capitals to show a change of facet and lower-case otherwise. It is similar to the class-marks found in early editions of the English Electric Company's faceted classification for engineering.

More revolutionary and in many ways more interesting is the idea of retroactive notation. Mills[1] has shown that an embryonic form of this exists in DC and indeed that scheme's creator and subsequent editors have long been at least partly conscious of the need for what we now call facet indicators – witness the special use of the zero to introduce standard sub-divisions. The idea of retroactive

[1] Mills, J. *A Modern outline of library classification*, Chapman and Hall, 1960, pp. 44–45.

notation supposes that the notation is allocated so that the principal facets in a subject field follow minor facets as far as the notational sequence is concerned. (This has advantages, in any case, from the point of view of the principle of inversion and the maintenance of correct general to special order, as was hinted in discussing the syllabic notation of D. J. Foskett's *London Education Classification*.) Then, assuming an alphabetical notation is used, primary facets can be accommodated towards the end of the alphabet and each facet can be qualified by any facet preceding it. No special facet indicators are needed, since each change of facet can be shown by a reversion to an earlier letter. If we have a planned fully retroactive notation then and see a class-mark SXLMHRY, we know that there are three facets in this imaginary example with foci represented by SX, LM and HRY. Some special faceted schemes have already experimented with this idea for, although it requires careful allocation of notation and perhaps has more scope within the greater capacity of a letter notation than it has with numerals like Dewey's, it does help to reduce the length and complexity of notation while still displaying the faceted structure of the scheme.

In Britain, Mills has been an enthusiast for retroactive notation and there are many examples of its skilful use in the new BC, for instance:

DD	Astronomical bodies
DDF	Stars
DD*JW*	Dwarf stars
DD*K*	Variable stars
DD*KJW*	Variable dwarf stars

or

VW*CO*	Military music
VW*L*	Instrumental music
VW*L CO*	Military instrumental music

In this way, the expression of compound subjects through notational synthesis is greatly encouraged. There are now many such examples, amply explained and applied by Mills, in BC. In an earlier chapter, Ranganathan's analogy between synthetic classification and a Meccano set was mentioned and it was suggested that Lego is a more modern equivalent. If we pursue the dual comparison, it might be said that facet indicators, like the nuts and bolts of Meccano, link elements together, but that efforts are now made – and retroactive notation is a major one – to link the elements, as in Lego, without such awkward aids.

A completed class-mark is not synonymous with a 'call-number'. When we apply our scheme of classification we find that it is often desirable to make a further addition to the notation; this is necessitated by the fact that when several books have exactly the same subject class-mark they must be sub-arranged in author order. Thus we find that most librarians, apart from those with very small collections, find it necessary to attach to the end of the notation on the spine of each book further symbols to complete a full 'call' mark or 'call' number which identifies the individual book and not simply a specific subject. In many cases these symbols are merely the first three letters of the author's surname; they enable us to achieve, within any particular specific class, an exact and convenient arrangement. We realize that BG 7 SMI comes before BG 7 STE, although both notations appear on books dealing with exactly the same topic. We may say then that arrangement within a specific subject class is mechanized by means of such author marks, or that they enable us to have a 'call' or request number from which we can determine the exact position of an item on the shelves. In the United States, more elaborate systems have been conceived to denote the author's name after the class-mark and represent an entire call-number. The most famous of these is that devised by Charles Cutter and subsequently revised by Kate E. Sanborn. These Cutter-Sanborn numbers really involve the provision of a table which enables us to translate the first three letters of authors' surnames into a sequence of figures; the result is that the same author order within a class is achieved, but the author marks are numbers rather than letters.

Arrangements such as this, however, are extremely elaborate. Indeed, even the usual author marks are of slightly debatable value – although one finds that a young student with some experience of work in a library will sometimes argue far more fervently about this comparatively minor matter than about controversies of major importance in our subject. It may be said that author marks of any kind add to the complexity of notation, fail to distinguish between writers with the same surname, and may be odd or ridiculous – to write ROT, for instance, after a class-mark on the spine of a book is hardly the best way to commend the volume to the potential reader. It can also be claimed that the author's name usually appears on the spine of the book and will enable us to achieve an alphabetical sub-arrangement within a class more easily than contractions or figures representing this name. Yet many libraries find these marks worth while, and it is unwise to be too dogmatic about them; we may nevertheless say that, if they are required, it now appears simpler to use the first three letters of the author's name rather than Cutter-Sanborn numbers or similar systems devised by L. S. Jast, J. D. Brown, or the great American classifier, W. S. Merrill. If the student is interested in these, or in the Biscoe Time Numbers – devised to secure final chronological arrangement within a class – he can read about them in more detail in the chapter on 'Book And Work Numbers' in the third edition of this *Manual*, or in other texts.[1] We must stress, however, that author marks are a comparatively unimportant part of classification theory; they are, for instance, of much less significance in our studies than the principles considered.

Finally, it must be said that a great deal has been written, here and elsewhere, about the qualities and functions of the symbols that serve most library classifications – ways of achieving brevity and hospitality, ideas such as retroactive and syllabic notation, mnemonics and so forth. It is well worth repeating that the notation is not the classification: some classifications function well without one or with symbolism of a very rudimentary kind, but this is not so in the case of the bibliographical systems in widespread use. There is a danger that some notational manipulations could distract us from the more basic question of achieving a helpful and hospitable classification. One firm rule is quite evident; notation must be determined by the nature of the scheme and the needs of the libraries to which the scheme is to be applied. With this in mind, we must make sure it is the servant and not the master of our classifications. As B. C. Vickery says,[2] 'The only purpose of classification is to put subjects in a helpful order . . . We must make our preferred arrangement before we can mechanize it . . . We must use symbols as Humpty Dumpty used words "so that they mean just what we choose them to mean, neither more nor less".' The features of notation discussed in this chapter must be reviewed carefully with this sound advice in mind; all we can say with certainty is that the two vital attributes are the ability to convey order clearly and the power to accommodate new subjects in their correct place in the existing classified arrangement.

[1] W. H. Phillips provides a good account, *Primer of book classification*, 5th edition, A.A.L., 1961, pp. 50–54.
[2] *Classification and Indexing in Science*, 2nd edition, Butterworth, 1959, p. 72.

Appendix to Chapters 1–5
A Synthetic Classification for Literature

1) A further example of several of the principles discussed in this part of the *Manual* may be useful. Literature scarcely needs a faceted scheme and this outline is intended only as a theoretical exercise to demonstrate synthetic classification in a non-technical subject field. There is a frank and obvious bias towards *English* literature. The order for the combination (citation order) of facets is:

> *Language*;
> *Date* (followed by individual authors);
> *Literary form* (usually only needed if a writer employs more than one form);
> *Method of presentation*.

Through the use of synthesis, a great deal of potential detail is encompassed in a brief schedule. There is, inevitably, some scattering relating to the facets which come last in the combination order.

2) The notation has been deliberately chosen to show when a change of facet occurs, as each facet has its own distinctive notation. There are some literal mnemonics (see for example the 'University wits'). Classmarks for compounds are not very brief, but neither are they unduly complicated when one considers the precision of classification that is offered. Numbers file before letters, eg, B209 before BA.

3) *Phase relationship.* Some subjects draw on elements from *more than one main class* and are said to be *complex*. A colon is used here to link notations for such subjects (this is very different from Ranganathan's use of the colon).

Thus we have:

> B: SB The influence of the Bible on English Literature.
> B: SS The influence of the Sea on English Literature.

The influencing phase has been shown by a capital letter not used to represent a language. B: files after B09 but before B1.

4) *Intra-facet and intra-array relationships.*
These expressions may be distinguished from phase analysis. They involve the influence or impact of one topic upon another topic from the *same* field, eg, in this literature classification:

> Bjm: ev The influence of Henry Vaughan on William Wordsworth.
> Bmb: ds The influence of Shakespeare on George Bernard Shaw.

5) *Differential facets*

This can be a problem for a faceted scheme as the chronological facet shows. Sometimes a primary facet has foci which cannot all be qualified by the same foci from a secondary facet. The secondary facet must therefore list several sets of foci because of the varied needs of the primary facet. Literature offers a good example of such 'differential facets'. The foci provided in this scheme for the chronological facet are based on the needs of *English* Literature. They might need to be varied or an alternative list might be required for the reflection of the literary movements of *other* countries. (Such alternatives would demand enumeration of detail as in LC.)

TABLES

Note: Most classes are shown in outline only, but some have been more fully developed.

Language facet
Foci   A   Literature as a whole (world literature)
       B   English
       (Other letters represent the various other languages.)

Chronological facet (based on the requirements of English Literature. Only some of the possible foci have been listed).

Foci				
a	Pre-Chaucerian Literature		ee	Marston
as	Anglo-Saxon Chronicle		ef	Jonson
b	Chaucer and his contemporaries		eg	Middleton and Rowley
c	1400–1558		eh	Heywood
d	1558–1610		ej	Beaumont and Fletcher
da	General poetry		ek	Webster
db	Sidney		el	Tourneur
dc	Spenser		em	Massinger
dd	Hooker		en	Ford and Shirley
de	Drama (General Elizabethan)		ep	Poetry of this period (General)
df	Arden of Feversham		eq	Carew
dg	Greene		er	Cleveland
dk	Kyd	University wits	es	Suckling and Lovelace
dl	Lyly		et	Herrick
dm	Marlowe		eu	Donne
dn	Nashe and Lodge		ev	Vaughan
			ew	Herbert
dp	Peele		ex	Crashaw
ds	Shakespeare		f	1642–1702
dx	Bacon			

Foci	e	1610–1642		g	1702–1745
	ea	Authorized version of Bible		h	1745–1798
	eb	General prose		j	1798–1832
	ebr	Browne		jm	Wordsworth
	ebu	Burton		jn	Coleridge
	ec	General drama of this period		k	1832–1856
	ed	Dekker		l	1856–1900
				m	1900–

Facet denoting literary forms	*Facet denoting method of presentation* (based on the standard sub-divisions of the Decimal Classification)

Foci		*Foci*	
1	Drama	01	Theory and criticism
11	Comedy	02	Outlines
12	Tragedy	03	Dictionaries
2	Poetry	04	Essays
3	Prose	05	Periodicals
4	Fiction	06	Societies
5	Essays	07	Bibliography
6	Letters	08	Biography
7	Oratory	09	History
8	Satire		
9	Miscellany		

Examples of class-marks obtained

B07	Bibliography on English Literature
B21	English Lyric Poetry
Bd01	Critical work on Elizabethan Literature
Bd101	Critical work on Elizabethan drama
Bdm08	Biography of Marlowe
Bdm1	Plays of Marlowe
Bdm101	Critical work on Marlowe's plays
Bdm104	Essays on Marlowe's plays
Bdm2	Poems of Marlowe
Bds1 : dx	Did Bacon write Shakespeare's plays?
Beh3	Thomas Heywood 'Apology for actors'
Beu3	Prose writings of Donne
Bjmn2	Wordsworth and Coleridge 'Lyrical Ballads'
D05	A periodical on Italian literature
E16	19th-century Spanish Letters
R407	Bibliography on Russian fiction

Principle of inversion

It is now recognized that, in any scheme, the combination (citation) order should be one of *decreasing concreteness*, the most important facets being to the fore for combination purposes, eg:

B	ds	I	04
English Literature	Shakespeare	Drama	Essays

But if we have *Essays on English Literature* (B04) it is clear that this document should come before *Essays on Shakespearian Drama*. Thus 04 must file before I or ds; that is, the filing order of elements should be one of *increasing* concreteness for a sequence of the optimum value to be attained. *This means that the classified sequence stresses the major subject relationships and confines scattering of allied information to minor facets.* If we changed to a pure notation of (say) numbers, we would need an *inverted schedule* – one in which the chief facet comes last notation-wise, the next most important one is next to last and so on. This would involve retroactive notation, eg:

9	67	I	04
English Literature	Shakespeare	Drama	Essays

CHAPTER SIX

Other Factors to be Assessed: Evaluating a Classification

Before turning from pure theory to a study and appraisal of individual classification schemes, it is important to ensure that we know what is required of a sound classification. Obviously we would like any scheme to display a sequence of the optimum helpfulness and to be supported by a suitable relative index. We can also evaluate a system by examining its full notation or call-numbers, its provision through synthesis, or by other means, for compound and – to a lesser extent – complex subjects, and the degree of detail offered. We can check to ensure that classification by discipline is correctly observed and ask ourselves whether the classification in question takes due recognition of literary warrant. In weighing up all these factors, we should also take into account the fundamental purpose and objectives of a scheme; the aims of UDC, for instance, are not the same as those of DC and realization of this must affect a critic in his examination and assessment of those schemes according to theoretical principles.

In addition, there is one minor but not altogether unimportant point not yet considered. This is the place of 'form' as opposed to 'subject' in our classifying. Form is usually very much a secondary factor in arrangement. We rightly classify *a dictionary of chemical terms* under chemistry and the *history of logic* under logic. To the basic subject class-mark we usually add, by synthesis, a common division to note that this is an historical form of presentation or that our work is in the form of a dictionary. In DC, this has long been one of the methods of synthesis permitted and indeed the appropriate table was originally dubbed 'form divisions'. It was renamed 'standard sub-divisions' in recognition of the fact that it embraced aspects and viewpoints as well as forms of presentation as such. All the other schemes have a similar table, except LC, which does provide also for a work on a given subject presented in a particular form by treating subject as the primary and form as a secondary factor; the difference here is that the effect is achieved by enumeration rather than synthesis. Thus there is no 'common' number, as in other schemes, for a form of presentation such as *dictionaries*. In DC, dictionaries are represented by 03 and the historical form of presentation by 09 continually – thus achieving mnemonic effect. UDC, CC, and BC also opt for synthesis and the resulting notational mnemonic for any recurring form of presentation, when classifiers obey the long standing general rule – classifying a work by subject and then by form of presentation.

There are some exceptions to this rule; instances where the form of presentation is more important than the subject content. In literature, we ignore the subject of plays, novels and poems in favour of arrangement by literary *form* (along with facets for language and literary movements or periods). Some novels can be classified usefully by subject and some drama may illuminate history, but usually in *belles lettres* it is form which must have precedence over subject. So this is a *Form Class*. Form too may be considered paramount in areas such as *biography* or *bibliography*. If we keep all bibliographies together, we class first by the form 'bibliography' and sub-arrange by subject; if we prefer to distribute bibliographies by subject appeal, however, we reverse the process and presumably add, through synthesis, symbols which denote the bibliographical form of presentation. Likewise great lives may be collected as a biographical form class or distributed wherever possible by subject appeal. Much will depend here upon the nature of the library, with regard to the best arrangement of biographical material. If a helpful grouping is sought for a general library, then classification by form, that is, the making of a separate biography class, may be best; on the other hand, large scholarly libraries, including public libraries with several separate subject departments, may find it best to distribute biographies by subject interest whenever possible. This will leave a small form class – Biography – for those lives which cannot be linked with one subject field and for collective biography. Most general classifications provide alternative arrangements for a topic such as biography, although LC (and latterly DC) favour the distribution of biography by subject interest. So, biography and bibliography if appropriately treated offer us examples of form classes along with the great form class – literature. A further example of primary arrangement by form may be seen in parts of the generalia class; encyclopaedias on a subject go with that subject, but general encyclopaedias and similar polytopical works go into generalia. Here they are arranged by their form, since they cover too many topics to make their subject classification a feasible proposition.

Finally, on the subject of form, we may return to the usual cases where form is a secondary feature, for *form classes* are relatively few. If we classify by subject and then by form, we may note that the term 'form' covers two rather different things, although it is rare for our classifications to attempt to distinguish between them. *Outer form* is the term which denotes dictionaries, essays, serials; it is a physical form or a mode of presentation that we can immediately recognize. *Inner form*, on the other hand, is a term used to denote forms such as Philosophy, History and Theory. Here the form is less clearly discernible, being closely interwoven with the subject of the book. Outer form may thus be regarded as the literary shape in which a volume is presented; inner form is subjective, the method by which the subject is presented, or the viewpoint from which an author regards a subject in his text. C. D. Needham points out that *inner form* restricts or helps to define subject content, but *outer form* does not. The distinction is interesting and may possibly merit some further investigation and analysis.

We can thus, if we wish, add a consideration of 'form' in its various manifestations to the principles involved in the theory of classification. Along with all the theoretical canons, however, a solid streak of pragmatism should exist in any criticism and assessment of a classification. Criteria of a rather more 'practical' nature[1] include the following.

1) Adaptability and alternatives offered. Many libraries will insist on a certain number of alternative arrangements in any classification, or else will make their own. Biography (as we have seen) and geography are two subject areas which come to mind as being especially vulnerable to the improvisations of individual libraries. In BC, of course, the virtually unique *alternative locations* increase the scope for expressing different modes of thought within the systematic arrangement at various levels of the classification hierarchy. Such provision of two or more locations for a topic, from which a single one must be chosen and the other left blank, is more radical than alternative arrangement and should be distinguished from it.

2) The ease of use of any classification is an important practical

---

[1] Several of these factors are considered in more detail in Chapters 16–17.

factor. This depends largely on the explicit and implicit guidance within the scheme's introduction and schedules, but obviously a well-planned faceted system with a predictable citation order could score here.

3) The acceptance of a system as an acknowledged standard will become of increasing significance. It is already almost vital to several librarians that a scheme should be recognized firmly as a standard in central indexing services so that some, or even much, of the work of classification can be carried out at an appropriate centre with class-marks appearing on a machine-readable bibliographic record. A. C. Foskett[1] has mentioned that the MARC record has 'places for not only DC and LC class numbers, but for UDC and BC as well . . . as many subject designations as are economically feasible'. The burning question is – *how* many is this?

4) The time and cost spent in classifying is also of relevance. Some systems may demand more intellectual input than others, but costs can often be reduced by re-examining and changing the flow of work within a technical processes sector or department or by joining more fully in a centralized classification programme. Simplified or broad classification may even increase costs by impeding such participation. Many items are easy to classify, but a few are not and these add significantly to labour costs. Once again, the advantages would seem to rest with a well-guided, predictable scheme.

5) Another and most important practical factor which arises in a critique of any classification is the scheme's policy with regard to the important matter of updating the schedules and providing new editions at suitable intervals. It has been suggested that an ideal classification would appear in loose-leaf form, so that it could be constantly amended to keep pace with new developments. The one existing instance of this may be seen in the German edition of UDC. The plan has not been generally favoured, for although it might prove a boon for the schedules, it gives rise to serious problems with regard to the attendant revision of the index. All schemes that hope to survive must, however, make some provision for their perpetuation. Most have taken the precaution of setting up an editorial board and acquiring financial support. They try to steer a sensible middle course between the one extreme of being deemed out of date and the

---

[1] *The Subject Approach to Information*, 2nd edition, Bingley, 1971, p. 392.

other – that of drastic, hasty change that might alienate established users because of the reclassification it undoubtedly implies. A sensible policy, assuming the necessary funds are available, is a new edition at fairly regular intervals (ten years or less) with an interim periodical bulletin service announcing developments and proposed changes or new schedules. DC offers such a policy and so does LC, except that, in the case of the latter, new editions are of appropriate classes rather than of the scheme as a whole. LC revision is gradual but continual; that of DC results in the relative (but necessary) upheaval occasioned by the arrival of a new edition at intervals of seven or eight years. Change, by one method or the other is vital: the history of classification shows that to remain static is to invite obsolescence and that gradual change is best. The longer change is postponed, the more dramatic, radical and upsetting it is likely to be when it does eventually arrive.

So all these points of pragmatism and principle ought to be carefully weighed and balanced. An ideal scheme would combine them. In reality, all our systems can be faulted; some of the most used systems lack the rational categorization of concepts afforded by faceted classification, but they may have other assets which offer at least partial compensation for this. A brief digression is necessary to point out that all the above factors, both theoretical and practical, could be expanded in number, and indeed they would be if it is a *special* classification rather than a general one that is being evaluated. Here the emphasis of the institution and the ability of the scheme to incorporate important peripheral material may be significant. We would expect a modern special scheme to consider the use of retroactive notation and to have an *inverted schedule*, with major facets coming last in the notational filing sequence because they must come first in the sequence of combination or citation. Likewise, if a general classification is applied to a *special library* or collection, it must be evaluated carefully with regard to the detail and order provided for the special subject area, the amount of notation allocated to the subject, the place given to the subject in the system as a whole, and the extent to which adaptation is necessary.

There is thus a very definite onus on an individual or group who make a classification scheme. Due care should be paid to order, detail, notation, opportunities for synthesis, and what some see as more practical factors – such as revision policy, adaptability, and guidance for the classifier. The classificationist must also refrain from placing some subjects in 'critical' fashion – he ought not to allow any private scepticism with regard to, for example, a certain political or religious viewpoint, or a subject like *Flying saucers* to intrude upon the placing of the topic concerned. Classificationists have not always been immune from this weakness; Dewey treated Spiritualism severely in the early editions of DC and Bliss, in his writings on the structure of the field of knowledge, makes it plain that he viewed Jazz as a degenerate form of music! Strong personal attitudes and indignities similar to this kind have been eliminated from the modern editions of schemes, although others of a slighter yet more insidious nature can creep into any scheme unless vigilance and liberality of viewpoint are allowed to prevail.

As the classificationist has responsibilities, so there is an onus on the individual classifier. He too must beware of critical classification. He should also strive to become thoroughly familiar with the scheme in use and ought to seek advice, if necessary, when dealing with subjects from areas which are difficult or unfamiliar to him. The consistency in application of any scheme and recording of 'decisions' is a point which the classifier or the person who supervises and co-ordinates the work of classification, needs to bear in mind. Classifiers must also see that they distinguish the true specific subject of each book or document and must beware of classifying by title only – titles are often accurate, but can at times be notoriously vague or mis-leading. It has been stated already that the classificationist ought to provide guidance for the application of his scheme; here too there is an equivalent for the classifier – he and his colleagues need to provide generous guidance both at the shelves and at the catalogue to make the helpful systematic order readily useable and intelligible to the library user. Finally, it can be said with justice that classifiers, whether they do all the classification themselves or rely in part on centralized bibliographic services for class-marks, ought to 'step back', from time to time, and look at the end product of the classifying process to try to discover how well it is doing its job. Although heads of large cataloguing departments sometimes grumble about the amount of time their staff spend on relief at reader service points, all classifiers and cataloguers benefit from *some* continuing experience involving employment of the system they apply. Such experience, together with the ability occasionally, to view objectively and analytically, the value or defects of a classi-fication in practice, is a valuable part of a classifier's work; likewise *some* experience in classifying inevitably improves any librarian's general knowledge and knowledge of his stock.

Classification and the consumer. A real sign of the achievement of helpful order in practice would be a customer vote of approval. What *is* the reader reaction to the class-marks and call-numbers of the various classifications in our libraries? This is a subject on which it is difficult to obtain hard and reliable evidence and upon which very little concrete work has been done, the latter fact being perhaps a consequence of the former. Research has, of course, been carried out on testing the benefits of rival information retrieval systems and this is considered in a later chapter, but if we look for a justification of shelf classification in terms of expressed consumer satisfaction, or even an attack upon it in terms of consumers' doubts, we find an almost complete silence. Shelf classification is, of course, of potential value as a great time-saver both for those who search for information on a known subject and for those who wish to browse advantageously, but seeking out reader opinion of its success is complicated by the overlapping of these functions and the difficulty of defining 'browsing'.

A valuable recent study by R. J. Hyman, cited at the end of this chapter, strives to illuminate this area of darkness, although his work concentrates on the views of librarians – from libraries of various sizes and types in the United States – on the value of shelf classification rather than on the opinions of their readers. Dr Hyman notes the serendipity factor of desirable but unsought finds through browsing, and wonders if sociologists and psychologists could help to throw light on the extent to which shelf classification is appreciated and used advantageously by the reader. But the result from the 152 questionnaires which he analysed give us the voice of our fellow librarians supporting our own inner conviction that shelf classification is well worthwhile, rather than the opinion of the uncommitted reader. Equally inconclusive, is the small impressionistic survey carried out in two regions of the United Kingdom during late 1971, which involved the putting of suitable questions to readers within a group of libraries where different classifications are employed. The search for the customer viewpoint is complicated by the number of variables that exists, but this tentative and exploratory survey convinced the present writer at least that readers appreciate that 'a system' must and does exist and that most will accept the one offered, if at all reasonable, provided that it is well presented so that the reader can reap the benefits of systematic grouping without encountering its complications. While there is still much to learn about the reader viewpoint in shelf classification, the little we do know reinforces the earlier plea for good guiding. One is reminded of R. R. Freeman's perceptive remark to the effect that a system may be technically and theoretically excellent and yet the final product will make little impact on users. Guiding of various kinds and personal assistance are surely the ways to combat this danger.

Classification and post-co-ordinate indexing. It is worthwhile to digress here to introduce very briefly a possible alternative to classification in information retrieval rather than in a shelving context. During the last twenty years a form of alphabetical indexing for information, chiefly for use in a special library environment, has made great strides. This is co-ordinate indexing, or post-co-ordinate indexing, as it is often called, and the customary method of its application should be grasped. In such indexing, the documents – usually periodical articles or technical reports – are given a running accession number. Each subject is then analysed and expressed as a series of verbal concepts. Cards are made out for these verbal concepts and the document number is recorded, sometimes manually, but usually by a punched-card system, on the body of each card. Thus a report on the *colouring and perfuming of soaps* would have cards made for each of these three concepts with the number of the report punched into the three cards. To obtain this or similar documents later, one must extract the cards from the file, arrange A–Z by the concepts, and search for common numbers, using the optical coincidence, or peek-a-boo, facilities offered by the body-punched cards. The documents themselves are retrieved via their numbers.

In evaluating classification, it is necessary to remember the emergence and challenge of post-co-ordinate indexing, which in some situations may be complementary to a classification, but in others can be viewed as a rival. The advantages of the alphabetical indexing procedure that has just been concisely described include the following:

1) There is less of a problem in coping with the physical forms of media, in that we can file reports, articles, patents, etc. in separate numerical or chronological sequence without worrying about the need to integrate them in a single classified file;

2) the problem of long class-marks for highly specific subjects disappears;

3) in classification, as indeed in alphabetical subject headings within conventional catalogues, concepts are pre-co-ordinated in a fixed, chosen order. In post-co-ordinate indexing the problem of a fixed citation order which shows only some subjects association, ignoring others, disappears. Concepts are kept separate and uncombined until the actual time of retrieval, when any subject association can, it is claimed, be quickly displayed. Thus the paradox is that by showing *no* fixed association at the indexing stage, we can show *any* association at the searching stage. Both faceted classification and post-co-ordinate indexing rely on concept co-ordination, but the latter postpones (hence its name) the linking of concepts until the actual time of retrieval;

4) multi-topical documents can be fully analysed without reference to the inhibiting influence of order on the shelves.

Some problems or restrictions of post-co-ordinate indexing are:

1) choice of vocabulary is crucial if we are to retrieve all wanted information and avoid the retrieval of unwanted data. A systematic guide in the form of a carefully compiled dictionary or, as it is usually called, a *thesaurus* is thus a necessity. Classificatory ideas can be of enormous assistance here[1] – as R. A. Fairthorne puts it: 'the first step is to ensure that different things are called by different names, the same things by the same name, only one name, and a helpful name'. A sound thesaurus is essential to the success of any indexing system of this kind.

2) post-co-ordinate indexing is usually irrelevant for the needs of shelf arrangement;

3) it is difficult to browse in a post-co-ordinate system. It is true that we can broaden or narrow searches simply by adding cards (to make our search more specific) or by rejecting cards (to make our search more general), but the cards only give us concepts and numbers or concepts and punched holes. They do not identify or describe individual documents. Thus the searcher needs to be able to define with precision that which he is seeking. Then, when the items are retrieved with the aid of cards, he must scan retrieved items to determine their relevance. Browsing and speedy 'relevance determination' may be better served by a pre-co-ordinate classified sequence of documents or by a conventional classified catalogue.

---

[1] This is discussed in some detail in Chapter 19. But note the emergence of the idea of a combined thesaurus and faceted scheme of concepts as a *thesaurofacet*.

The intellectual effort and time demanded by such indexing is no less than that required by classification. However, post-co-ordinate methods have been introduced into classification theory here only briefly for comparative and introductory purposes; their basic merits and problems are considered at much greater length in other texts.

In comparing classification schemes with each other, or even with systems of post-co-ordinate indexing, it is clear that we need to look at many factors, both practical and theoretical. Modern theory offers us an integrated and coherent body of principles, with many features dove-tailing to support and complement these principles. Both recent and older general or special classifications can be assessed to some degree by an individual examining the arrangement and detail offered by two or more of them in an area of his own interest and this can prove a very interesting and worthwhile exercise. Without yielding at all in the firm presentation of theory, however, it is clear that several other matters, some of them administrative rather than strictly classificatory in character, are important in assessment too. In addition to contemplating both theory and practice, we need to consider the *raison d'être* of the individual schemes and to take account of historical perspective. The latter part of this statement does not mean that the older schemes can necessarily survive the arrival of improved concepts and techniques, but it does mean that, in our computer age, there are many factors to take into account in striving to evaluate any one system. We should remember always that technical excellence ought to be, as has been stressed already, supported by acceptability of the end product and by staff scrutiny and appraisal – what F. W. Lancaster has, in fact, within a rather different context, referred to as 'continuous quality control'.

General Bibliography and Bibliography on Section One

The bibliographies at the end of sections endeavour to provide suitable further readings without being too long and tedious. General works on classification include:

Foskett, A. C. *The Subject Approach to Information*. 2nd edition, Bingley, 1971.
A good text on the 'integrated' subject approach, thus dealing with post-co-ordinate indexing and alphabetical subject headings, in addition to classification.

Foskett, D. J. *Science, Humanism and Libraries*. Crosby Lockwood, 1964.
A collection of papers and lectures, many of which concern classification. The paper on 'classification and systematic arrangement', for instance, is useful reading at an early stage in one's studies. See also this author's chapter in W. Ashworth (editor), *Handbook of Special Librarianship and Information Work*. 3rd edition, Aslib, 1967.

Langridge, D. *Approach to Classification for Students of Librarianship*. Bingley, 1973.
Elementary, but very helpful at the start of classification studies.

Mills, J. *A Modern Outline of Library Classification*. Chapman and Hall, 1960.
Not so modern now, but well worth examining despite the crowded, verityped pages.

Palmer, B. I. and Austin, D. *Itself an Education: Lectures on Classification*. 2nd edition, Library Association, 1971.
Complements textbook reading and is thought-provoking, eg, on 'notation' or 'classification as a foundation study'.

Palmer, B. I. and Wells, A. J. *Fundamentals of Library Classification*. Allen and Unwin, 1951.
Dated, but gives a good description of facet and phase analysis.

The above are all British texts. From other countries, there is, for example:

Dunkin, P. S. *Cataloguing, U.S.A.* American Library Association, 1969.
Illustrates the view of classification taken by many librarians in North America. It is presented here in purely pragmatic terms and as an appendage to cataloguing.

Metcalfe, J. *The Subject Classifying and Indexing of Libraries and Literature*. Angus and Robertson, 1959.

Ranganathan, S. R. *Elements of Library Classification*.
The simplest of his many books. Prefer the 2nd (British) edition, edited by B. I. Palmer. Association of Assistant Librarians, 1959.

Wellisch, H. and Wilson, T. D. (editors). *Subject Retrieval in the Seventies: New Directions.* Greenwood Publishing Co., Connecticut, 1972.
Several interesting papers by appropriate specialists.

Note that some other texts have useful sections on classification. They include:

Needham, C. D. *Organizing Knowledge in Libraries.* 2nd edition, Deutsch, 1971.

On faceted classification, there is:

Bakewell, K. G. B. (editor). *Classification for Information Retrieval.* Bingley, 1968.
Includes papers by J. Aitchison and A. Maltby on faceted schemes.
Vickery, B. C. *Faceted Classification: a guide to the making and use of special schemes.* Aslib, 1960.
There is also this author's longer work, *Faceted Classification Schemes.* Rutgers University, 1966.

On PMEST citation order and a critical view of its problems one can read:

Moss, R. *Categories and Relations.* American Documentation, October, 1964, pp. 296–301.
Roberts, N. *An Examination of the Personality Concept and its Relevance to the Colon Classification Scheme.* Journal of Librarianship, July, 1969, pp. 131–48.

On the 'consumer' viewpoint there is very little, but one can consult:

Hyman, R. J. *Access to Library Collections: an inquiry into the validity of the direct shelf approach, with special reference to browsing.* Scarecrow Press, 1972.
Maltby, A. and Hunter, E. J. *Readers and Classification.* New Library World, October, 1972, pp. 411–13.

Outline History of Classification

CHAPTER SEVEN

Classification before Dewey

The gradual development of classification, and especially of bibliographical schemes, is a natural preface to the study of modern book
classifications, since these owe much to the experiments made by
classificationists of the past. The history of classification, effectively
written, would almost necessarily be a history of all attempts to
organize human thought. Since man began his long endeavours to
distinguish and understand the parts of his universe, he has consciously or unconsciously formed some system in which those parts
were related to one another. There are thus hundreds of systems
which have either been written down in schedules by their makers
or can be inferred from their writings. The most compact and
convenient account of the older schemes is the valuable appendix
'Systems of Classification', which appears in Richardson's book
Classification (3rd edition, 1930). Here are registered, with useful
bibliographical material, no less than 161 theoretical systems, as
opposed to practical or library systems, beginning with the scheme
somewhat uncertainly abstracted from Plato's *Republic* (428–347 BC)
and concluding with late nineteenth-century classifications. These
compilations, designed to aid the mental plotting out of the universe
of thought and of objects and not intended for practical library use,
range from those of Aristotle, Zeno, Pliny and Porphyry down to
the near modern ones of Karl Pearson's *Grammar of Science* (1900)
and E. Barthel's *Zur Systematik der wissenschaften* (1910). The study
of such schemes can be defended on the grounds that modern
systems reflect earlier ones and some of the terminology associated
with library classification has been inherited from the past. However, the student of librarianship can rarely afford the protracted
study which this side of the subject demands and our account is
therefore limited to systems most relevant to librarianship.

Quite apart from systems of a non-bibliographic kind, such as the 'classifications' which exist in the life sciences, our earliest traditions of libraries bear their account of classification. We are assured that the clay tablets in the Assyrian library of Assur-ban-i-pal were divided at least into two main classes – those dealing with knowledge of the Earth and those dealing with the Heavens – and that these were sub-divided. How the libraries of Greece and Rome were classified we do not know, but it seems safe to suppose that a race which produced the classifying mind of Aristotle would keep its books in some sort of order, and that the massive orderly mind of the Romans would also use classification. 'With regard to Aristotle, Strabo has preserved the tradition that he was the first who made a collection of books, and taught the Kings of Egypt how to arrange a library' – words which may be taken to mean that Aristotle was the first to work out the arrangement of books on a definite system which was afterwards adopted by the Ptolemies at Alexandris.[1] However that may be, the earliest recorded system of any dimensions was that designed by Callimachus, the greatest of the librarians of Egypt, for the library of the Pharoahs' at Alexandria (260–240 BC). The scheme as a whole is lost, but Richardson has picked out for us certain facts and the main classes.[2] The latter appear to have been:

Poets
Law-makers
Philosophers
Historians
Rhetoricians
Miscellaneous writers

There are hints of form and subject sub-divisions and of the fact that some of the classes at least were arranged chronologically by periods and, in the shorter subjects, alphabetically by the names of authors.

There is a wide interval in our knowledge after this. Schemes for the arrangement of mediaeval monastic libraries existed and are recorded by Richardson. They need not detain us, except to remark of the later ones that Mr W. R. B. Prideaux[3] in a paper on 'Library Economy at the end of the Seventeenth Century', says it was usual 'to divide the books into a certain number of general classes and

[1] Clark, J. W. *The Care of Books*, Cambridge University Press, p. 5.
[2] *Classification*, p. 89.
[3] Library Association Record, 1904, pp. 132–3.

then to place them in fixed location according to size, in the shelves set apart for each class . . . The books were sometimes put under the classes in alphabetical order of the authors' names. Century and nationality were also used as the basis of division.' He tells us, further, of the system favoured by the Jesuits: on entering the library, if you turned left, you beheld the resplendently bound collection of choice and exquisite authors; if you looked in another direction, you saw 'the unhappy books of the heretics placed in mourning and dirt, and indeed bound in black skins or black parchment'. The 'fixed location' here mentioned has also been referred to briefly in our very first chapter. It is an impracticable method in any growing library; we may best consider it as a form of the once common collegiate press-marking system.

Edward Edwards made a distinction in the types of library classification which is helpful, and which brings us to the central theme of the present chapter. There are, he says, library classification systems which have a metaphysical basis, and there are those which are merely practical and convenient arrangements, made without reference to any ideal order of knowledge. A system with a metaphysical origin is clearly one based upon a mental order of the things it covers existing in the mind, it is therefore one in which its maker had laid out some ideal order for his classes before he began to put books or other material into them. The second category of classifications observed by Edwards, 'schemes directed, more or less specifically, to the practical arrangement of books', begins, we may say, in 1498 with that of Aldus Manutius and proceeds through the systems of Naudé, Garnier and others to that of Ismael Bouilliau[1] (1605–98), which is generally considered to be the foundation of what is called the French System, or, alternatively, the System of the Paris Booksellers. This system, worked out in great detail and with excellent scholarship by Jacques Charles Brunet (1780–1867), became the most influential and widely used of all bibliographical schemes, especially on the continent of Europe.

France has always been essentially the home of bibliographers; indeed, it may be said that until comparatively recently the best works on the subject were French. The seventeenth century saw catalogues which have points of interest, amongst which may be mentioned those of Gabriel Naude, 1643, whose *Advis pour dresser une bibliothèque* was translated by the great diarist, John Evelyn; it is a work of such liberality of ideas that it would do honour to the

[1] '*On écrit aussi, mais moins exactement, Bouillaud*'. A. Cim, *Le Livre*, Vol. 9, 1907.

modern librarian. It has twelve main classes, which, because of the eminence of the compiler, deserve transcription:

Theology	Military art
Medicine	Jurisprudence
Bibliography	Council and Canon Law
Chronology	Philosophy
Geography	Politics
History	Literature

But we must return to the System of the Paris Booksellers, which is almost contemporary with Naudé's system and is more important from our point of view. 'The honour of originating it has been claimed,' writes Edwards in his *Memoirs of Libraries*, 'sometimes for the learned Jesuit, Jean Garnier, and sometimes for Gabriel Martin, for so long a period the most eminent of the Paris Booksellers; but the claim which is best authenticated seems to be that of Bouilliau, the compiler of the sale catalogue of the famous library of de Thou.' Edouard Rouveyre, on the authority of Gustave Brunet, claims that this outline was originated by Gabriel Martin, a bibliographer who between 1705 and 1761 had compiled 147 library catalogues. The point does not seem to be important; we must notice, however, that the system was modified and extended enormously by Brunet, who made it the basis of the classified part (volume 5) of his *Manual de Libraire et de l'Amateur de Livres*, an important bibliography, which first appeared in 1804 and has been revised and extended many times since. The scheme has five main classes only:

1. Theology
2. Jurisprudence
3. History
4. Philosophy
5. Literature

In the hands of Brunet, the scheme had for its object the arrangement of a great general bibliography, in which the books are classified by their predominating characteristics. French bibliographers have been almost lyrical in their praise of the system, as is natural, seeing that so many of their bibliographies are classified by it, and it is the scheme with which they are most familiar. 'It has been reproached,' remarks Gustave Brunet, 'for not being philosophical enough or rigidly scientific. On the other hand, it is clear, simple, easy, and as Charles Nodier says with reason, "It embraces, without too great an effort, all the innumerable and capricious sub-divisions which human ingenuity has been pleased to introduce into the literary form of books, and it is sanctioned by excellent catalogues which have become classics of their kind." ' Rouveyre compares it with Dewey, greatly to the disadvantage of the American scheme, of which he contends, 'en Europe, en France particulierement, son emploi serait désastreux.'

The full tables of the Brunet classification comprise some eleven thousand sub-divisions, but a reasonably detailed outline of this famous system, with considerable literary warrant in its day, is apparently not available in English. It has had, nevertheless, great vogue in France, especially for the arrangement of bibliographies and for booksellers' stocks and private collections. So far as it is classified, the Bibliothèque Nationale bases its arrangement upon Brunet. The great and well-administered public library of Sainte-Geneviève in Paris has also been arranged, with success, by an expansion of it. It may be noted that the system proposed to the Trustees for the classification of the British Museum in 1825 is a modification of the French scheme, the adaptations being based on the needs of the library and the experience of the proposer, T. H. Horne. The arrangement of that great library now bears only a remote resemblance to the Brunet classification, but there is sufficient to suggest that it was an influence. Criticism of Brunet's scheme is very easy from the standpoint of today and yet difficult because, without practical experience of the system, it is likely to be merely academic. The obvious remark is that it is old-fashioned and conditioned, as one might expect, by the state of knowledge in its day. The tables are far too brief for modern needs and many important subjects are relegated to various appendices; for example, Australia and New Zealand are merely an appendix to the History of Asia. The notation of the scheme is mixed, extremely cumbrous, and obsolete; it uses upper and lower-case letters and also numbers, but combines them in a fashion which has no attraction for the modern librarian. The classification also lacks an index. In short, the interest for us nowadays lies not in the possibility of applying it to the organization of knowledge, but in its value as a clue to the labyrinthine arrangement to several continental bibliographies.

A French system of some appeal because it was based on a determined attempt to seek out and reproduce what would now be called an evolutionary order of nature, was the scheme devised by R.

Merlin for the catalogue of the Bibliothèque de Sylvestre de sacy (1842–47). It is not profitable for us to survey this or other systems at length, nor can the fertile and interesting fields of German and Italian bibliographical classification be scanned in detail, as their vogue has not been great outside the countries of their origin. A German classification that has been favourably regarded is that of Otto Hartwig (1888). This is an extensive scheme with a complex notation and has some considerable emphasis on law; it has had, nevertheless, some influence on the course of classification in the United States. In Italy, R. Bliss once told us, 'Bacon has been especially influential, but Battezzati's system... which Dewey says stimulated his study most, was an adaptation of Brunet's.' There was also once an interesting attempt in that country to combine the schemes of Dewey and Hartwig.

We must now examine one or two important examples from the other category of classifications distinguished by Edwards – schemes having a metaphysical or a philosophical basis. Such systems would seem to deserve priority of treatment in a survey of this kind, but in chronological order schemes which do not possess this basis are found first. When we come to consider philosophical schemes we are obliged to pass over several centuries with a quiet mind, because nothing that can be so described occurs until approximately 1550. It may, nevertheless, be noted that the order of studies evolved by the universities found early reflection in Duke Humphrey's Library, the early part of the University Library at Oxford, in about 1431. Here the statutes ordained that books for the study of 'the Seven Liberal Arts and Three Philosophies were kept apart in a chest, and might be borrowed by Masters of Arts lecturing in those subjects.'[1] But the first important early philosophical system is that which is called by some 'the first bibliographical scheme;' it was created by the German-Swiss scholar, naturalist, and author, Konrad Von Gesner (1516–65). Gesner's life is one of the romances of the history of learning. Son of a poor furrier in Zurich, who died when his son was fourteen, Gesner at that age started out in the world in the hope of relieving the dire poverty of his mother and many brothers and sisters by the use of his pen. Coming to Strasbourg, he entered the service of Wolfgang Fabricius Capito, with whom he studied Hebrew; whence, returning to Switzerland he was granted a small travelling scholarship which enabled him to continue his studies in France; later he became a schoolmaster in

[1] Gibson, S. *Some Oxford libraries*, Oxford University Press, p. 15.

his native city. A course in medicine at Basle followed, and in 1537 he received the appointment of Professor of Greek at Lausanne; but this he relinquished to continue medicine at Montpellier, to graduate at Basle, and to return to Zurich in order to commence practice. The University of Zurich made him Professor of Physics and Natural History in 1541, and this office he dignified until his death, which occurred prematurely, as a result of devotion to his medical duties, in a plague which swept the city in 1565.

In a life of little more than forty-eight years, his industry was enormous and his learning has rarely been surpassed in its width and comprehensiveness. George Cuvier, himself a master of zoological classification, called him 'the German Pliny'. Gesner published no less than seventy-two works on grammar, botany, pharmacy, medicine, natural philosophy and history, and was working on eighteen others at his death. His claim to remembrance, however, rests mainly upon his *Bibliotheca Universalis* (1545), which is a catalogue of Latin, Greek and Hebrew books, with critical notes and extracts from the most important ones, and its supplement *Pandectarum sive partitionum universalium Conradi Gesneri Ligurini libri XXI* (1548), of which, however, only nineteen of the twenty-one books indicated in the title were published, the books on medicine and theology not having satisfied the compiler. In the *Pandects*, Gesner classified the entries according to subjects and in such manner as to make the system employed an immense advance upon its predecessors. It is classification of knowledge according to definite principles and Gesner obviously had the progressive order of studies in his mind. Philosophy, in his system, stands for the whole sum of knowledge which is to be approached through the arts and the sciences. Of the arts and sciences there are two kinds: (1) those which are primary or preparatory, and (2) those which are fundamental. Of the preparatory sciences he finds some to be (*a*) necessary and others to be (*b*) embellishments or enrichments. His necessary arts are (*aa*) those of discourse, (*bb*) mathematical sciences and arts. What he terms (*b*) ornates (a word for which an exact English equivalent is difficult to discover) form a curious class, but are clearly a progression of studies through divination and magic, geography and history to the illiterate or mechanical arts. From these the prepared mind may proceed to his great class (2) *substantiales*, which holds the higher forms of knowledge, and connotes all forms of philosophy, metaphysical, natural, moral, civil, economic, political, legal, medical and theological. The result is a hierarchy of knowledge of an ideal kind in no way dependent upon the fortuitous appearance of books in this or that subject. Brunet remarks that the system sufficed in its time for the arrangement of a library *bien composée*, and that Gesner, being a man of good sense, had avoided those arbitrary combinations of different sciences into one class which have seduced so many savants. In any case, it is the great mediaeval attempt to relate the arrangement of books to the educational and scientific consensus of the day.

There are several other philosophical systems; the only other we shall describe here and the one which is of most importance to us today is the chart of human learning which formed the framework of Francis Bacon's treatise on *The Advancement of Learning* (1605). The origin of this scheme may be outlined briefly. Bacon, in laying the foundations of his philosophical system, commences with a review of what has been accomplished in the field of learning, and of the documents in which that accomplishment has been recorded. The ambitious character of his project will be observed; he is the prototype and in all ways the greatest British example of those remarkable men of whom the world has produced about a dozen, who take the whole field of knowledge as their province; his mind was encyclopaedic. The *Advancement of Learning* is therefore the history of the record of thought as it was at the date of its appearance; but it is also rather a discussion of the state of knowledge than of the books or methods themselves. Bacon rarely, and only then by allusive methods, mentions the names of books. His treatise is still notable, not only as an example of the classifying mind, but because of the clarity of its logic and the magnificence of its prose. One cannot refrain from quoting the beautiful reference to libraries –

'The shrines where all the relics of the ancient saints, full of true virtue, and that without delusion or imposture, are reposed'

not because any librarian of this workaday world regards it as a statement of the purpose of his library, but because there is a nobility in the utterance which strikes something responsive in us all.

Bacon's method is subjective and he proceeds upon a definite principle of division that we can recognize and appreciate. In fact, as applied to books, he is the first of all the classificationists who is consistent in the characteristics on which he bases his outline. This follows the idea that there are three distinct mental faculties, or fountains – Memory, Imagination and Reason – and that from these flow the three emanations – History, Poetry and Philosophy. Now *memory*, according to Bacon, produces History and this is of two kinds. One records the works of nature (Natural History): the other (Civil History) the works of man. The second class shows the *imagination* working on the materials provided by our senses, 'combing, magnifying and idealizing them at pleasure', from which we obtain Literature and the Arts. The third class, Philosophy, is the product of *reason*. It includes the sciences and Bacon's civil philosophy comprehends our modern sociology, politics and economic science. Yet there is no place for theology, as we understand it, in this class. Bacon says that theology consists mainly of sacred history and it goes mainly under Ecclesiastical History in the History class.

Bacon's recognition of three mental faculties has long since been superseded by the findings of scientists and psychologists. The scheme of classification which he proposed is, like many other classifications, a reflection of the state of knowledge in the age when it was created. However that may be, the influence of the Baconian classification has been profound. It formed the basis of the great French encyclopaedia of Diderot and D'Alembert in the eighteenth century. 'If', wrote Diderot, 'we emerge from this vast operation, we shall owe it mainly to the Chancellor Bacon, who sketched the plan of a universal dictionary of sciences and arts at a time when there was not, so to speak, either arts or sciences. This extraordinary genius, when it was impossible to write a history of what man already knew, wrote of that which they had to learn' – Bacon's chart also influenced, apparently, the early classification of the Bodleian Library; it was the outline of the first classification applied in the Library of Congress; in 1870 it became the plan for the famous inverted Baconian classification of Dr W. T. Harris and this, in turn, strongly influenced the Dewey *Decimal Classification*. No other philosophical system has had such important results or led to such significant bibliographical developments.

The study of eighteenth- and nineteenth-century schemes which are metaphysical or philosophical in origin could be pursued further with profit and interest. Leibniz, himself influenced by Gesner and Bacon, anticipates bibliographical classification and our frailties are his frailties.[1] He can be regarded both as an early enthusiast

---

[1] He tells us, for example, that the classifier is often 'in suspense between two or three places equally suitable'. Quoted in L. M. Newman, *Leibniz and the German library scene*. Library Association, 1966.

for a form of faceted classification and as an important forerunner of H. E. Bliss. The schemes of Prosper Marchand (1704), S. T. Coleridge (1826, as amended by editors), Comte, Wundt, Spencer and Pearson may occur to those with some knowledge of the subject. Indeed, of the classification of Comte (1822), Richardson writes: 'this much abused system, to which its enemies grudge any pretention to originality of merit, has nevertheless been almost the chief stimulus to progress in classification during this [nineteenth] century'. Yet all these, valuable and suggestive though they are, have not exercised a direct influence upon modern bibliographical classification as a whole, although they have played their part on the path leading to the rational construction of an effective order of the major classes of knowledge at which Bliss and his supporters arrived. The present enthusiasm for prefacing classification studies, in many instances, by some investigation of the structure of the universe of knowledge may well lead to some revival of interest in the better and more influential of these older systems.

The real beginnings of library classification, as we know it today, took place in the nineteenth century and most of the important steps forward were made by librarians in the United States. At the beginning of the nineteenth century, the arrangement of books in the Congress Library was according to size. This is exhibited in the earliest catalogue put forth by the first Librarian of Congress, John Beckley, in April 1802; it is what might have been expected from a librarian who also held the office of Clerk to the House of Representatives. At that date, the United States, as a nation, possessed in all only 964 volumes and nine maps; and the order of the catalogue ran: folios, quartos, octavos, duodecimos, maps. This system remained in vogue until 1812, by which year the Library had increased to 3,076 volumes and 53 maps, charts and plans. In this year, the second Librarian, Patrick Macgruder, ventured on a catalogue, the fourth issued, of much more ambitious design, in which the works were classified under eighteen headings which reflect those of a few well-known scholastic systems, and subarranged in each by size. In August 1814, occurred one of those war tragedies which occasionally scar the history of libraries. The British soldiery, under General Ross – who appears to have been unaware of the existence of the Library – burned the Capitol, and the greater part of the Library with it. At this juncture ex-President Thomas Jefferson sold to Congress his private library of nearly 7,000 volumes, a collection which was, according to A. R. Spofford, 'an admirable selection of the best ancient and modern literature up to the beginning of the present nineteenth century'. After a Congressional wrangle, in which little of the modern American library spirit, but much of the average step-motherly English attitude to books, was shown, the library was acquired. This collection was catalogued and classified by Jefferson himself, and his Catalogue of the Library of the United States, published in 1815, was based upon a modification of Francis Bacon's divisions of knowledge; forty-four divisions were employed and the arrangement of titles under each was alphabetical. It is interesting to note that this system, with further modifications, was in use until the end of the century. The modifications were made by the Librarians, John Silva Meehan, in 1861, and A. R. Spofford at a later period, but their contributions were revisions of detail alone; essentially the classification of the Library of Congress for the first century of its existence was that of Francis Bacon.

At this stage, it is worth while for us to move on in time in order to survey the preparatory background to the Decimal system. Decimal arrangement, as applied to book-shelves, did not begin with Melvil Dewey, nor does he claim such priority. Cim[1] tells us that in 1583 the learned Lacroix du Maine presented to Henry III a curious and singular project for the arranging of a library 'perfect in all ways'. This library was to consist of 10,000 volumes (100 books in each of 100 bookcases). The first order of these cases, numbers 1–17, was devoted to Religion; the second, numbers 18–41, to Arts and Sciences; the third, numbers 42–62, to the Description of the Universe; the fourth, numbers 63–72, to the Human Race; and so on. It will be seen that this is a vague decimal system applied not to subjects but to bookcases or shelves. All decimal systems before that of Dewey seem to have this peculiarity – they number the shelves and relegate subjects to shelves so numbered; they do not number the subjects themselves decimally. Other early systems involved giving each book a fixed place in a numerical or alphabetical sequence. The modern arrangement of a library, of course, rejects all such methods of fixed location, which are either completely impossible for a growing library or result in an order reflecting the order of accession of books rather than a helpful subject classification. It is far better to be able to move the books about freely, so that all books on the same theme can be located together and new volumes can be inserted at the most appropriate

[1] *Le Livre*, Vol. 4, p. 309.

place in the sequence of subjects. Another primitive, although much later scheme than that of du Maine, is described in a small manual of library economy by Nathaniel B. Shurtleff. This is the *Decimal System for the Arrangement and Administration of Libraries* (Boston, USA, 1856), which employs alcoves with ten bays, each bay having ten shelves and both bays and shelves being numbered from 1 to 10. The notation was of a non-expansive kind not essentially related to the shelves. It bears no relation to that of Dewey.

A glance at the systems in vogue in 1874, the year in which Dewey became librarian of Amherst College, shows very little to the advantage of the librarians of the time. In England, the British Museum was classified by a free adaptation of Brunet, which still survives; at the Bodleian Library were a series of partial classifications which appear never to have been resolved into a coherent whole; the Bibliothèque Nationale had been arranged partly by Brunet, but was to a large degree unclassified; the Library of Congress possessed a variant of the system of Bacon. Dewey almost immediately realized the need for some more competent classification than appeared to be available. He therefore made a comprehensive study of existing schemes and devised his own. He tells us in the introduction to it that he was most indebted to Natale Battezzati's *Nuova Sistema di Catalogo Bibliographico Generale* (Milan, 1871), and to the systems of Jacob Schwartz (1879) and W. T. Harris, the last of which was devised for the public school library of St Louis in 1870. It is not clear, however, to what extent Battezzati and Schwartz influenced Dewey's work; its relation to that of Harris is more obvious. In fact, with the appearance of Harris's scheme we reach the vital formative years of American library classification.

Harris's system was the first of the 'inverted Baconian' schemes, of which there have been several. With modern connotations of the terms, Harris took Bacon's outline and inverted it. In its details this system was expanded in the Peoria Public Library version, which is later than the original scheme, but the outline – Science, Art and History – remains the same. A comparison of the outline structure of the schemes of Bacon, Harris and Dewey indicates sufficiently the origin of the last system, see table on facing page.

Such a comparison has its purpose in our studies. It is true that Richardson remarks: 'the system itself is supposed to be in some way an adaptation of Bacon, but the relation is hardly to be discovered and it should really be counted as independent'. On the other hand, certain points in the order are susceptible to criticism

BACON		HARRIS	DEWEY
Original	Inverted		
		Science	General Works;
History	Philosophy	Philosophy and Religion; Social and Political Science; Natural Sciences and Useful Arts	Philosophy and Religion; Sociology; Philology; Science and Useful Arts
Poesy	Poesy	*Art* Fine Arts Poetry Pure fiction Literary miscellany *History*	Fine Arts Literature
Philosophy	History	Geography and Travel Civil history Biography *Appendix* Miscellany	History Biography Geography and Travel

from the modern standpoint, and can only be explained by a reference to its pedigree. For example, the separation of Sociology by five great classes from History, to which it is more closely related than it is to any other major subject, can be understood only in this way. Again, in the Peoria classification, Philology is a sub-division of the Social and Political Sciences and ranks immediately before Natural Science, exactly as it does in Dewey; and is therefore separated in the latter system by three classes from its natural partner, Literature, although Dewey suggests that some libraries might find it convenient to bring these two classes together. This debt to Bacon must be stressed, to a certain extent, because the Dewey outline does not seem to be explicable on any other ground; yet efforts have been made by writers on classification to give it a philosophical basis of its own.

CHAPTER EIGHT

A Century of Library Classification

The title of the present chapter is not meant to imply that the earlier systems of arranging libraries or their catalogues are of no consequence, but it acknowledges the fact that it was Dewey's work which really began library classification as we find it today. Indeed, by looking at the crucial years in the latter part of the nineteenth century, we move – in Leo La Montagne's phrase – from the 'prehistoric' to the 'historic' period of our studies. A bare listing of the major milestones could easily degenerate into a tedious chronology, but it is useful to see the path to the present with each significant system or event related to the time and environment from which it sprang. In compressing the story here, gaps have doubtless been created and many more historical facts can be accumulated; just as important, however, is the interpretation of those facts – the noting (with the benefit of hindsight) of errors and false starts, the observation of the ideas which have proved worthwhile or enduring or which have appeared in embryo to be fully developed at a later date.

Whatever its philosophical origins may have been, the *Decimal Classification* was, from the first, an outstanding success. It represented an enormous advance on earlier systems; it was based on Dewey's own survey of the needs of libraries and, no doubt, in part – in its early editions – on the 'literary warrant' of the Amherst College Library. It had a flexible notation and an excellent index; above all, perhaps, it appeared at a most opportune time in public library history, when, with the gradual introduction of open-access, librarians needed a system based on relative rather than fixed location. These reasons for its initial popularity and rapid development are considered in more detail in the chapter on the scheme. Here, it is sufficient to say that the impact of the *Decimal Classification* – the first of the modern bibliographical systems – was tremendous. It is incredible, and indicative of the genius of Melvil Dewey, to reflect that it was drawn up in 1873 and first published (like many great works anonymously) three years later, when its compiler was only twenty-five years of age. The introduction to this first edition contained much advice, some of which is still valid. Ranganathan justly described this introduction as 'almost prophetic'. The second edition of 1885 gave the scheme its distinctive name, greatly enlarged the schedules and index and made some alterations in the sequence of classes. It was this edition which cast the basic mould of the *Decimal Classification* as we know it today, establishing the DC mnemonics and the provision of some scope for number building. The 1885 assurance of no drastic structural change was doubtless unanimously regarded as a further commendation for the scheme at the time. Ranganathan suggested that, in a sense, the newly created DC was too good in that it inhibited further thought on the subject of library classification, but its very creation gave a great impetus to the development of librarianship in the United States and, in fact, the initiation of rival schemes owed much to the achievement of this pioneer classification which made relative location on the shelves of libraries the rule rather than the exception.

Another important system, which has not endured nearly so well as the *Decimal Classification*, is the *Expansive Classification* of Charles Ammi Cutter. Cutter is now best remembered for his *Rules for a Dictionary Catalogue*; he was, by about fourteen years, Dewey's senior and his experiments were with a scheme having an alphabetical notation. Yet his arraignment was not of the decimal notation only; he had his own definite ideas on the order of subjects in a classification. In due course there appeared a slender volume entitled *Expansive Classification*, 1891–93. It consists of seven separate classifications; the first one extremely broad; the second less general; the third less still, and so on in progressive stages of minuteness. Cutter's recommendation is that when a library is small and likely to progress slowly, one of the earlier classifications should be applied and, as the library develops, a later expansion can be used. He says: 'I have been led to prepare a scheme applicable to collections of every size, from the village library in its earliest stages to the national library with a million volumes.' The first expansion has, in fact, only seven classes, represented by the letters A, B, E, F, H, L, and Y. The successive expansions develop this outline considerably; by the time we reach the fifth, the whole of the alphabet is employed, many classes being quite minutely subdivided. Cutter actually carried the method as far as six stages in the 1891–93 volume and later to an uncompleted seventh stage. The idea of a classification that can be developed in this way is extremely interesting, when one considers the requirements of libraries of different sizes and character.

Unfortunately there are difficulties with this 'expansive' programme; Cutter's advice to the classifier to 'be minute, be minute, be not too minute' is rather vague.[1] Another problem is that, as the Relative Index sometimes shows, the notation often changes as we move through successive expansions; thus the librarian may find that class-marks may need to be completely altered as his collections increase.

Plants   L ^{2}M ^{3}N

Apart from the expansive principle, the most interesting feature of this classification is perhaps the idea that the order of classes reflects an order of development in nature. Cutter claims that 'The Expansive Classification follows the evolutionary order throughout, in natural history putting the parts of each subject in the order which that theory assigns to their appearance in creation. Its science proceeds from the molecular to the molar, from number and space, through matter and force, to matter and life; its botany going up from cryptogams to phanerogams ... The book arts follow the history of the book from its production, through its distribution, to its storage and use in libraries ... Economics, too, has a natural order – population, production, distribution of the things produced, distribution of the returns, property, consumption ... There are many such transitions ... They are not merely ingenuities pleasing only to their contriver; they have a certain practical value, since they bring together books which one may wish to use at the same time.' There were several efforts to justify ideas such as these at the turn of the century; J. D. Brown claimed an order of development for his *Subject Classification*, although he does not use the phrase evolutionary order. Cutter's fellow-countryman, E. C. Richardson, of course, also placed great reliance on the need for a book classification to follow the arrangement of the sciences. Nowadays, however, less stress is placed on this; classifiers recognize that the value of a scheme must be assessed solely on its practical achievement and not according to its success or failure in revealing a real or supposed

---

[21] Ranganathan has suggested that better advice would be: 'Be minute, be minute, be most minute'.

'natural' order of progression which, in any case, may be inapplicable to certain subject fields.

Cutter's notation has been quoted as a pure one, but only to a degree is this the case; his Local List (a series of common divisions to indicate geographical regions) is numerical, as are his form divisions. Apart from these, letters are used throughout. Numbers from the Local List may be added directly to subject class-marks; form division numbers may be added to them when necessary, by means of a point. Thus:

IU   Schools
IU.4   History of schools (.4 denotes history in the common form divisions)
IU 45   English schools
IU 47   German schools (these being the appropriate numbers for England and Germany from the Local List)

The form divisions and the Local List give the notation mnemonic value; they are, of course, mnemonics of the systematic kind. But Cutter also uses literal mnemonics, where he is able to do so without strain. He claimed that his scheme was 'ten times as mnemonic' as the *Decimal Classification*. More important, probably, is the fact that the letter notation has a great capacity for accommodating subjects with brief class-marks. He also developed the idea of author marks for final A–Z grouping by author within each subject class.

Dewey once said that he wished to see a notation of letters fully tested and, at one time, it seemed that the *Expansive Classification* would fulfil that wish. The scheme, alas, was never completed; it has been steadily abandoned by those libraries using it in the United States today because it is now obvious that it will never be finished or brought up to date. Yet its historical importance is tremendous. The system received tribute from both Richardson and Bliss. The former regarded it as a 'really scientific work of high value'; the latter at one time attempted to develop and revise it, but abandoned the task and was content to recognize it as 'a stepping stone to the future'. Its help for both the Congress classification and for Bliss's own system has been strong. This influence can also be discerned in an important twentieth-century special scheme – the *Harvard Business Classification*, which owes much to the work of W. P. Cutter. La Montagne suggests that although most classifications at this time attempted to follow an inverted Baconian arrangement, Cutter's is nearer to the spirit of Brunet. It is, he says, 'the best classification of the nineteenth century'; this, coming from a modern and well-informed writer, is praise indeed. Eric De Grolier also points out the merits of this scheme and the influence of its auxiliary tables. Yet today the system has no vogue at all.

Cutter's scheme has been discussed at comparative length because it may not be readily accessible. However, we shall not survey systems of lesser stature in any detail here. It will suffice to say that, among other systems of this period, those of Lloyd P. Smith, of Philadelphia; J. C. Rowell, of the University of California; and F. B. Perkins, of San Francisco, are probably of the greatest significance for us today. Indeed, the last-named of these classificationists was a descendant of one Thomas Clap, who had done much to establish classification in the Yale Library in the middle of the eighteenth century. For our purposes, however, it will be more useful to examine the changes in the method of classification at the Congress Library that were taking place towards the end of the century.

By this time, the Library had reached a very high position, in number of volumes as in character, amongst the national libraries of the world; the Librarian thus determined to commence the formidable task of providing his great collections with an entirely new and minute classification. Older libraries have made such effort and experiments, but no national library of long history has yet accomplished the gigantic task of classifying its books according to any modern system of knowledge, or to any plan that the science of today would accept. Indeed, the task is incredibly great and could only be accomplished by such a fine organization as that of the Library of Congress, where there is a large team of well-qualified classifiers and adequate financial resources. Even in these happy circumstances the work has been long and arduous. The new building, completed in 1897, plus the fact that the stock of books and pamphlets by this date was in the region of a million items, brought about the decision to reclassify. The use of either the scheme of Dewey[1] or that of Cutter was considered carefully. Of these two, the latter was preferred, but it was decided that in view of the special requirements of the Congress Library and the nature of its collections, an entirely new scheme would be most appropriate. The final decision was made right at the end of the century and work on a new system, which was to be shaped by the 'literary warrant' of the

[1] Charles Martel's summary of the advantages and disadvantages of using Dewey's system is given by La Montagne, *American Library Classification*, 1961, pp. 223–5.

vast Congress collections then began. It is strange, in retrospect, to reflect that at the time when this system was being drafted under the direction of Herbert Putnam, Richardson was writing what was to be virtually the first textbook on bibliographical classification, for the principles which he extols are very different from the essentially pragmatic ideas which motivated Putnam, Charles Martel, and the other librarians who contributed to the discussion and planning which preceded the formation of the Congress system. A provisional outline of the Congress scheme was ready by 1901; this early draft reveals the influence of Cutter, but the system is essentially an independent and utilitarian one moulded around the stock and departmental structure of the library.

Meanwhile, in Britain progress was relatively, but perhaps understandably, slow. Edward Edwards had proposed a system of classification for public libraries, but it had defects – the greatest perhaps being that it was too far ahead of its time. A few broad groups represented the usual arrangement in the newly created municipal libraries. The potent attack of Jevons on the classification of books doubtless delayed the proper introduction of that process and a further calamity was the invention of the ingenious and seductive 'indicator', a contrivance for use in libraries where the public were not admitted to the shelves. It consisted of columns of numbers in a glazed frame standing on the library counter. These numbers were on a blue ground if the books were available and on a red ground if they were not. The would-be reader found the number of the book he required in the catalogue, and consulted the indicator before calling for the book by that number. The number was really written on the turned up ends of a small metal slide which fitted into a little shelf in the column of the indicator, and one end of the slide was red and the other blue. This slide held the charge when a book had been borrowed. The whole machine was thus a remarkable help to the librarian; it threw the finer work of librarianship upon the reader himself, and saved brain wear effectively. As far as it concerned classification, it seemed to make it quite unnecessary. As the indicator was arranged by a continuous number, from one to the number representing the last book added, it seemed to be the best method, as it certainly was the easiest, to arrange the books by accession numbers. Such was the magic of the indicator that the Library Association actually passed a resolution commending it to local authorities, and by so doing put back the calendar of library progress by some thirty years.

It was some time before the *Dewey Classification* made any real progress in British public libraries. In the 1890s, however, L. Stanley Jast, then librarian of Peterborough, came out as a champion of the scheme, and at much the same time Basil Anderton and T. W. Lyster were also its advocates. But generally there was a great fear of the difficulty and complexity of Dewey, a fear founded partly upon ignorance of the scheme itself, and partly upon the fact that until 1900[1] there were hardly any trained assistant librarians in Britain to apply it. This, in fact, led to the issue of several broad classification schemes in which some such arrangement as follows constituted the *whole* classification:

A	Religion and Philosophy	G	Useful Arts
B	History	H	Language and Literature
C	Travel	J	Poetry and Drama
D	Social Science	K	Fiction
E	Science	L	Miscellaneous
F	Fine Arts		

– classifications which did not classify, and by their incoherence were expected in some way to make things easier for librarian and reader. Some think that it was unfortunate, too, that J. D. Brown, the most influential librarian of the time ('the eager moving spirit' of the agitation for classed libraries, as E. A. Savage called him) never viewed the *Decimal Classification* as kindly as he might have done, holding it to be too American.

Although he did not consider DC suitable for British public libraries, Brown was certainly no opponent of classification as such. His strenuous and – at the time – daring efforts to promote open-access methods were bound to be allied with a wish to classify efficiently. Two schemes produced by him in the 1890s proved unsuccessful; one was an effort in collaboration with J. H. Quinn and the second was the ill-named *Adjustable Classification*. Undeterred by these setbacks and no doubt provoked by the American bias of the DC and the hold which it was gradually gaining in British libraries, Brown set about the compilation of an entirely new system; SC was thus presented to the world of librarianship in 1906. A second edition was published in 1914 (the year of Brown's death), the alterations in which are of no radical importance; and a third after

---

[1] Jast informed us that, about the turn of the century, about 12 per cent only of English public libraries applied systematic classification, but that the process was gaining ground rapidly.

many years of experiment and application appeared in 1939, edited by the classificationist's nephew, J. D. Stewart. This is the latest edition and revision has again been extremely conservative; indeed, it retains every feature that Brown devised or adopted and carries the stamp of a single, strong personality.

The object of SC is to provide a simple 'one-place' classification, selecting basic 'concrete' themes and grouping material around them. The idea has superficial appeal, but the goal is not a feasible one since it ignores the very fundamental notion of classification by discipline. Brown practised what has sometimes been called 'classification by attraction'; some of his chosen concrete themes act as magnets which pull to them a host of concepts which should really be distributed under several disciplines. Thus Brown, for instance, regarded subjects such as the *human body, money, speech, women,* and *ships* as 'concrete' topics, material about any one of which should be kept together. This analysis ignores, for instance, the difference in context between bodily exercise and funerals; between numismatics and monetary economics, between oratory and ventriloquism; between sea transport and shipbuilding. (As for 'women', the reader may care to consult the SC schedules!) Such differences, although fundamental to accurate classification, are ignored in SC. The pursuit of a system with one place only for each concrete subject (as defined by Brown) led also to what Berwick Sayers once called the 'specific' or one-place per subject A–Z index – a defective tool which largely ignores the problem of revealing associations that are ignored in the schedules. Allied to the one-place theory is Brown's attempt to link science and technology. This is sometimes done in SC with a skill which won the admiration and support of Bliss; the linking of pure and applied chemistry and of the theory of electricity with electrical engineering can certainly be tolerated and perhaps commended. Brown, however, overworked this idea and often made unorthodox judgements as to what constituted theory and associated practice. Thus, in the SC schedules the principles of heat immediately precede the work of the fire service, while the concept of time is followed by clock and watch making.

These amusing examples are admittedly extreme cases, but they demonstrate the defects of Brown's subject analysis and collocation. His scheme is also of interest for the odd and unsatisfactory generalia class and for the claim – so characteristic at the turn of the century – that the main classes are arranged in a developmental sequence which mirrors, however vaguely, the chronological order of evolutionary progression. (Brown tended to avoid the expression 'evolutionary order', but his broad sequence of Matter and Force, Life, Mind, and Record approximates to this.) One of the most interesting of all the SC features, however, is the list known as *categorical tables*, a synthetic device by which nearly a thousand aspects, forms or viewpoints can be added to the 'concrete' subjects from the main schedules. The categorical tables consist of numbers introduced by a point, which is not a decimal but simply a splitting device. Thus we have, for example:

I 750   Leather
I 750.I Bibliography on leather manufacture (.I is the constant categorical table number for bibliography)
and D 705   Physical chemistry
D 705.954 Essays on physical chemistry (.954 is the categorical table number for essays)

These numbers give considerable opportunity for synthesis and this is enhanced by the fact that, if necessary, class-marks from the main tables can be directly combined, if appropriate. The latter idea is especially useful for the regional qualification of a subject, for example:

The irrigation of Ireland Ioo3Uo36

There are also facilities, albeit somewhat cumbersome, for the specification of time periods. Official rules are somewhat slack and thus alternatives abound, for Brown did not realize the full significance of synthesis in classification. Yet by the application of modern theories and sterling common sense a consistent citation order emerges and the principle of inversion can be applied. SC, despite defects in its order, thus had considerable potential for the expression of compounds, although the categorical tables really needed pruning and reorganization.

On the other hand, it has never had a worthwhile revision policy or the funds for such. It has only been used in its entirety in British public libraries and the few which employed it have now ceased to do so. Despite its great emphasis on British history (including local history) and geography, which receive a disproportionately large slice of notation, Brown did not seem to expect great success for SC even in Britain, but hoped it would be 'simple and practical'. It was probably never really practical, but has often been praised for its simplicity. There are even those that would argue that its simple order was a great asset in public lending libraries and that the earlier arrival of DC, plus Brown's failure to provide for the perpetuation of SC, were the real reasons for the latter's decline. When we examine it now, we see faulty order, antiquated language, and poor apportionment (the same amount of notation given to domestic cats as to aeronautical engineering, for instance) which, like the lack of revision facilities, serve as a warning to individuals who aspire to be long classificationists. Revision would now be futile, but one should look for the praiseworthy as well as the defective or even ludicrous in SC. It foreshadows modern theories remarkably well and in Brown's idea of concrete themes being qualified by less concrete concepts from the categorical tables the careful retrospective 'listener' can perhaps catch Ranganathan's terminological echo – the expression 'decreasing concreteness' with regard to citation order. One could speculate long on such points; suffice it to say that it is largely Brown's powers of anticipation which the French writer, De Grolier, has in mind when he declares SC a good scheme provided the time of its origin is remembered.

SC was not the only influential system which has some roots in the early twentieth century and others in the nineteenth. In Belgium another scheme of a far more ambitious nature, had been initiated. This was the work of the Institut International de Bibliographie, now known as the International Federation of Documentation, and two great Belgian enthusiasts, Paul Otlet and Senator Henri La Fontaine. One of the aims of the Institut, which was initiated following an international conference of bibliographers held in 1895, was to compile a universal catalogue that should include, in a classified arrangement, every book in existence and every article of worth in periodical literature. It seems quixotic enough an enterprise; by the 1920s it was estimated that about 150,000 books were published yearly and there were at least 72,000 periodicals. Otlet also calculated that, if one included books and the principal articles published in journals the world over, there had appeared from the discovery of printing to the year 1900 some 25 million bibliographical units! Nevertheless, the conference entered upon the project; the Belgian Government, no doubt through the high influence of La Fontaine, provided funds and so became the first government to sustain bibliography; and, for the gigantic catalogue envisaged, work began on an extension of the *Decimal Classification* for documentation purposes, for which special permission was received. This was the *Universal Decimal Classification*, a system which has been since published in many languages and has proved extremely useful in large or specialized libraries where the exact classification of literature, especially scientific literature, is demanded. UDC, as it is usually known as, was first published in the French language in 1905. As an important living classification, and one which is extremely popular in special libraries in Europe and, to a lesser extent, throughout the world, it is a system which must be described in more detail later. Here it may simply be said that, with the possible exceptions of the system of Brunet and that devised for the University of Halle by Hartwig, which had some influence in the USA, this was the first important European classification aimed at organizing knowledge in libraries. It was bold enough to practise synthetic classification before the requisite theory was forged and this factor, plus its necessarily piecemeal development and the fact that the editorial burdens rested for too long on the shoulders of a few dedicated individuals (notably Donker Duyvis), handicap its present and future potential to some extent. Yet it was and is a remarkable achievement and the scheme has much merit and no lack of support today. It is salutary to note that the kind of thorough-going subject analysis and specification which UDC demanded from the start for the world of documentation is, due to the knowledge explosion, now increasingly applicable to books.

Two individuals with different ideas from Otlet and La Fontaine may be considered next. The itinerant German, Julius Otto Kaiser, was an indexer rather than a classificationist, but in his attempt to establish principles for an alphabetical subject retrieval system, he inevitably encountered the problem of citation order. Kaiser in his *Systematic Indexing* – and in other writings – distinguishes between *concretes* and *processes* and urges that the latter should qualify the former in a subject heading. Thus a piece of information on the 'moulding of plastics' might be indexed under Plastics – Moulding. The analysis (quite unconsciously akin to Brown's in some ways) is insufficient, but Kaiser worked hard to establish rules and consistency. He looked also at the problems of filing headings, of incorporating place headings into the system adequately and above all at the need for cross-references. The latter, he advocated, should be provided liberally and should be specific to general as well as general to specific. His ideas of categories and his distinction between entities (concretes) and processes (operations) are important and represent a simple form of the analysis which now, of necessity, taxes the mind of modern designers of indexing systems. His work was largely ignored for some time, but has now received due recognition; this is perhaps partly due to the praise given to Kaiser by Metcalfe in his *Subject Classifying and Indexing of Libraries and Literature*, 1959.

Contemporary with Kaiser's work and chronologically the next writings of importance in Britain are the periodical articles of Wyndham Hulme, whose ideas about the distinctive nature of book arrangement have already been briefly mentioned. Historically, Hulme's work is the natural antithesis to that of Richardson; whereas the former stressed that a map of knowledge adapted to fit the needs of books might well neglect their 'literary warrant', the latter thought that such a map was the essential basis of bibliographical classification. Hulme's ideas, as put forward in 1911, are that classification in libraries must essentially be 'a mapping-out of areas pre-existing in literature'; these he put into practice with his deputy at the Patent Office Library, H. V. Hopwood. For many years his work, too, was neglected; this was most unfortunate as it contained some very important theories. The late E. A. Savage[1] was to support him in the provocative and even amusing work published in 1946, and Metcalfe also pays tribute to the principles expounded by Hulme. Savage indeed, in extolling the merits of literary warrant, made a direct attack on schemes which owe a debt to the old philosophical classifications – 'when the Gods want to destroy classifiers', he says, 'they first set them to play somersaults with Bacon!' But Hulme's place in the history of library classification is now fully assured. In fact, some of his leading ideas have been incorporated with modern theories and it is interesting to note that, in the twilight of Hulme's life, he met and conversed with Ranganathan; their talk is mentioned in Ranganathan's moving tribute to the British classifier.[2] Their ideas may have been somewhat different, but like all enthusiasts for this subject, they found plenty to discuss when they met.

In any chronological account, there is little to record in the decade following the work of Hulme and Kaiser. In 1918, the *Introduction to Library Classification*, by Berwick Sayers was first published as an elementary work on the subject; it was followed in 1926 by the first edition of this *Manual*. These works in their early editions tend to support Richardson's theories on the need for a book classification

---

[1] *Manual of Book Classification and Display.* Allen and Unwin, 1946.
[2] Library Association Record, March, 1956, pp. 120–22.

to be founded on a classification of knowledge. These are essentially textbooks; on the other hand, the *Code for Classifiers* of the United States librarian, William S. Merrill, is essentially a guide for the practical classifier. It first appeared in 1928 and its intention was to show the main decisions which the classifier has to make, regardless of the scheme which he is applying, and to give advice to enable him to make these decisions wisely. A year or so later, we have the writings of another great librarian from the United States – Henry Evelyn Bliss. He more than any other is the inheritor of the ideas of Richardson, but he brings to these notions a new status and dignity on account of his erudition and his extensive study of the philosophical systems of earlier centuries. His two books – *The Organization of Knowledge and the System of the Sciences* (1929), and *The Organization of Knowledge in Libraries* (1933) are not easy reading, although Ranganathan once coped with them in a single sitting! The first of these shows Bliss's debt to the philosophical schemes; the second discusses notation, the principles of classification and the faults of existing book classifications. This latter work appeared in a second edition in 1939; Bliss was thus able to add a critique of the *Colon Classification* and to revise his own theories as he prepared his own *Bibliographic Classification* (1949–53), which was later to be revised by others. The depth of Bliss's learning and the extent of his research is evident from a perusal of these two large volumes, although his rather pedantic and over-precise use of words tends to serve as a stumbling block to the potential reader. Nevertheless, he has contributed a very great deal to our subject, especially in the realm of helpful order. He emphasized the idea that classification in each subject area should reflect the opinions of specialist consensus, while at the same time providing alternative locations where there were seen to be rival and legitimate schools of thought. The Bliss concept of gradation by speciality (described in the BC chapter) is in full accord with the ideas of several modern classification theorists and the recent attempts to use the philosophical theory of integrative levels of knowledge as the basis for an order in a new general scheme would doubtless have won Bliss's support, for – in the words of one obituary notice – his constant concern was to seek an arrangement so that 'subject matters are inter-related as the existent realities evidently are in the universe'.[1] His limitations seem to be the direct result of his attempt to establish the 'consensus of opinion' almost single-handed, rather than as

[1] *New York Times*, August 10, 1955.

a member of a team of experts (although his efforts were based, it is true, upon a vast amount of study and investigation) and of the fact that he devoted so much time to a consideration of principles and to destructive criticism of existing schemes that he began to prepare his own classification too late in life. In some respects, these writings certainly anticipate modern theories; in others they cling to notions of the past. But Bliss, in any case, did not live to see the modern theories of classification firmly established, although in some ways he prepared us to receive them. We might describe him by means of the phrase used so aptly, by the poet Cowley, of the pioneer of scientific method, Francis Bacon, and say that Bliss is like 'the bell-ringer who is up early to call *others* to church'.

From India, in 1933, came the first edition of the *Colon Classification*. No other bibliographical classification has aroused either the enthusiasm or the severe criticism that have been accorded to Ranganathan's scheme. This mathematician-turned-librarian has shaken what many thought were the very foundations of book classification; no matter what our opinions of *Colon* may be, its influence cannot be ignored. Indeed, if one is not positively hostile towards the scheme, it could be regarded as the greatest stride forward, with regard to the principles of bibliographical classification, in the twentieth century. The chief ideas of Ranganathan, which were only dimly perceived in this first edition, but which were developed considerably in succeeding editions, are: the creation of an entirely synthetic scheme, the provision of a distinctive class-mark for each book in a library, the making of a scheme with the maximum of flexibility and mnemonic aids, and the provision of autonomy to the individual classifier for the creation of new class-marks. It must be stressed that, although *Colon* is the only general classification that is completely synthetic (for it relies entirely on the piecing together of standard unit parts to construct class-marks), the older book classifications do have, to a greater or lesser extent, an element of synthesis. Facet analysis *as such* is something that they do not recognize; but the synthetic idea occurs in their notion of common form and geographical divisions and elsewhere. Yet the full impact of the ideas which Ranganathan has either unearthed, or developed and crystallized, is almost incalculable. Metcalfe, who has been perhaps his most severe critic, suggests that few Indian librarians have been influenced by his theories. Despite the fact that Dewey's scheme is still the most used classification in that country, the number of articles in Indian library journals these days which owe so much to those theories, would seem to refute this particular argument or, at least, to indicate that it is true no longer. Metcalfe is certainly on firm ground, however, when he suggests that Ranganathan's greatest influence has been on British classifiers and classificationists.

Along with innovation, ideas and principles there is, in the historical growth of any subject, the need for consolidation and the development of sound practice. It would not be unfair to say that in the first half of the present century, while men like Bliss and Ranganathan planned new schemes, others were well content to apply and develop the earlier ones, thinking possibly that – if greater subtlety was required – the answer would eventually lie in mechanized information retrieval systems. In some countries, perhaps particularly in the United States, the DC became well established in public and academic libraries – although more recently the academic libraries of North America have led a swing towards LC, prompted doubtless by the thought of facilitating participation in centralized cataloguing programmes. The impact of BC in North America has been negligible and even the UDC, which (much more than LC) enjoys great vogue in many parts of Europe, has had difficulty in making progress in view of the monopoly position which DC and LC gained and held in the United States. Yet, along with the rock-like position of those schemes (some might say because of it) there grew a certain amount of disillusionment with specific classification. The favouring of the alphabetical subject catalogue and the tendency in many quarters to view classification as a mere hand-maiden of cataloguing led to some questioning of the value or success of the great enumerative classifications. Dr Grace Kelley's important study of 1937 drew attention to numerous elements which affected the usefulness of systematic arrangement and advocated a 'wise simplification of classification' with more reliance on the subject catalogue. It is nevertheless interesting to note that the simplified standard edition (the fifteenth) of DC in 1951, which was really the only edition to abandon tradition in a search for broad arrangement and which urged users to give it 'the benefit of their criticism', was very badly received and was exposed to extensive criticism. Perhaps in simplifying classification, anticipation is better than realization. Alternatively, some might say that there is a law in library classification which suggests that any degree of change in a scheme should be inversely proportionate to its degree of use and that no widely accepted system can afford to recast its basic framework. One would not wish to present a wrong impression of the development of classification in the United States; the prevalent philosophy with its emphasis on the utilitarian and the practical, has largely complemented the quest for new principles and schemes which has so characterized the recent history of classification in Britain. Much of the research in the United States has had demonstrably pragmatic ends and where there has been some scepticism it is healthy, for any critique of detailed classification must spotlight faults and may promote improvements.

One, comparatively late, event which is at least partly indicative of that philosophy and scepticism deserves to be remarked upon. In 1961 there appeared, almost unnoticed, a new general classification. The lack of publicity or enthusiasm for it was due in part to the fact that any new scheme with the avowed aim, as its sub-title says, of providing solely 'for the arrangement of books on the shelves of general libraries' has little chance of driving out old favourites which can be thought of as standards, but also in part to the very modest claims made by its author. Dr Fremont Rider was a scholar of distinction whose contributions to micro-records and storage problems alone would ensure him of a deserved place in library history, but his *International Classification*, although interesting, is something of an anachronistic curiosity. It shuns close classification and 'divide like . . .' advice as unnecessary complications and enumerates some 16,000 topics, taking full account of contemporary literary warrant and providing a pure notation of capital letters. No class-mark has more than three letters and the size of the single volume testifies to the bulk which is the inevitable result – even in a broad classification – of full reliance on enumeration. Rider does acknowledge the merits of precise classification in some contexts, but avows that it is too complex for shelf order. (He might have been warned by the lesson of DC 15.) His own, commendably simple, scheme has good balance and apportionment by and large, plus some sequences and divisions to which other classificationists or compilers of thesauri could refer as a check on broad headings, but it remains unused. IC is at once both a testimony to the difficulty of introducing change into established present-day shelf arrangement of books and to the futility of one man attempting to row alone against a stream of time and opinion. In addition, any classificationist who, however commendable his motives, states baldly that his scheme will not be revised and that libraries of the future which use it (if there are any such) should accept its unchanging structure's growing limitations or switch to a new and better scheme, is likely to have a system which attracts dust rather than adherents.

Since 1950 at least, there has developed a British tradition in classification which has been, as already hinted, to seek out new principles and to clarify those which underlie existing schemes. This has been attested to by the formation of the Classification Research Group in 1952 and the subsequent work of its members, the making of numerous special classifications on fully-faceted lines, the growth of chain indexing and the writings of various enthusiasts. Currently we have the development of PRECIS as an indexing language for the BNB and British MARC and the construction of a new general scheme for a computer-based system. If Ranganathan's work influenced the British theorists, there have certainly been other influences too and, in some cases, the ideas of CC have been partly rejected as new facts have been generated by research. The research, however, is by no means restricted to Britain and the general enthusiasm for investigation, of one sort or another, into the principles of classification, is reflected not only in the ever-growing literature and proliferation of systems of indexing which use some ideas of a classificatory nature, but also in the international conferences on classification – at Dorking in 1957 and at Elsinore in 1964. The Dorking Conference had representatives only from France, Germany, India, Italy, the Netherlands, the United States and the United Kingdom, but sixteen nations were represented in Denmark. A third conference has been arranged for 1975 in Bombay. Post-co-ordinate indexing and thesauri too have their own intriguing history of research and development.

Meanwhile, new problems – and some that have been long with us – constantly rear their heads. Will project MARC and the boost it gives to centralization change classification theory and practice? Can classification be tested with regard to its usefulness in general libraries as it has been in an information retrieval context in the Aslib Cranfield experiment and elsewhere? Should stability take precedence over innovation in an established scheme? What classification should be used for the newly integrated national service of the British Library? Can a computer measure statistically the frequency of word-use and word-associations and thus promote mathematically-generated classifications based on impartially selected keywords and clusterings? When is reclassification justified? History cannot give us dogmatic answers to questions like these, but can often illuminate our thinking. (Perhaps too, in examining the work of people such as Karen Sparck Jones, Elizabeth Moys or Jean Aitchison, we may at last be witnessing the emergence of the female classificationist.)

A skeleton outline of library classification can do scant justice to the theme, but may act as a useful preface to the study of individual schemes; the latter provides further insight into the development as well as into the present position and prospects of each one. The total history of systematic subject order in libraries shows many interesting ideas, some of which have a perennial attraction. The early bibliographical schemes are naturally influenced by philosophical charts of knowledge (the Congress system being an important exception) and, like philosophical classifications, tend to be relatively broad. They soon increase the amount of detail provided, however, and pay more attention to helpful order within classes as the growth of libraries demands a more exact arrangement. The idea of 'literary warrant' challenges the notion that book classification is merely a classification of knowledge with certain adjustments and, in the twentieth century, we find the older classifications breaking down in principle, if not in practice, and increasingly the recognition dawning that only the fully-faceted scheme can cope with the complex problems of subject analysis which arise in dealing with so many modern documents. As in other subject fields, we discover that the early history of book classification reveals the emergence in a crude form of certain fundamental principles which, like a river, may disappear underground for a time, only to return in a fuller torrent later on. The ebb and flow of theories and ideas has left us with much on which to speculate: the possible value of 'expansive classifications', the need to recognize 'literary warrant'; facet analysis and citation order; phase analysis; Bliss's ideas on alternative location; integrative levels and so forth. Many of these notions are certain to be crucial in the development of new schemes, but all these and other ideas revealed in the comparatively short history of library classification will repay careful study. Several will be utilized by the classificationists of tomorrow and by those who revise the systems of today.

Bibliography on Section Two

La Montagne, L. E. *American Library Classification*. Shoe String Press, 1961.
An excellent historical account: a detailed history of the LC classification is given.

Older schemes or less successful ones may be examined, eg, Rider's *International Classification*. J. D. Brown's *Subject Classification*, 3rd edition, 1939, has a useful introduction. The books of Bliss and Ranganathan put the development of their respective theories into historical context.

On the development of the Classification Research Group, 1952–62 in Britain there is D. J. Foskett's paper in his *Science, Humanism and Libraries*, 1964.

One can also read:

Wilson, T. D. *The Work of the British Classification Research Group*. In Wellisch and Wilson (editors), *Subject Retrieval in the Seventies* (cited in full at the end of Section One).

On classification and thesauri there is the interesting paper:

Jones, K. Sparck. *Some Thesauric History*. Aslib Proceedings, July, 1972, pp. 400–11.

The Major General Bibliographical Schemes

CHAPTER NINE

The Dewey Decimal Classification

Introduction. A classification scheme which is used in all five continents, has been translated, at least in part, into several European languages and into Chinese, and has reached an eighteenth edition in English, must take priority of place in our discussion of modern library systems. That, briefly, is the record of the *Decimal Classification* of Melvil Dewey. Its cardinal virtues are universality and hospitality, a simple expansible notation which is now almost an international classification vocabulary, excellent mnemonic features, first-class machinery for its perpetuation, and an admirable index. It has many defects, but nevertheless has such adaptive qualities that it has survived much cogent and seemingly unanswerable criticism and has progressed in spite of it; indeed, for some years, to meet a real demand, the Library of Congress has printed the DC (some prefer the abbreviation DDC) numbers as well as its own on its catalogue cards. Shortly after Dewey's death the editorial office was housed in the Congress Library and editions from the sixteenth onwards were in fact produced by the Congress staff. As the introduction to the latest edition points out, the scheme's enormous popularity is attested to by the fact that 'titles in thousands of reading lists, book guides, and bibliographies have been arranged or their subjects identified by the *Dewey Decimal Classification*'. Perhaps equally significant is the fact that the main classes and divisions and the essential parts of the notation of DC form the basis of the *Universal Decimal Classification*.

DC regards knowledge as unity, which is to be divided into nine large classes; works too general in scope for any of these form a tenth class. These are properly written thus:

0.0 General works   0.2 Religion
0.1 Philosophy   0.3 Social Sciences

0.4 Philology	0.7 Fine Arts
0.5 Natural Sciences	0.8 Literature
0.6 Useful Arts	0.9 History

The ten units of decimal division are thus reached. In practice, however, the initial o and point are assumed and the classes are written merely: o General works, 1 Philosophy, 2 Religion, etc. An extract from the introductory explanation to an abridgement of the schemes will give the salient features of DC in the words of its author: 'The classification divides the field of knowledge into 9 main classes, numbered 1–9. Cyclopaedias, periodicals, etc., so general as to belong to no one of these classes, are marked o (nought) and form a tenth class. Each class is similarly separated into 9 divisions, general works belonging to no division having o in place of the decimal number. Divisions are similarly divided into 9 sections and, it may be said, further sections, sub-sections and sub-sub-sections, without limit other than that imposed by the material to be classified, can be devised. Thus 512 means class 5 Natural Science, division 1 Mathematics, section 2 Algebra, and every algebra is numbered 512. Its class number, giving class, division and section, is applied to every book and pamphlet in the library. Since each number means a definite subject, all material on any subject must, if physical form permits it, stand together. The schedules show the order of subjects. Thus 513 Arithmetic follows 512 Algebra and precedes 514 Topology.

The first edition appeared in 1876, and consisted of 12 pages of prefatory matter, 12 of tables and 18 of Index, a total of 42 pages; and of this modest work 1,000 copies were printed. It is curious to reflect that it was immediately challenged by librarians as being too minute in its sub-divisions for the arrangement of any but very large libraries. The fourteenth edition (1942), however, consisted of 1,927 pages, including index; its elephantine nature brought forth some protests and the reaction was seen in the unorthodox edition (15). Later editions returned to the conventional pattern, but offered the index in a separate volume. Indeed, the current edition (the eighteenth) provides three volumes. The first consists of introductory material and the various auxiliary tables for synthesis; the second accommodates the schedules; and the third offers the relative index. This growth suggests the enormous number of sub-divisions that are possible, because literature exists or may exist upon them, and are necessary when minute classification is undertaken. It reveals also the flexibility of a scheme which has permitted such expansion.

Features and Principles. Although the tiny tables of 1876 were considered to be too complex by their earliest critics, who had not yet applied them, the development which followed their use, especially by larger libraries, brought out the most enduring comment, some of it adverse, to be made of them. Yet there can be no doubt that much of the criticism of DC is the direct result of its enormous popularity; no other scheme has been tried and tested in so many libraries and so minutely scrutinized by members of our profession. The great merits of the system lie in the simplicity and universal appeal of its notation, the ease with which it can be understood and applied, the fact that it is regularly revised with an awareness of customers' needs, and the assurance, given in the second edition of 1885, that no drastic changes in the allocation of numbers to subjects would ever be made. This last promise is, in many ways, a two-edged sword; it means that the librarian does not have to contend with the problem of drastic changes in the location of subjects each time a new edition of DC appears, but it also means that a really thorough overhaul of the sequence of topics is out of the question, unless this long-standing assurance is violated. Yet, by and large, the 'integrity of numbers' policy is pleasing to users of DC, who rarely welcome relocations of topics. It might also be said, when endeavouring to explain the phenomenal success of this classification, that the fact that it appeared at the ideal period in the history of librarianship, a time when libraries were about to change from closed access (with its reliance on fixed-location systems) to an open-access principle, is a major reason for its popularity. It is certainly true that DC was firmly entrenched by the time its earlier serious rivals began to appear and that classifications, once adopted, are not to be lightly abandoned. But it is also true that DC had – and has – definite advantages of a more positive kind over many of these rivals. Cutter's *Expansive Classification*, although excellent in some respects, was never completed; LC is really chiefly for the huge Congress library itself; SC has some odd features and has never been regularly revised; UDC is mainly for special libraries and for use in bibliographies and complex retrieval systems; and BC in its nature and intent is the obvious challenger, but it arrived very late and the notation is hardly an international one. The emphasis, merits and limitations of other schemes are considered later; here it is sufficient to say that Dewey's DC has been favoured in the majority of public, college and school libraries because of inherent qualities, plus historical and administrative factors. Among the latter is the increasing convenience of employing a system which is accepted in national and international centralized cataloguing and has its class-marks safely incorporated into a taped record for machine-readable catalogues. The wise and continuing emphasis on 'classification by discipline' is also welcome.

It must be stressed that the early editions of DC represented a tremendous improvement upon earlier methods, for when this scheme first appeared, many books in libraries were still arranged solely by size or some such artificial feature. DC has not only proved more successful than its later rivals, it has influenced them greatly. For the best features of this classification and its index have been copied by most schemes; even the modern stress on the value of synthetic classification was anticipated by Dewey, although he does not fully recognize the possibilities of this idea. Another excellent feature of his scheme lies in its adaptability. DC can easily be modified to meet the needs of different libraries and various modifications and minor rearrangements are authorized in the introduction to the schedules. Recent editions point out that the scheme offers reasonably close, or detailed, classification for general libraries, if the synthetic possibilities are taken into account. Any library not requiring a great deal of detail can use the abridged version, or 'cut back' quite easily the notation of the full schedules. Thus we see that the abiding merits of the system are those of simplicity, ease of comprehension and application, universality of appeal, susceptibility to modifications, and regular production and overhaul.

The system is certainly not without fault; some critics suggest that it is lacking in scholarship and detail, that the notation is a mixed blessing and has often been allocated with insufficient care, and that order and collocation are sometimes more than a little suspect. A few extreme supporters of synthetic classification would have us abandon DC, although they find it difficult to suggest a suitable alternative. Weaknesses in Dewey's classification include faulty order in certain classes (650, for example, from which many subjects have been recently transferred), the separation of closely allied disciplines, such as Social Sciences and History or Language and Literature; the failure to bring the history and geography of a country together; and the American terminology and general bias towards the needs of Western civilization. Recent editions try to come to the rescue with this last point; provision is made for other cultures and nations to be brought to the fore, if so desired. DC has also been criticized as being unsuitable for the special library, but this is really true of almost all general classifications. A serious fault perhaps, as we have already briefly mentioned, is inherent in the 'number integrity' idea. The removal of drastic defects in the DC sequence of topics is certainly hindered by the refusal to introduce radical change; the difficulty is that such change is impractical in most established libraries and the policy of conservative scrutiny and gradual rearrangement of the schedules to keep pace with the growth of knowledge is the one which commends itself to practically all librarians who are committed to the scheme. Of course, newly created libraries will insist upon a modern organization of knowledge, so overhaul of the tables cannot be too conservative. But the traditional policy has been one of evolutionary rather than revolutionary development, relocations taking place just in sufficient quantity to prevent, in the words of the editor, 'an outmoded past from tyrannizing over the future'. DC's severest critics would also point to the scheme's debt to the Baconian chart of 1605. True, this makes it seem that the roots of this classification are in the remote past, but the constant attention of experts has succeeded in overcoming many defects in the order of classes without violent upheaval and the links between Dewey's scheme and that of Bacon can be overstressed.

To sum up, the features of DC are such that it is still, on balance, the best scheme for public libraries and many other general libraries will also unhesitatingly accept it. When Fremont Rider, in the introduction to his *International Classification*, described DC as 'the most marvellous bibliographical tool ever devised for the use of the library world', he was bestowing praise on a rival system, which is rare among classificationists, but he was surely expressing the enormous debt of the profession, and this on a truly international scale, to the genius and tenacity of purpose of Melvil Dewey.

Notation. This illustrates well some of the merits and defects of a great classification. The choice of numerals, although making the scheme universally acceptable, placed a great barrier on its capacity to house subjects. DC has always attempted to reveal its hierarchy in the notation; this restricts it to nine places at each stage of division (assuming that the zero is used to introduce standard sub-divisions, or form divisions as they were formerly called). This 'decimal procrustean bed' has received a great deal of criticism. The cramped nature of the notation is intensified by the fact that the original apportionment of numbers to subjects was in many cases faulty.

Recognition of this and also of the difficulty of change is clearly shown by the editor, Benjamin Custer: 'To reapportion the notation so that it would be equally hospitable to all disciplines and subjects held by libraries today would require the development of a wholly new system and would only establish a base for other inequities of a future that today cannot be imagined, just as much as the [modern] world . . . could not be imagined in 1876.'

Because of this faulty apportionment, in the light of modern needs, many subjects, especially in sciences and technology and in other rapidly developing fields of knowledge, are burdened with long numbers – a direct result of the overcrowding in the classes concerned. Other classes, in more static subject areas, are relatively empty and provide concise notations for the topics concerned. The scheme offers advice, however, for coping with long numbers; we are shown how and where to make cuts, if we so wish. There must never, of course, be a number which ends with a zero to the right of the decimal point. It must be confessed that the notation could be expanded indefinitely in chain and that the average class-mark is easily recollected – the pure notation may contribute something to this. Although the scheme, like two others, was named after a notational feature, we would not necessarily agree with the editor of the system that this is its 'greatest strength'. It is, however, despite the acknowledged lack of capacity of numerical notations, a good feature in many respects. Dewey may have restricted the development of his scheme in some ways on that eventful morning in the Amherst College chapel when he decided upon the decimal system, but his choice did much to make his classification internationally acceptable.

Synthesis and Mnemonics. Synthesis has always been present along with the enumeration in DC, but has often appeared only in an embryonic form. Possibilities for notational synthesis have been greatly increased in recent editions. The introduction now even accepts terminology such as 'faceted' and 'citation order' (a glossary being provided). The problem of phase analysis and allied matters also emerges in the introduction to the eighteenth edition, although the term is not used, with a consideration of the classification of 'the influence of Shakespeare on Keats'. The main use of synthesis, however, is through the use of special tables, now seven in number – and akin to some of the synthetic apparatus of BC and UDC. These tables are:

1) Standard sub-divisions (once called form divisions; these cover a miscellany of recurring concepts – forms of presentation, aspects, viewpoints, etc.).
2) Area Table (a very full 'common geographical facet').
3) For sub-division, by appropriate synthesis, of individual literatures.
4) For similar treatment of individual languages.
5) For specification of racial, ethnic or national groups.
6) To specify the language in which a document appears.
7) For sub-division to specify persons – usually distinctive groups of persons.

The use of these is naturally optional. Table 1 can be employed at any point in the main schedules where its detail is appropriate, but the others are all dependent on the instruction to use them. If the area table cannot be applied directly because of possible notational ambiguity, it can be employed indirectly via 09 from the standard sub-divisions of Table 1. Most of these tables are somewhat specialized and limited in their application in shelf classification, but Tables 1 and 2 deserve further scrutiny.

A short sample may serve to illustrate the scope of Table 1, which now goes far beyond the original concept of nine divisions of 'form' specified by 01–09:

-016   Indexes and bibliographies
-017   Professional and Occupational Ethics
-018   Methodology
-0182 Statistical method
-0184 Operations research
-019   Psychological principles

These can be used, as appropriate, throughout the scheme and are always to be introduced by their one initial zero, unless they are added to a class-mark ending with a nought; in such cases the zero of the form divisions usually disappears. But if subject sub-divisions are introduced by .o under a particular number, then .oo introduces the standard sub-division. Thus a *history of pharmacology* is 615.09, but the *history of management* is 658.009 as 658.01–658.09 are partly consumed by subject sub-divisions.

Synthesis is also achieved by the use of the area table. Its divisions are based on the country numbers of class 900. At various points in the main schedules we are invited to build up numbers by specifying the region to which a subject is restricted and this means involvement of the area notation. *Music festivals*, for instance, are at 780.79 and we are invited to sub-divide further, if need be, via the area table. In this table, the distinctive number for London is 421 (because the History of London in class 900 is at 942.1). So *Music festivals in London* can be classed specifically at 780.79421. Likewise the *military situation in Vietnam* can go at 355.0332597 (597 being the precise area notation for Vietnam). It must be pointed out that the area tables can only be used in this form where an invitation to employ it appears in the schedules. If no instruction is given and the classifier wishes to divide a subject by a geographical region, he must introduce the regional number by 09. Failure to do this will lead to serious muddle and ambiguity, for without the 09 in such instances the regional number will coincide with a *subject* sub-division. Such ambiguity is largely a result of the fact that this synthesis has been grafted on to the original Dewey framework and has evolved piecemeal rather than been planned or applied 'at a stroke'. There is thus, alas, no clear indicator digit which can *consistently* introduce a geographical facet.

In addition to the use of these and, where necessary, the other tables for synthesis, there is frequently to be found in the main schedules the instruction 'add to', which is an invitation to number build. An example is at 623.812 *Design of Craft*. In this division of naval architecture we are told that we may 'add to 623.812 the numbers following 623.82'. Thus, by synthesis, we can specify *The design of motor boats* at 623.81231. This 'add to' device (represented by 'divide like' in editions prior to the eighteenth), is a potent tool for synthesis and the frequency of its use has greatly increased in recent editions of DC. Another example is at 345.06 *Evidence in criminal law* (note .06 is a *subject* sub-division here, for this is another example of .00 being needed for standard sub-divisions). Here, to specify *use of scientific evidence in criminal law* we can 'add to 345.06 the numbers following 347.06'. Our specific number thus becomes 345.064. The 'add to' device is a useful way of avoiding the continual listing of recurring concepts and it thus helps keep down the size of a large enumerative system. Sometimes this type of advice covers the whole classification. For example, at 069.9 *Museums*, we can add numbers from the full range 000–999 to specify accurately the *type* of museum. A work on *geological museums* could thus be classed at 069.955. Again, at 016, *subject bibliographies* may be classified in this way. Thus a *bibliography of art* would be 016.7; a bibliography of architecture 016.72 and so forth. Of course, for those librarians who prefer it, it is permissible to distribute such bibliographical material by subject interest, adding in this case the appropriate standard sub-division for bibliographies to the subject class-mark.

There is clearly more opportunity than ever for number-building, although the 'grafting on' of such synthetic apparatus leads to some complications and – as has been shown – necessary exceptions to general instructions because of the late arrival of some of that apparatus. The main scope for synthesis undoubtedly lies in the standard sub-divisions, the area table and the 'add to' instructions. But the connoisseur of faceting should notice also the distinctly North American concept of general-special, which is a form of synthesis in a sense, but achieved by a device of the classificationist rather than by number building from the individual classifier. The general-special idea arises when a characteristic of division of wide application is used both for the sub-division of general topics *and also* of more specific and within the same class. It is clearly a device for enabling a basically enumerative system to cope with more compounds than might otherwise be possible. Thus, to quote a DC example, the Bible can be viewed from the standpoint of criticism and exegesis. It can also be divided into its individual books. Each of these also can be viewed from the standpoint of criticism and exegesis, so that we have:

Bible
> *Criticism and exegesis*
>> Individual books
>>> *Criticism and exegesis of individual books*

The rigidity of a fixed hierarchy is largely removed by this notion. However, if the concept is excellent, the execution is rather less so. For the division 04, freed from its former role as a standard sub-division, is often used for the task especially within certain technologies. This leads to *subject* sub-divisions of a class at 04 intruding most unhelpfully, between *forms of presentation*, ie, encyclopaedias and serials on the subject. Accurate subject specification *is* achieved but at some expense of helpful order. One reviewer has even suggested, with some justification, that the discerning classifier should, in such instances, employ .00 for the standard sub-divisions in order strictly to maintain a suitably correct general to special sequence.

The scheme is still to be thought of as basically an enumerative one, but all the synthetic devices have the effect of adding to the memory value of the notation. For it is clear that, by means of their constant repetition with the same significance, the standard subdivisions and area divisions will have mnemonic effect. 42 is not always England and Wales in the scheme, nor does 73 always denote the United States.

But England and Wales and the United States are constantly denoted by 42 and 73 respectively when these geographical areas are to be added to a subject number. Thus we have here an example of systematic mnemonics. The DC notation also achieves mnemonic power by the similarity of the numbering used for certain kindred classes. Thus 913-919 are the numbers used for the geography of various countries; this block of numbers has divisions which are based on those of 940-999, which cover the history of the same countries. So we find that in class 900 the History of Switzerland is 949.4 and the Geography of the same country 914.94. Or, to look at this in a different light, if we imagine 9 as denoting History and 91 Geography, we merely need to add to these the appropriate area table number (494 in the case of Switzerland). The common area table is based on these numbers. The Language and Literature classes show a similar parallel structure in their major divisions; likewise we find that the divisions of the various languages and literatures are based on those of English Language and Literature. One should look carefully at classes like these and note the mnemonic effect gained by the similarity of the notational pattern.

Index. The eighteen pages of the first Relative Index had expanded to 738 by the time the fourteenth edition was reached, and it had become a vast alphabet of about 80,000 terms. It is now published as a separate volume, but following some criticism of the index to edition 16, the seventeenth edition tried to reduce the bulk of the index somewhat. Many of the entries of the sixteenth edition were replaced by see references, thus:

Gaseous
    fuels, see Industrial gases
    illuminants, see Industrial gases

The revolutionary character of the new index led to a flood of complaints and a revised index, more in the traditional mode, was published. The index to edition eighteen combines the features of the two forms, but is basically conventional and unlikely to offend any librarian who can use a good relative index and who realizes that one cannot classify by the index alone. Cross-references are frequently made and the use of bold typeface indicates topics that are sub-divided in the main schedules. Economy dictates that certain proper names and other terms are omitted (eg, entries for some, but by no means all, subjects specified through synthesis are shown), but the current index runs to over a thousand pages and is not so very much shorter than the schedules of the classification.

It should be added that, notwithstanding the outcry concerning the original index to edition seventeen, the DC indexing tradition has been generally excellent. The indexes to all other general schemes are, to a greater or lesser extent, indebted to the influence of the Relative Index as devised and lauded by Melvil Dewey.

Use and Revision of the Scheme. The most striking testimony to DC lies in the fact that it is by far the most used general library classification in the world. The standard edition (1951) indicated that, in the United States, DC was used by about 96% of public libraries, 89% of college and university libraries and 64% of the special libraries. This position of near monopoly has not changed a great deal in the last decade or so; there was a definite tendency for North American academic libraries to move away from DC to LC in the late 1960s, but this appears to have lost some momentum. As far as the revision of the system is concerned, we find that new editions are published approximately every eight years. Revision of detail and relocations in these are rather conservative in comparison with, say, the *Colon*, *Universal Decimal* or even the *Congress* schemes; on the other hand, there are users who complain about the alterations which are made and, by and large, DC seems to steer fairly well the difficult course between the Scylla of introducing drastic notational alterations and the Charybdis of failing to keep pace with knowledge. The bulletin issued to subscribers between editions and entitled *Decimal Classification* Additions, Notes and Decisions is a useful pointer to changes which will be incorporated in the schedules as soon as possible. The editorial body of DC is especially attentive these days to the complaints and suggestions of practising librarians and will gladly listen to the advice of the scheme's users; there is every opportunity for the consumer to put forward his ideas with regard to proposed improvements – witness the surveys of the *use* of the scheme within and without North America.

A word about the preparation of the last four or five editions may be in order. Dewey left actual library work some years before his death in 1931, but he kept the management of the scheme, although other editors supervised the various editions. A feature of DC, at least from the sixth edition, was the use of a phonetic simplified spelling, which increased in unlikeness to that of ordinary folk with each successive edition. This did much, we are certain, to interfere with its acceptance by some would-be users. The Lake Placid Club Educational Foundation, which was another enterprise of Dewey's, has cared for the classification during the years since 1924, and for some years after Dewey's death, until ill-health prevented, his policies and practices were continued by his chosen editor and loyal fellow-worker, Dorcas Fellows, who produced the thirteenth memorial edition in 1932. This was a considerable expansion of the twelfth in parts. The revisions, however, were never radical and balanced; its editors made expansions to meet the obvious needs of knowledge, but side by side with some of the most modern schedules, as, for example, the alternative tables for Psychology in the 1932 edition such obsolete schedules survived as that for Photography. The bulky fourteenth edition may be passed over, but a word must be said about the 'Standard' fifteenth edition. A new editorial committee was given 'the difficult task of modernizing DC' and 'in 1945 the pattern of the new revision was furnished by instructors in library schools and by librarians in a variety of libraries in North and South America and in Great Britain'. Nevertheless, the policy of reducing the size of the schedules and seeking uniform expansion of classes for the needs of medium-sized libraries was not very successful. Nor was the index to the Standard edition satisfactory; in fact, it had to be reconstituted at the last moment to satisfy librarians in the United States. This edition must be regarded as a brave attempt to modernize DC and has been described as its first true revision, but the general reaction to it is well reflected by the article from the pen of Thelma Eaton[1] suggesting that it was virtually a new classification and that DC, as Dewey had conceived it, was thus dead.

Edition 16 returned to the traditional pattern, dropped most of the relocations and restored details which its predecessor had rejected. It tried to reconcile the conflicting aims of stability of notation and provision for new topics, but is more successful with regard to the former goal. It was in two volumes and was the first edition to be actually prepared by the staff of the Library of

[1] Library Association Record, November, 1956, pp. 428–30.

Congress. Work had taken place under the Congress roof for the perpetuation of DC since edition 13, but editions from the sixteenth onwards are the product of a team resulting from the combination of the staff of the Dewey Editorial Office and the DC section of the Library of Congress Subject Cataloguing Division. Edition 17 also continued the traditional pattern of DC, but contained many new and interesting features which are developed further in edition 18. For smaller libraries there is an abridged version. A feature of recent editions has been the determination to break away from rigid notational integrity to the extent of completely recasting one or more schedules to conform with modern needs. The disciplines in edition 18 for which the traditional pattern has been destroyed, with 'phoenix schedules' rising out of the ashes, are Law and Mathematics. Some librarians, loath to recognize and implement any change in DC may shudder at such treatment, but there is very much to commend and little to criticize in these new schedules. Those who advocate intensive reform and recasting might argue that this kind of process, with only one or two major disciplines having their arrangement remoulded in each edition, is too slow. Slow it is, but it does enable some real revision to take place without over-annoying established users – and one might argue that the speed at which a general classification can afford to accept radical change depends largely upon the number of users. There are fewer re-locations in the eighteenth edition than in its predecessor, but interesting innovations include the freeing of 999 to accommodate 'extra-terrestial subjects'. More ambitious changes sometimes advocated, such as the use of a two–digit base for interdisciplinary topics, would involve drastic remoulding of schedules and re-allocation of numbers at a rate guaranteed to make practical classifiers shudder. To return from speculation to fact, it must also be stated that the classes to which the 'phoenix schedule' treatment is meted out are presumably those which scrutiny and user opinion show to be in most dire need of reform. A mention of user opinion serves as a reminder that no system has done as much as DC to try to discover via surveys the wishes and attitudes of its librarian users. There is now more and more editorial awareness of international attitudes and viewpoints towards many subjects and their arrangement in DC.

Conclusion. It will be seen that the system still inevitably lags behind modern theories; the wholehearted supporter of the clear analysis of the elements which make up a subject into definite categories, or facets, is likely to be tempted to regard such an enumerative system as almost antediluvian in many respects. Yet no classification devised in the nineteenth century and at all concerned with number integrity could hope to be completely abreast with modern theories of classification or with modern knowledge. The fact remains that DC works well in a very large number of libraries. Some librarians may be lethargic or apathetic (although we often find that those who bandy these words about are the very ones who are not faced with the enormous task of reclassifying a collection of books but are anxious that others should reclassify) but the profession as a whole is too concerned about efficiency to make do with a tool that is hopelessly inadequate. Thus DC survives and thrives because, despite the arguments of its critics concerning real or imaginary faults, it seems to many to be still the best classification for public and probably for college libraries. No other system has yet been able, in practice, to offer a decisive challenge or to prove its theoretical superiority for the arrangement of such collections.

That the Bacon-Harris schemes, to which Dewey was partly indebted for his order of subjects, do not coincide with the modern view of subjects and studies is admitted, but any scheme of the so-called enumerative type cannot move its classes with every shift of knowledge.

The scheme certainly reflects the needs of a capitalist society and a Christian culture, although recent editions do attempt to provide for a library to bring its own nation and culture to the fore if it so wishes. Again, the limits of the decimal base are continually proclaimed and the British users sometimes still grumble about American bias and terminology. A formidable critic was Bliss, who attacked what he called the subject index illusion; the inverted Baconian order as unphilosophic and impractical; the important main sciences as separated and mangled; the notation as ill-proportioned and uneconomical. The scheme has also been criticized, in more recent years, by D. J. Foskett, who complains about the rigidity of its framework, and by Coates.[1] On the other hand, many critics insist that the great merits of DC be recognized also; as the American, H. H. Young,[2] points out, it has many excellent and lasting qualities.

No one now rushes to defend DC on the grounds of the modernity

[1] Library Association Record, August, 1959.
[2] The enduring qualities of Dewey. In Allerton Park Institute. *Role of Classification in the Modern American Library*, 1959.

of its order or the brevity of its notation. The curious fact remains that more and more libraries throughout the world are coming to use it, many of them modifying it; somehow it works. We should certainly fail in our appreciation of services rendered if we did not say that a scheme which has survived for a hundred years in growing currency, in spite of merited criticism, must have virtues which in practice outweigh our most powerful theoretical objections. These are chiefly its accessibility, its use in national cataloguing services, its constant revision by a large group of zealous and well-qualified workers, and the ease with which it may be applied in part or entirely to collections of books and expanded as these collections grow. The notation, despite the restricted base, has been most successful and influential. Ranganathan[1] writes: 'The most potent and lasting contribution of DC to the philosophy of library classification is the demonstration of the practicability of securing hospitality of notation by the simple device of decimal fraction notation.' The scheme is also much better equipped than many of its rivals with advice for the practical classifier; in the eighteenth edition this is shown by the long editorial introduction, by the reprinting of Melvil Dewey's original introduction, and by the usual very generous use of scope notes and definitions throughout the schedules.

Edition 18 strives to rationalize as well as to improve the scheme and to lay down a logical plan with more predictability for the individual classifier. It represents, on balance, an increased gain in the use of principles and clarity of subject analysis (although the gain is not as big as some theorists would wish) without any sacrifice of the pragmatism for which Dewey was renowned. After carefully considering the DC and listening to very many comments, both favourable and otherwise, we are convinced that the oldest and most persistent one comes from the expert who wants all material together on his subject, whatever that may be and from whatever angle he may approach it; it is the most understandable one and, to those of us who know what library classification entails, the least reasonable. Powerful opposition to DC has been noticeable in recent years from the supporters of the new theories; one can appreciate their zeal in extolling the merits of these theories more readily than the tendency, in certain quarters, to evaluate DC solely in the light of these principles and pronounce it obsolete when, in fact, no readily usable general faceted scheme yet exists to challenge it. Meanwhile, the decimal notation remains an obvious reason for the world-wide

[1] *Philosophy of Library Classification*, Munksgaard, 1951, p. 20.

use which the system enjoys, that it is an international 'language' understood by all nations. It will need a good shelf classification indeed to drive out DC in libraries. Some day it may disappear, as do all human efforts, but we now look ahead to the next edition, confident that the scheme has sufficient intrinsic merit, and certainly enough support, to endure as the popular favourite, in well-established general libraries at least, for many years to come.

CHAPTER TEN

Universal Decimal Classification

Many factors combine to make this a most interesting classification to study, perhaps especially at the present time. Of all the general schemes, UDC is the one aimed specifically at retrieval rather than at shelf arrangement or at fulfilling a dual purpose. It is, apart from CC and notwithstanding the changes in the new BC, the most synthetic of these schemes; certainly the most synthetic among the 'big three' in terms of use – DC, LC and UDC. It is, moreover, in process of some quite turbulent and dramatic review and development, with some disagreement among specialists and users as to how much reconstruction is needed for it to have a valuable future role in information science. Thus the emphasis in this chapter is on the sections designated synthesis, revision and use, and conclusion.

This system of classification was initiated by the International Institute of Bibliography, which was formed towards the end of the nineteenth century. The Institute (now International Federation of Documentation, or simply FID) hoped to collect bibliographies published throughout the world and to build up a vast classified catalogue covering all literature. Although the task was from the start a colossal one, early omens were encouraging; financial support was given by the Belgian Government, the IIB and its Bibliography Office were given premises in the Musée des Beaux Arts, and Paul Otlet and Henri La Fontaine, the originators of the IIB, became the secretaries. Later, the collections, which became extensive, were moved to larger premises in the Palais Mondial, where they remained with an interregnum of exile in Paris during the German occupation of Belgium 1914–19, until the Belgian government were seduced from bibliography by the British promoters of a rubber exhibition in 1923, who were allowed to turn out the Institute in order to use the Palais. No doubt in any but an ideal state *caoutchouc* will oust learning![1] The work came to a standstill for a while; then the League of Nations proposed to base its intellectual activities on the work of the Institute, so that what two nations failed to appreciate had a chance of being appreciated by the nations in concert. Meanwhile, the Institute had changed its name, to express more comprehensively its purpose, to the International Institute of Documentation; and in 1937 another World Congress of Universal Documentation was held in Paris, which determined that the Institute should be the world authority on documentation and its classification scheme the standard one. The name was changed once again to the title now used by the organization.

The arrangement of the cards in the vast classified catalogue obviously required a more detailed type of cataloguing than was commonly in use, wherein analysis could be carried to an almost extreme fineness. Moreover, to accomplish arrangement by subject a minute classification of infinite expansibility was a primary necessity. It was recognized that such a classification, in order to show such *nuances* as the relation of books to subjects, places, languages, epochs, etc., would demand a series of common sub-divisions much more comprehensive than those in any then existing system. The DC was adopted as the parent of the envisaged scheme, and this, in its adapted and extended form, was reaffirmed in 1937 to be the standard classification by the World Congress referred to above. In spite of the interruption of the war years, the great card catalogue contained in 1921 over 12 million entries; the FID were, however, forced to abandon this, but the UDC, as the 'Expanded Dewey' was called, continued to thrive and to prove most useful for the exact classification of the highly specific subjects encountered in documentation. The first edition of UDC (in French) appeared in 1905 after ten years of development and experiment; it was based on the fifth edition of DC. The second edition, also in French, was produced in 1927–33. A third full edition in German and a fourth in English were begun in 1933 and 1936 respectively.

The great success of this scheme in special libraries and information bureaux has created a need for national organizations to supervise its development and publication in the various languages. In Britain, the appropriate organization is the British Standards Institution, which took over the responsibilities for production of English editions in the 1940s. The full English edition has been

---

[1] So small was the interest in the fate of this patiently built-up enterprise that *The Times* refused to accept a short letter of protest.

published in fascicules and has concentrated mainly on schedules relating to science and technology. These fascicules appear as British Standard 1000, an example being:

617 Orthopaedics, surgery, opthalmology. BS1000: 1968

The delay in the completion of BS 1000 has caused considerable concern, but the rate of production has fortunately increased greatly in the last year or so and at the time of writing most of the schedules are becoming available. While awaiting them, or for the classification of material in 'fringe areas' the special librarian or information officer in English-speaking countries has been able to use the excellent abridgement BS 1000A: 3rd edition, 1961. This covers all the subject classes in a volume, which is slim but can, on account of its use of synthesis, provide much more detail than one associates with an abridged version if such detail is wanted. There is also a tri-lingual abridgement (BS 1000B) and J. Mills's valuable Guide to the use of UDC (BS 1000C). There are abridgements, and parts of the full schedules, available in other languages and it may be added that the tardiness in the production of full schedules has not exactly been a monopoly of the British Standards Institution.

Features and Principles. It must be stressed that UDC is a practical classification, based on the demands of pamphlet, report and periodical literature rather than on the framework of theory. This fact, together with the piecemeal development of the schedules over the years means that despite the work of national organizations, the yeoman service of men like the late Donker Duyvis, and the co-ordinating influence of the FID Central Classification Committee, the scheme contains certain anomalies and inconsistencies which, as we shall see, are increasingly coming to the fore. In addition UDC lays more stress on the detailed specification of each document's subject than the achievement of a sequence of optimum helpfulness. The emphasis on detail, actual or potential, is understandable and commendable; the apparent relegation of helpful order is less so. The aim is stated in the Abridged English Edition:

'UDC is essentially a practical system for numerically coding information, so designed that any item, once coded and filed correctly, can be readily found from whatever angle it is sought. It should not be regarded as a philosophical classification of knowledge, *nor is the order of subjects of primary importance* [our italics]. What is of greater moment to a scientific classification is that the introduction of an auxiliary apparatus of connection and relation signs,

6

lacking in the original Dewey system, has made UDC really universal . . .'[1]

The point about the order of subjects is one to which we shall return. The detail (achieved by synthesis) and universal application of the scheme are freely admitted.

The choice of the DC as a basis for the new classification was a notable one in view of the antipathy to the system in French-speaking countries and the ascendancy of the system of Brunet. The wisdom of this decision is still warmly debated; the instrument was certainly there to hand, although in its existing form it might be inadequate. The universality of the significance of decimal numbers, plus the achievement of the early editions of DC, must have been decisive. Yet Savage has suggested that this choice 'heavily mortgaged' the future of UDC and several other writers have suggested that it is folly to attempt to build a system for the exact classification of scientific literature on an unscientific basis.

The decision having been made, and permission having been received, to base UDC on DC, the earlier classification system as a whole was taken and examined critically by a number of specialists, who 'completed, amended, rehandled, according to the necessities of their specialities', while preserving the general order and character of the Dewey original. But there has, over the years, been gradual divergence between the main divisions of the two systems and G. A. Lloyd and others have drawn attention to the considerable differences that exist now, even at a basic three or four digit level.

Notation. In the main tables the 'three minimum' method of writing numbers, which is invariable in DC, is abandoned for the logical contracted form. Thus class 5 Science and class 54 Chemistry are so written and not 500 and 540 as in the original. This sets free the zeros for use, together, with other indicator symbols, in the special system of common facets and other forms of synthesis that are such a feature of this classification. The notation is often far from brief and may not be simple due to the range and variety of the auxiliary devices for number building. It is, of course, designed for arranging entries in catalogues and bibliographies rather than for the spines of books. An interesting feature is the breaking up of longer numbers by the frequent use of the point which does not occur once only in a class-mark, as is the case with DC, but which is employed after every three digits to provide convenient 'pauses' in a notation which, although commendably specific, could prove a

[1] BS 1000A: 1961, p. 6.

burden in a manual, as opposed to a mechanized, retrieval system. UDC has explored various methods of notational hospitality; one method associated with the scheme is the achievement of much more capacity in arrays of co-ordinates through the use, if necessary, of centesimal notation in which topics are denoted by .11–.99 rather than .1–.9.

Synthesis and Mnemonics. The scheme has a most powerful synthetic apparatus available in a series of auxiliary tables which may be regarded as a detailed development of the notation contained in DC's standard sub-divisions and area table. These auxiliary tables are supported by a series of signs of combinations and indicators. The range of the synthetic devices is as follows:

Symbol	Name	Significance
+	Plus sign	Document deals with two topics.
/	to	Document covers several topics which are consecutive in UDC.
		Ordinary UDC number from main tables, eg, 623.433.3
:	Colon	Shows relationship between two subjects.
[ ]	Square brackets	Relationship sign used when one of two subjects is obviously of secondary importance.
=	Equal sign	Language sub-divisions.
(o)	Parentheses	Sub-divisions of form.
" "	Inverted commas	Time facet.
(1/9)	Parentheses 1/9	Space facet.
.oo	Point double zero.	Standard points and points of view.
-	Hyphen	
.o	Point zero	
'	Apostrophe	

Common facets[1] brackets the group from Equal sign through Point double zero.

These do not all represent synthesis in the truest sense of the word; the use of final alphabetical order, for example, can hardly be described as a synthetic device. But the full range of the signs and auxiliary tables does provide the UDC with an extra dimension for the analysis of documents in bibliographies, catalogues and abstracting services. Each of the signs, therefore, deserves further explanation. The plus sign is used when a work joins subject matter of about

[1] These are given in an approved filing order, but the space and time facets may change places, ie, it is permissible to file a geographical concept before a time division.

equal interest from two classes; for example, 622 + 669 is the combination for Mining and Metallurgy. Its use is chiefly in the catalogue, for of course in shelving books the work can go only under the first of these numbers. The oblique stroke / is a connective symbol which is used to mark the fact that such a sequence as 592/599 indicates a document covering Systematic Zoology. It is an expedient to save writing 592 + 593 + 594, etc., to 599. In filing entries arranged by UDC, a number followed by a plus would file before the same number followed by a stroke; we would then have the main table number alone without any synthetic attachments. Next in sequence comes the colon which, to use modern terminology, enables many multi-phased subjects to be specified. Thus agricultural statistics are 31:63 in the library where statistics is the main interest, but if agriculture is predominant, the class-mark may be written 63:31. In a classified catalogue entries could be made under both topics. The square brackets are used instead of the colon on rare occasions; they are only required when the relationship between two subject fields involves one of the topics in a role which is definitely a subordinate one. Thus if, in a technical library, we classify Scientific education as 5[37], this would indicate that we did not wish to reverse the relationship in the catalogue, as we considered that education was the subordinate subject on this occasion.

The equals sign for languages is very important and is often employed in documentation. It virtually replaces the 4, Language, of the Main Tables, eg, = 2 works in English, = 3 in German. Modern languages in general are represented in the appropriate table by = 083, and artificial languages by = 089; the other languages are as in Class 4. The form sub-divisions correspond to the standard sub-divisions of DC, but are always placed in parentheses. Thus 53(03) is a Dictionary of Physics, 53(09) a History of Physics. In addition to the employment of the DC numbers in this way, ingenious developments and extensions have been made. Thus a novel dealing with socialism could go at 335 (0:823). Within brackets also go the numbers from the auxiliary table dealing with geographical areas. These are distinguished from the form divisions in that they are never introduced by a zero. The geographical divisions are based on the numbers from DC's 900 class, with extensions. Thus 385(4) denotes European railways, 385(42) railways in England and Wales, 385(73) railways in the United States. The Race numbers operate in very similar fashion, except that they are distinguished by an equals sign within the parentheses. Thus (= 95), for example, would stand for the Mongolian peoples.

The inverted commas as the time symbol are used to indicate the period covered by a work or, less frequently, the date at which it appeared. An example of use is 62 "18" (05) a periodical on nine-teenth-century engineering. The classifier can be much more specific than this with the auxiliary table for time, if he so wishes. Years, months and days can all be shown in logical sequence; thus "1906.12.25" stands for Christmas Day, 1906. Centuries are indicated by the use of two or three figures, as "03" the fourth century AD. Dates BC have the minus sign prefixed, eg, —"55" the year 55 BC. There are also many other sub-divisions of time, as seasons, months, days, hours, and even minutes; we can also use numbers for concepts such as sunrise, "414.21".

The A–Z division simply indicates the use of a letter in the notation to allow an alphabetic arrangement of subjects already specifically classed, or for making alphabetic sub-classes in such cases as chemical elements, or in popular subject fields where it is thought to be convenient. More interesting is the auxiliary table for view-points introduced by a double zero. This table can be used through-out the schedules where necessary and can often be taken up with great profit. To take a few examples from it: 001 represents the theoretical point of view, .007 (a useful mnemonic, perhaps, for some students) the staff viewpoint, .009 the moral point of view. Lastly, we may briefly add that the hyphen, apostrophe and .0 are used in many places to provide special extra specialized sub-divisions of a subject; the .0 cannot be confused with the common divisions of form as the latter always appear in parentheses. Piece-meal development in the scheme has led to some confusion between these symbols which needs to be rectified. Unlike the auxiliaries of form, place, race, time and language, the divisions are limited to the areas of the scheme for which they were designed.

At first view these symbols and tables give a sense of bewilder-ment, but their apparent complexity dissolves to some extent when we remember that they are optional and need not be used unless the topic to be specified cannot be dealt with via the enumerated detail in the schedules. We must remember that shelf arrangement was a minor consideration in the compilers' minds; minute indexing on an illimitable and infinitely expansible scale was sought, and has been achieved. The auxiliaries are remarkable when we consider the early date of their creation and they have accomplished a great deal. The most used numbers and symbols provide us with distinctive unambiguous systematic mnemonics – France is always (44) and in UDC this can have no other meaning; the French language is always = 4; the present century is always "19"; pocket dictionaries always carry the form number (033); the theoretical viewpoint must always be expressed by .001 – and so forth. As always with a rational synthetic system, it is the constant repetition of single number or symbol to designate a familiar and recurring concept that provides the information officer with his memory aid. (The mnemonics are more consistent than those of DC, where 44 can mean France – but does not always do so).

Despite the great and enduring success and considerable seminal influence of this extensive synthetic apparatus, it can be criticized on certain points.

1) Some notational devices, although apparently logical and satisfactory, cause problems in a computer retrieval system. Some necessitate the recognition of more than one character to distinguish them; others would have no meaning in a machine-held file. (The point after every third digit falls into the second category.) Various proposals for change, some of them radical, have thus been made.

2) Symbols such as — and .o have been associated with ideas which developed in somewhat haphazard fashion and this in turn leads to confusion and overlap in the functions of these indicator symbols which needs to be put right. In addition, the symbol + appears superfluous in practice to some critics.

3) Naturally, in many examples, more than one of the auxiliary tables for synthesis is needed. We thus have the important problem of citation order; should we have, for instance:

338.585.3 (729) "324"   or
338.585.3 "324" (729)?

We are told in BS 1000A that time and place are interchangeable in citation and filing. This generosity in acceding to users' wishes certainly offers flexibility and may seem to some to be a just example of 'the perfect law of liberty', but it must make for important differences between individual information centres employing UDC. The more facets a subject has, the more important it is that a firm citation order should exist. So is the scheme, with its permitted variations in citation, *truly* a universal one?

4) Allied to this is some prevarication on the important principle of inversion, which must rear its head whenever we look at citation and filing problems in a synthetic scheme. We are told[1] that the 'internal order in a compound number (citation order) is *approximately* the reverse of the "vertical" order, in which a series of compound numbers is filed or listed, though *no definite standard order is prescribed*' [our italics]. The desire to offer choice to users is commendable, but when a citation order *has* finally been chosen, the failure to use the inversion principle for filing will lead not to the mere violation of theoretical precepts, but to practical muddle and unhelpful order. Order does not seem too important to many UDC users, who merely want to pin-point information on a specific theme, but we all widen or narrow our searches from time to time, even if it is only to clarify thought or define our topic clearly, and then helpful order is very valuable. It seems futile to bend rules and let good order partly slip away when it is there for the taking.

Nevertheless, the synthetic apparatus is generally to be commended. Criticisms such as the above are offered largely with the benefit of hindsight and with that view of modern classification theory and the needs of information work which enables weaknesses to be pointed out and reform suggested.

Index. The indexes to UDC are of the relative kind and are highly satisfactory. The one most likely to be encountered by British librarians and students of librarianship is that of British Standard 1000A. This has over 20,000 entries, including details of numbers from the auxiliary schedules. We are often referred in a helpful manner from one part of the index to another related heading. There is the usual omission of personal names and the customary, and thoroughly understandable, warning regarding the folly of attempting to use the index as more than merely a key to the classified schedules.

Use and revision. It is possible to find many varying estimates as to the number of UDC users – the highest being a figure in the region of 100,000. Users include not only specializing libraries and departments, but also many journals and abstracting and indexing services in the sciences. Among the serial publications which are users, we

---

[1] BS 1000A: 1961, p. 10.

may note, to draw a few examples from the field of electrical engineering and electronics, *Radio and Electronic Engineer*, *Mullard Technical Communications*, *Post Office Electrical Engineers' Journal*, and *Ericsson Review*. There are several more that could be cited, both in this and other subject areas – most of them technical ones. The *Russian Journal of Physical Chemistry* and other titles in that field, published as cover-to-cover translations in Britain by the Chemical Society, carry UDC numbers on their articles. The system is also used to classify United Kingdom Atomic Energy Authority reports and the publications of technical organizations, such as the Cement and Concrete Association. Technical libraries using UDC are heartened by the fact that numbers appear in these publications; such evidence of its appeal acts as a great fillip to 'pre-natal' classification. Users of UDC come from many parts of the world, but the peak of its popularity is found in certain European countries. In Russia its use in scientific and technical libraries was made compulsory.[1] In certain libraries and in some subject fields UDC is not used alone, but is employed in conjunction with other systems. The best example of this can be seen in the way it has been combined with the Swedish *Samarbetskommitten för Byggnadsfragor* (sfB) scheme for architecture and building. Here the sfB schedules have been published along with the relevant classes of UDC and the integration may well prove extremely useful to those engaged in classification in this sphere.

On an international scale, revision is carried out by the various national committees and users are informed of change and expansion in the publication *Extensions and Corrections to the* UDC, which appears every six months.[2] Information also appears at times in the FID *News Bulletin*. Those who take an active interest in revision work will scan the so-called *P notes* which are circulated for comment and which indicate proposals for development or for the recasting of certain schedules. An interesting feature of the long-term revision policy of the scheme lies in the idea known as revision by starvation. This means that if a topic is badly located it can be transferred to a more suitable part of the classification and the old number can be starved of material for at least ten years. After this period has elapsed, it is considered that the association of the subject with the old number will be extremely tenuous and the number can thus be

[1] See *American Documentation*, July, 1964, p. 226.
[2] This is now to be replaced by an annual volume of supplements with five-year cumulations.

set free to be used, if need be, with a different significance. This idea has been criticized, but is certainly not without merit; interesting parallels can be found in walks of life quite remote from librarianship and documentation.[1]

Many users would argue that UDC revision is, although necessarily very slow, on the whole extremely good. The size and complexity of international involvement, with the FID Central Classification Committee ultimately controlling development, acting as an international clearing house and seeking opinions from many users, inevitably inhibits radical or speedy change. The system does, however, permit the calling in of specialist helpers in many subject fields. In Britain, such helpers have included the United Kingdom Atomic Energy Authority and the British Iron and Steel Research Association. Despite the great complexity of the revision network, UDC – perhaps because of its character and purpose – has always been ready to consider widespread change and reorganization. We now have a period when some radical changes are being contemplated with the recasting of many subject areas and much relocation of topics. The interesting idea of the transfer of Class 4 Language to Class 8 Literature is being implemented, so that 4 can act as a bridge between the sciences and social sciences and relieve some of the overcrowding in 5 and 6.

One hesitates to be critical of UDC revision because the scheme is on a relatively sound footing in terms of finance and well off in terms of editorial attention; if this is coupled with willingness to consider changing with the times, UDC might be said to have the best revision policy of all. But at present there is some internal conflict as to how drastic change should be. Established users tend to resist dramatic innovation, but we are currently witnessing a more vigorous manifestation of a trend that has appeared also in the past[2] – an attempt to give the whole scheme that modernity and scientific basis which new users demand.

Whatever one's thoughts about the extent and degree of UDC schedule revision, there is also the question of speed and method of schedule revision. The production of full editions in their entirety, as opposed to parts, medium editions or abridgements, has often been slow. The full schedules in English have, for instance, benefited greatly from a recent BSI acceleration in schedule production, but the full English edition was started in 1936. One possible future

[1] For example, J. A. T. Robinson, *Honest to God and the Debate*, 1963, pp. 7–8.
[2] See W. H. Phillips, *Primer of book classification*, 5th edition, AAL, 1961, Appendix 2.

solution is the use of a computer to up-date the schedules, as discussed in the writings of R. R. Freeman. The idea of COM (Computer Output Microfilm) in terms of speed and costs has been advocated, with some vigour, by A. C. Foskett.[1]

Conclusion. UDC is extremely important as the most truly international of the general schemes and as the system which first clearly demonstrated the potential of synthesis. Its unscientific structure, inherited from the DC base, is undoubtedly a handicap and Brian Vickery and Barbara Kyle, in articles cited at the end of this chapter, have drawn attention to its shortcomings. Vickery writes: 'a thorough survey of the technology schedules is needed, to pick out sections in which facet analysis can usefully be applied ... Its size and universality will not save UDC if it is unable to advance with science and technology'. It has nevertheless the great and continuing advantage of being recognized and used as a 'standard' and is qualified as few schemes are to assemble, sort and identify the most minute material, to show subjects in all forms – physical and intrinsic – in all languages, of all times, and in all aspects. This detail through synthesis is optional and can be used selectively or even disregarded if the scheme is employed for shelf arrangement.

Apart from structural problems arising from imperfect subject analysis and the lingering influence of DC macro-order, there is the question of the superimposition of an extensive synthetic apparatus on an enumerative base. Ranganathan has pointed out that UDC 'did not go the whole hog' in redesigning the nature of bibliographical classifications and suggested that the 'new attachments were so attractively elastic as to hide the rigidity of the *Decimal Classification* which it had indolently adopted as a readily available core'. A charge of laziness here is difficult to justify, for the use of DC and its international notation in a suitable developed form must have seemed obvious at the start of the century and the pioneers worked very hard to make their choice succeed. As an actual or potential international standard the system will not be easily replaced, but several writers think that it must be developed and revised more extensively and quickly if it is to survive the challenge of the newer systems of organization in special libraries and that its notation needs some remodelling for use in conjunction with the machine searching of literature. Post-co-ordinate indexing in relation to classification is discussed in chapter 19, but it is not

[1] *UDC: the history, present status and future prospects of a large general classification scheme.* Bingley, 1973.

necessarily a suitable replacement for UDC, nor is it necessarily superior. The two may, at times, be used in complementary fashion and UDC can help other indexing vocabularies by lending its own terminology, displaying hierarchical structures, or acting as a thesaurofacet. It can also render valuable service as a linking device or switching language between the indexing thesauri of different countries, since it is independent of any one tongue. Indeed, some critics now see the function of a switching language as a most necessary and important UDC role.

As far as mechanization is concerned, there are problems but these are fewer than in most other classifications. Research on the UDC in computer based retrieval systems has been carried out, in the United States, by Freeman and Atherton in the AUDACIOUS (automatic direct access to information with an on-line UDC system) project of the late 1960s at the American Institute of Physics, by Rigby – most especially in *Meteorological and geoastrophysical abstracts*, and by T. W. Caless and others, who tried to evaluate UDC as a tool for computer retrieval and discussed strategies for its manipulation. Such research is by no means limited to the United States, as some quite recent articles show.[1] There are some difficulties arising from the occasionally imperfect revelation of hierarchies in the notation and others resulting from the auxiliary symbols, their filing problems and the requirements for computer filing. With the CRG scheme still awaited, UDC is certainly the general classification most suited to retrieval by computer; it may itself benefit from the fruits of CRG/BNB research.

The UDC is consciously aimed at what Ranganathan has called microthought – the world of highly specialized packages of literature in reports, periodical articles, standards and the like. Thus the pressure for rapid and continual change is stronger here than in the case of any other general system. There is, however, the same problem to be faced in this as in any other widely used scheme; established users do *not* want radical alterations. Yet, apart from the challenge of post-co-ordinate rivals and the needs of mechanization, there is now a new impetus towards recasting of the UDC basic framework for a suitable system is needed for the proposed United Nations world scientific co-operative information system, known as UNISIST. Supporters of UDC naturally see it as a strong candidate for the role of an 'unspoken meta-language with lexical and syntactic signs of

[1] For example – Halm, J. Van. *Use of the UDC in a mechanized system* (in Holland). Special Libraries, *63* (10), October, 1972.

its own',[1] which is wanted as a general roof or superstructure under which more specialized systems can be accommodated within UNISIST. If it is to serve the UNISIST project as a broad form of SRC, which means to some a standard 'roof' classification and to others a standard reference code (the definitions are virtually synonymous), the UDC must be presented as a modern, well-balanced scheme. This need is resulting in more drastic change being mooted, especially in the general outlines – since the idea of a 'roof' is to provide a relatively broad umbrella of about 5,000 terms as an international code for information systems under which more detailed special classifications and thesauri can be 'sheltered'. Writers such as J. Perreault, H. Wellisch and A. F. Schmidt have argued the case for radical reform, stating that UDC now undoubtedly needs this and that the opportunities afforded by UNISIST and by mechanization pose a challenge which *must* be faced. More adventure in the moving of disciplines and a great speeding up of the revision programme, through COM or by other means, is thus being argued. Others, aware of vast files of classified entries which would be affected by change, favour making haste more slowly. They press for the streamlining and overhaul of classes in a genuinely evolutionary way rather than by a radical upheaval of the existing structure and argue that FID finance is better directed by promoting steady change and growth rather than seeking new UDC roles, which might dissipate valuable funds. There is much to be said for the maintenance of a high degree of *status quo* when so much is obviously at stake – no existing and committed user wants a classified file of high proportions in which many numbers are about to become erroneous or redundant. Yet the challenge of UNISIST and the concept of a 'roof' classification remains and it would be surely futile and expensive to have an entirely new scheme made for this purpose. Would the changes needed in the UDC superstructure be *so* radical and costly?

This is by no means the only contemporary UDC question to be resolved; queries and problems come thick and fast. There is the question of the alteration and refinement of certain relationships to facilitate future computer searching; proposed changes in the pattern of UDC's management structure to take executive functions from the FID Central Classification Committee and vest them in a small editorial body; and the problem of deciding how far the

[1] Unesco. *Unisist: study report on the feasibility of a world science information system,* 1971, p. 73.

scheme can be truly universal – can it be so at the 3 or 4 figure level only, allowing latitude in more detailed arrangement for the requirements of individual institutions or publications? Should there be more effort concentrated on the provision of full editions with their estimated 200,000 concepts or do medium editions (with about 30% of these concepts) and abridged editions (with about 10% of the concepts) serve a useful purpose – especially with the advent of an SRC – when made available in various tongues? There is certainly controversy here, since some critics argue that abridgements have deflected attention from the need to press on with full editions, while others contend that they have been a blessing. What is to be the place of UDC within the MARC record? (It seems that UDC numbers will only appear for certain when the item concerned is published carrying such a number.) Can liaison between UDC and other classifications and thesauri be more effectively promoted?

Perhaps – among all these queries which jostle for attention in our minds – the question of the rate of change is the most pressing. It has been said by conservatives that the radical remoulding needed for the change in the UDC outline demanded by the international roof classification would be so prohibitive as to lead to a split and the existence of two distinct UDC's, or that this development would swallow up vital finance needed for other improvements. All that need be said by way of commentary is that, although this is a very difficult issue, UDC must face the problem of more vigorous change sooner or later and it would be foolish to ignore the opportunities for its own promotion which UNISIST now affords. Change for the sake of change and dislocation cannot be commended, but some suitable restructuring at this time, especially at the broad level where the DC framework lingers on most clearly, may have enormous implications for the future benefit and prospects of the brainchild of Otlet and La Fontaine.

CHAPTER ELEVEN

Library of Congress Classification

Introduction. For ninety-seven years after its foundation in 1800, the Library of Congress was housed in the Capitol at Washington; and at the end of this period, as may be readily supposed, its collections exceeded by far the space there available. It came into its new and magnificent home in 1897, a separate building of ample and handsome proportions, having the orthodox huge domed reading-room, something resembling that of Panizzi's at the British Museum, and ample space for marshalling the various divisions of the stock and correlating their contents, which consisted of about one and a half million volumes and pieces, with annual accessions approximating to over one hundred thousand. The first four years in the new building were years of organizing work of the first order. They saw, to quote the *deus ex machina*, Dr Herbert Putnam, 'the collections, formerly indiscriminate, divided into certain main groups and in large part arranged and digested; most of these groups conveniently located; and the physical equipment and personal service appropriate to each determined, and in part provided. They have seen determined also, and initiated into each group, a system of classification which not merely recognizes present contents but provides elastically for future development; and catalogues which, also elastic, when brought to date will exhibit adequately the collections as they stand and be capable of expansion without revision'.[1] They saw, too, the establishment of the Library of Congress printed catalogue card, a standard card which could be obtained by other libraries, and which made the Library the greatest bureau for the distribution of catalogue entries in the world; and, by combination of architecture, cataloguing, classification and an ingenious and effective book-carrier system, the most rapid book service in any national or other large library came into being at Washington. We

Report of the Librarian of Congress for the Fiscal Year ending June 30, 1901, p. 5.

are, of course, only concerned with one factor in this remarkable result, the book classification which came into existence during these four years.

It might have been expected that the Library of Congress would have adopted either DC or Cutter's *Expansive Classification*, when the decision was made to abandon the Jeffersonian system employed in the nineteenth century and to reclassify according to a more practical and flexible arrangement. No doubt the idea was carefully considered; however, the circumstances of the Library were thought to require special treatment and a largely independent classification – though influenced by Cutter's – was determined upon and gradually constructed. In the case of LC, all the books had their places in the scheme before the notation was constructed. This does not mean that the staff started the great task of classifying the Library of Congress without having first made a general plan; but it does mean that the plan was sufficiently fluid to permit of reconstruction when experience gained in the preliminary stages of arrangement demanded a reconsideration of the original design.

Features and Principles. It must be stressed that this classification is essentially a team product and that, in many ways, it is best thought of as a co-ordinated series of special classifications. Each major class is published separately and is virtually independent of the others, having, for example, its own form and geographical divisions and index. The classes formulated have largely been influenced by the Library of Congress building and by the needs of the various subject departments which it houses. The outline of LC was not published until 1904, although Class Z had appeared at a slightly earlier date; the scheme had thus been maturing for some five years. A comparison of the original edition of the outline with the latest version, indicates that several changes have since been made. One class – Religion – has been completely remodelled during the twentieth century; some sub-divisions have been transferred to other classes and important adjustments have been made to other divisions of the class. Such changes as these are demanded by the expanding collections. In the Report of the Librarian for 1901 Dr Putnam explained that 'The system of classification thus far applied is one devised from a comparison of existing schemes (including the "decimal" and the "expansive") and a consideration of the particular conditions of this Library, the character of its present and probable collections and its probable use. It is assumed that the departments of history, political and social science, and certain others, will be unusually large. It is assumed that investigators will be more freely admitted to the shelves.' It is clear, from a comparison of the two schemes, that the books in the Congress Library were first arranged in class groups corresponding to Cutter's Expansive system and this structural basis has been largely maintained in the final scheme. Yet it must again be stressed that the Congress approach is essentially a practical one; if at times, it leans heavily on Cutter's ideas, with advantage, it makes no claims at all to follow a 'scientific' or 'evolutionary' sequence; indeed, LC deviates, when necessary, from Cutter's notions quite readily in order to serve the special needs of the vast Congress collections.

Hints as to the general procedure followed by the team of classifiers are given in the prefaces to several of the published classes. These make it clear that the whole enterprise has been aimed at producing a scheme which is 'tailor-made' for the Congress stock, the work being done in these years of initiation under the direction of the chief classifier, Charles Martel, and ultimately under the supervision of Putnam himself. The classification as originally founded has been recast, when circumstances so demanded, in the light of experience. It has always been extended and remodelled with the actual books of the Congress Library under consideration. It still has the needs of that great library as its primary concern and has never been 'recommended' as such for other libraries, although it was recognized that several would, in fact, adopt or adapt it.

The fact that there is much to be said for the order of LC from the bibliographical point of view has resulted in the classification being praised by Hulme, Metcalfe, and others as the one widely used system which is based on the literary warrant of the library which it primarily serves. Other schemes have been made, of course, with the existing bookstocks of libraries in mind; yet no other general scheme that has been widely applied has actually been moulded and shaped so closely by the literature housed in a national library. The theoretical approach, whereby we map out knowledge first of all and then adapt the resulting map to meet the needs of books, was positively rejected in favour of a gradual building up of a classification which consistently regarded the character and use made of books in the Congress Library. Dr Putnam has stated: 'The system devised has not sought to follow strictly the scientific order of subjects. It has sought rather convenient sequences of the various groups, considering them as *groups of books*, not as groups of mere subjects.' The words which we have placed in italics are important, since this is just what Hulme meant when he first formulated the idea known as literary warrant in 1911. Putnam's words indicated that the way in which knowledge is presented in books should be paramount in a bibliographical classification. Many critics point out, however – and with much justice – that many areas of the scheme reflect the *literary warrant* of the age in which it was created rather than the bibliographical needs of today.

The original outline of the Congress system has been developed with great minuteness; and the method of that development cannot be exhibited by mere description. One can note particularly the enormous amount of space given to American history, to the Social Sciences and to Language and Literature. Classes A and B present little deviation from earlier schemes in their context, but one novelty in each is worth mentioning. AZ is the general history of knowledge and learning, and this scheme is the first to provide a place for such general works on the history of scholarship. In B, the finely conceived Psychology and Metapsychology section deserves close attention. C is general history and biography and introduces the historical classes proper, D, E, and F. Class G comprises Geography, Anthropology, Folklore, Manners and Customs, and Sports and Amusements. The inclusion of recreative arts here is unusual and noteworthy. The class acts as a link, by way of culture and customs, between the historical and social sciences. H to L are the important classes dealing with the political and social sciences. Of these, the arrangement of J Political Science may here be glanced at. It affords a 'national' method of grouping (familiar in the treatment of literature), conjoined with a chronological development, in complete contrast to the 'topical' method so familiar to users of DC. H is also well worth close study; Martel's 'favourite', it is, in effect, at least one-sixth of the total scheme. Classes M Music and N Fine Arts call for no comment, except that Landscape Gardening is omitted from the latter and appears as a division of Agriculture at SB. P Language and Literature is an excellent example of LC's insistence on practical convenience in arrangement; the major literatures are clearly defined and in almost all circumstances there is a wise preference for chronological division immediately after the division by languages. This helps to keep together the texts of a versatile writer.

Class Q Science is a strange companion for Literature; it follows the arrangement of the Decimal Class 500, but with the already quoted exclusion of Anthropology. R Medicine and S Agriculture are fairly orthodox, although the latter includes Hunting and Angling. The great class T Technology divides logically into four groups: Engineering and Building, Mechanical, Chemical, and Composite, respectively. The scheme is rounded off by Military and Naval Science – at U and V they merit separate classes in a system of this character – and by Z Bibliography and Library Science. This class might as well go first as last; it is comprehensive in character, serving the Library of Congress well, no doubt, although it is not particularly well developed; the letter notation here differs from the character of that in the rest of the scheme and the original notation was so closely numbered that the latter-day expansion of library science has resulted in considerable recourse to decimal sub-division.

An interesting feature of the scheme is its treatment of biography. This, as we have noted already is a controversial subject to classify, in that it may be collected or scattered at suitable locations throughout a scheme. In most classifications an alternative is provided; biography being distributed by subject interest or being collected in either an alphabetical or classified arrangement in a large class based on the 'form' biography. LC is not as liberal as other schemes in this matter; it insists on the distribution of biography by topic whenever feasible. The relatively small biography class, which is placed at CT as an auxiliary of History, accommodates only collected biography and those lives which are too general to be linked with any one subject field. This is an interesting attribute of the system, in that DC, under Congress influence, now favours the distribution of biography too. It is a procedure which offers obvious benefits in a special library or in a large general library which is broken up into subject departments; yet in many of our public lending libraries the idea of keeping all biographies together might well prove more useful to the reader.

Notation. The LC notation is of the mixed variety and usually employs two letters followed by a maximum of four figures. Sometimes only a single capital letter is employed. Thus main classes are marked with a single letter, as

A General Works   C History and so on
B Philosophy

Principal divisions are denoted by an added letter, as

BC Logic   BH Aesthetics
BD Metaphysics   BJ Ethics
BF Psychology

and this is the limit to the use of letters in the marking of classes and divisions. The letters I, O, W, X, and Y are not used in the main outline and there are some gaps left also for insertions at this second letter stage. The combination of two letters makes for an excellent and directive symbol for all the great sections of knowledge. It is very useful to be able to direct inquirers to such groups by clear labels. 'You will find books on Painting at ND'; 'Socialism you will find marked HX'; and so on. (It is noteworthy that the first completed schedule to be published, z – Bibliography, is numbered right through without sub-letter divisions and proves highly inconvenient for direction.) Further sub-division is secured by the use of arabic numerals read arithmetically, beginning at 1 in each of the main divisions. An example will serve to illustrate this:

TC   Hydraulic engineering   TC 361   Dry-docks
TC 353   Sea locks   TC 363   Floating-docks
TC 355   Docks   TC 365   Other special docks
TC 357   Piers, etc.

The numbering is rarely continuous; even where there is little anticipation of further intercalation, one or two places are usually left for future use. Where developments may reasonably be expected the numbering is open, and usually there are substantial gaps between the sections.

The notation does not end here, however, as one of the outstanding features of the Congress scheme is the frequent use of alphabetical order for the end-topics of a group. Indeed, the wide use made by LC of A–Z order by topic within a class, whenever this is the most practical method of arrangement will be gauged from the following examples:

QD   Chemistry. Metals   QK   Botany
QD 171 General works   QK 881 Metabolism
    172 By groups, A–Z   882 Photosynthesis
                                   887 Formation of new
    181 Special topics, A–Z   organic matter
                                   891 Respiration
                                   896 Fermentation
                                   898 Special Plant
                                        Products, A–Z

TL		Aeronautics, Airships	TS	Manufacturers. Leather
TL	650	General works	TS	1045 Imitation leathers
	654	Special projects to		
		1900, A–Z		1047 Special, A–Z
	658	Special makes, A–Z		
	659	Individual ships, A–Z		

Further sub-division can be obtained through the use of decimals if gaps between numbers prove to be inadequate. The very frequent use of alphabetical order by topic[1] seems at first sight dubious, although it has been highly praised by Metcalfe and some might claim that detailed systematic order sometimes reflects the classificationist's preferences or is based on a subjective view and that its purpose is thus not easily communicated to users. However, A–Z order has its own special problems in international systems, for it is often meaningless in translation. When LC, as it often does, employs a final A–Z order in a class with enterprise and discretion, the method must be commended; it is one which might be employed with advantage a little more often in some other systems, but less often in LC itself.

The notation of LC has received its fair share of criticism and not without reason. Despite the usefulness of the two-letter foundation and the fact that the majority of topics are denoted by a class-mark of two letters and three figures, or less, it is clear that the notation does not show the structure of the scheme and the hierarchy is sometimes difficult to discern clearly from the schedules themselves. It is extremely unfortunate that numbers have been employed in their 'arithmetical' or 'integral' sense rather than as decimals; this means that LC relies heavily on gaps for notational flexibility, although, as already pointed out, numbers are eventually divided decimally if these gaps prove insufficient. Ranganathan claims that only 'the liberal size of the gaps amidst integers is postponing notational crash'.[2] Elsewhere he repeats this criticism, but softens it by recognizing the many great historical features of the *Congress Classification* – 'the rigid, integral, notation came in to spoil what would otherwise have been the best scheme in existence, backed up by all the prestige, manpower and resources of the most library-minded government in the world'. While there is much truth in this particular criticism, and the flexibility of decimal rather than integral

---

[1] The student should search for some significant examples from the scheme, such as the long A–Z list of industries at HD 8039.

[2] *Philosophy of Library Classification*, 1951, p. 30.

numerical notations has been proved again and again, one is not altogether impressed with another common objection, that concerning the length of the LC notation. It is not fair to exhibit a few extreme examples which show great length or complexity, for such are rare, although inevitable, in a scheme providing for such minutiae as the Library of Congress houses and some of the detail is required for a precise call-mark rather than a class-mark as such. Some idea of this specificity may be gained from the consideration of the fact that thirty-one places are provided for editions of a single work of Thomas Paine, *The Rights of Man*, which forms part of a special table on Paine at JC 177. As it stands, the system is unlikely to be adopted by libraries other than extensive ones. Yet minuteness of detail need be no deterrent. Nothing is lost because one's library would use only a tenth (or less) of the enumerated places; smaller libraries can reduce the Paine numbers to ordinary proportions. Other examples of detail, and incidentally of final alphabetization, can be seen in the literature class P (under Chekhov for instance).

Synthesis and Mnemonics. This is by far the most enumerative of the general classification schemes. It does not employ notational synthesis through the use of common form and geographical divisions or their equivalents, nor does it make extensive use of the instruction to 'divide like . . .' followed by a reference to some other parts of the scheme. LC rather attempts to give to each country and subject its own set of geographical and form divisions; thus, instead of a common table, we have numerous sets of such divisions; a list is provided every time one is needed. It has been argued that, for example, a schedule for the Constitutional History of Russia would be quite inappropriate to that of Portugal, that a schedule for the History of Banking could not be made to suit the History of Insurance. This provision of separate sets of form divisions and geographical tables which are peculiar to the needs of particular classes has caused great enlargement of the schedules as compared with other bibliographical schemes. Indeed, the bulk of LC is only partly explained by its detail; much of it is due to the tendency to enumerate a special set of sub-divisions for forms and countries each time one is required, rather than providing a single common set that could be used to build up any basic class-mark. On the other hand, the compilers of LC might well defend themselves by drawing our attention to the trouble of devising a set of common sub-divisions which would be comprehensive enough to cover all circumstances and situations which might arise in a classification of such proportions. The examples below illustrate the individuality of the form and geographical divisions enumerated in the various classes of LC.

Example 1

HA Statistics	HB Economic theory	HD Economic history
1 Periodicals	1–9 Periodicals	*Land and Agriculture*
9–11 Congresses	21–29 Congresses	101 Periodicals
13–15 Collections	31–35 Collections	103 Associations
16 Comprehensive	61 Encyclopaedias	105 Congresses
works	71–74 Method. Utility	113–156 History,
17 Essays	75–125 History	General
19 History	151–195 Theory:	166–279 United States
23 Biography	General	301–1130 Other
29–39 Theory. Method	works	countries

Example 2

H Social Sciences	H Social Sciences	H Social Sciences
Periodicals	Societies	Congresses and
		Exhibitions
1 American and	10 International	21 International
English	11 American and	22 American and
3 French	English	English
5 German	13 French	23 French
7 Italian	15 German	25 German
8 Other	17 Italian	27 Italian
	19 Other	29 Other

This repetition of languages and recurring forms of presentation results in an excessive use of paper; on the other hand, it must sometimes save the classifiers time by avoiding frequent references to auxiliary tables. It must not be thought, however, that number-building is impossible with LC. It does occur, but not through the use of any table of *common* sub-divisions. Each class has its own complicated system of auxiliary tables. A selection of figures from the series of the tables at the end of this huge class H will give some idea of what these are like and how they are applied:

I	II	III	IV		V	VI	VII	VIII	IX	X
(100)	(200)	(300)	(400)		(130)	(200)	(830)	(840)	(420)	(1000)
(1)	(2)	(3)	(4)		(1:4)	(2:5)	(5:10)	(10:20)	(5:10)	(5:10)
42	81	122	161	Europe	44	52	281	251	136	421
43	83	125	165	Great Britain	45–48	54	291	271	141	431
47	91	136	181	Austria-H	49–52	66	331	301	151	471
48	93	139	185	France	53–56	70	341	321	161	481
49	95	142	189	Germany	57–60	75	351	341	171	491

The top line indicates the number of the table. The second line indicates the total of numbers allowed by the table. The third line indicates the number of divisions allowed to each country. In the text will be found such a direction as this:

```
  HV   Social pathology
1571–2220 Blind
         By country
1783–1796 United States
1800–2220 Other countries, Table IX
         Under each
(10 numbers)  (5 numbers) Documents
     (1)        (1)       State or province
     (3)                  City
     (4)        (2)       Associations
     (5)        (3)       History
     (6)
     (7)                  Biography
     (8)                  Policy
     (9)        (4)       By state or Province, A–Z
    (10)        (5)       By city, A–Z
```

To classify a book on the History of the Blind in France the classifier refers to Table IX and finds that France is allotted ten numbers, beginning with 161 (Germany is next, commencing at 171). The 161 is added to 1800, making 1961, which is the first of the ten numbers allotted to France. History, as shown by the table in our text, is (5), so that the precise number required is HV 1965. The smaller countries have only five places allotted to them in Table IX, Bulgaria, for instance, is 261–265, so that the History of the Blind in Bulgaria becomes 1800 + 263 = HV 2063. Yet even this elaborate system cannot provide for some of the extensions under country headings, and special tables to be applied in the same way, are given in the text. This occurs almost throughout HF Public Finance; similar auxiliary tables are appended to nearly all the classes.

In addition, there are also special geographical tables alphabetically arranged. These are notably to be found in classes G, H, T, U, and V. We give a simple form:

Abyssinia	A2
Afghanistan	A3
Algeria	A4

Argentine Republic A7, etc.

These are used after a point for dividing subjects according to the direction in the schedules: 'Local A–Z' or 'by country, A–Z'. The symbols have not a constant meaning; thus in three separate alphabetic tables A8 may mean Australia or Arkansas, A2 may mean Abyssinia or Alabama. To give an example of the application of these, we have at HJ 6082 'Texts in foreign languages issued by foreign governments' which is divided as

.A2 British	.A5 Spanish
.A3 French	.A6 –z Other, A–z
.A4 German	

It may be stressed, however, that although methods such as these may seem to loom large in the schedules, they arise comparatively infrequently in practice.

We have tried to show here that number-building can be carried out in LC through the use of a series of elaborate auxiliary tables. What the student of classification should realize is that classes in the Congress system have their own arrangements (some provide no synthesis of this kind) and the tables may vary greatly from class to class. This means that there is a great deal of enumeration of such details and the mnemonic value of the notation is small. For the chief way of introducing mnemonic features in traditional classifications is to have a few tables covering constantly recurring concepts, such as forms of presentation, and to denote each concept continually by the same notational symbols – these give rise to systematic mnemonic. Such common tables are just what LC lacks. However, there are certainly a few literal mnemonics to be found. The Generalia Class, for instance (modelled on that of Cutter's scheme and extremely orthodox), provides us with some; occasionally they can be discerned in other parts of the scheme. It may be considered also that, from a practical point of view, the frequent use of A–Z order by topic, for final sub-arrangement within a class, is the best memory aiding feature of all. Thus the regularly occurring alphabetical sequences, which are employed whenever systematic order of helpfulness cannot be discovered, may serve as a partial compensation for the lack of the usual kind of memory aid in the notational symbols.

Index. Each class is equipped with its own separate index. There is no index to the scheme as a whole, although the Library of Congress Subject Headings List acts, to some extent, as an alphabetical key to the classification in its entirety. The indexes are of the relative variety and a sample of their method must be given; this is taken from the fourth edition of Class T Technology:

Automobiles	TL 1–290
Alcohol	TL 217
Auto-Trucks	TL 230
Automobile Trains	TL 235
Biography	TL 139–140
Catalogues	TL 160, 200–229
Collections	TL 8
Compressed Air	TL 225
Congresses	TL 6
Design, construction	TL 9
Electric	TL 220–223
Endurance Tests	TL 290
Essays	TL 155, etc.

(some twenty more aspects are actually listed).

Thus great detail in indexing is provided; sometimes indeed the indexes do more work than is necessary for them, duplicating the sequence of the scheme itself by listing details which could easily be ascertained from the classified schedules. The indexes, too, sometimes fail to reveal all the aspects of a subject which the scheme has scattered, especially if these are distributed throughout several classes. In part, the schedules themselves compensate for this as they contain some 'see also' references, for example:

s 631–s 667 Fertilizers and soil improvement Cf. HD 9483; TA 710

On the whole, the very full indexing and detailed vocabulary of LC deserves commendation rather than criticism; when, as it is hoped will be the case, these separate indexes are finally cumulated, the result will be an instrument of value as a vast 'thesaurus' on the vocabulary of which other indexing systems can gratefully draw.

Use and revision. Many academic libraries and some others have adopted this classification, especially from the 1920s onwards. There has been a distinct trend also in the last seven or eight years for academic libraries in North America which use DC to switch to or consider using LC. One reason for this is the extra detail and scholarship offered; another lies in the Congress catalogue card service, which makes such an important contribution to standardization and economies in cataloguing. In fairness to DC, it might be added that this trend seems to have lost some of its momentum and that, for English language titles at least, DC numbers appear on a very large proportion of the Congress cards also. It is hard to count LC users accurately, for a few of the adaptations are so extensive that the result is almost a new scheme; some users employ it only in part, and there has been a flow of new users in recent years.[1] Outstanding British users include Edinburgh Public Library, the Department of Trade and Industry, the British Library of Political and Economic Science, and the National Library of Wales. LC ranks with DC and UDC as one of the 'big three' in terms of total use, although employment of LC is heavily concentrated in the United States and, to a lesser extent, in other English-speaking countries. The notation has not, of course, the international appeal of decimal numbers.

Revision has been very extensive and continuous in the sense of comparatively minor modification and addition of new detail, but probably somewhat conservative as far as genuine relocations and reconstruction of classes are concerned – there is certainly no equivalent here to the DC *phoenix schedules*. Although classes have appeared regularly since the start of the century and some have been revised several times, we still await the completion of the schedules for class K Law. Despite the problems involved, this is surprising when it is considered that the bulk of the scheme had appeared by 1920. This defect is now being steadily remedied as K appears in parts – for example, KD Law of the United Kingdom and Ireland, was published recently. The continuous changes, expansion and insertion in various other classes is reflected in the periodical bulletin, *Additions and Changes to the Library of Congress Classification*, which announces developments. If we think of the scheme primarily as a system for the Library of Congress itself, it may be noted that there is a unique factor which should be of great benefit in satisfactory revision, namely that classificationist and classifier are usually one and the same person. But, notwithstanding this and considering the needs of all libraries employing LC, revision is obviously balanced, adequately financed, and eminently satisfactory to those who support the existing LC structure and policy.

Conclusion. The theorist with a determined set of canons for the guiding of his judgement, in considering that structure and policy, is in a dilemma in his efforts to equate undoubted past achievement

[1] A powerful, but biased, plea for more is found in R. E. Matthis and D. Taylor, *Adopting the Library of Congress Classification*. Bowker, 1971.

with probable future potential. He is confronted by the realization that, despite many worthwhile and important features, the scheme has its own distinctive rules and sense of priorities. The Classification has had considerable and continuing success, especially in its own library – where, of course, classifier and classificationist are one and the same person – and it stands, to borrow a Bliss description of it, as a vast repository on which other indexing languages can profitably draw. It is a triumph for pragmatism, but at the same time the most difficult of systems to evaluate in accordance with the accepted tenets of modern classification theory. Perhaps the lack, for many years of a guide to the scheme has contributed to the opinion, sincerely held in some quarters, that the only way to come to really know it and learn *how* to use it is to start to use it and go on using it. This shortage of guidance has now been rectified, but the difficulty of reliably and consistently applying basic and underlying principles to this system remains. Its supporters might retort that practical classification, like politics, relates not to the ideal but to the art of the possible and would argue that demonstrable success in terms of thousands of items 'successfully' classified and the constant attention of a large team of experts more than compensates for the necessity to study the scheme empirically rather than in strict accordance with textbook theory. It can be argued too that, if enumerative schemes will continue to prevail in shelf arrangement, there is something to be said for wholehearted enumeration.

On the other hand, weaknesses – practical as well as theoretical – do exist. Scope notes are inferior to those of DC and there is much national bias in emphasis and terminology. Immroth, who has carried out important comparative work on the vocabularies of the schedules, indexes and the Congress List of Subject Headings, has drawn attention to gaps, ambiguities and inconsistencies in this sphere and has tried to point the way to chain indexing and a general rationalization of techniques. In addition, the failure to see subjects as compounds, the elements of which can be linked through synthesis, does not just mean repetition and a bulky schedule. It means, as Christopher Needham ably demonstrates, that many compound subjects are 'shut out' of the vast but rigid hierarchy and cannot be specified accurately. The problem of complex subjects too is tackled, in as much as it is tackled at all, by means of enumeration, which means that any multi-phased theme not yet enumerated cannot be classified with precision. The limited amount of synthesis that is provided (and this has been described above) is unusual, to say the least; indeed it is peculiar to the LC system. Clear facet analysis could obviously streamline classes and rectify many omissions and anomalies, but the result would not be the LC scheme as we know it at present.

Apart from the lack of synthesis and inconsistencies in vocabulary, there are features in this system that make one ask, as Phyllis Richmond once did – 'is it really a classification in the true sense?'. The structure often seems to avoid logical hierarchies and clear subject analysis to become a vast pragmatic pigeon-holing device. In a stimulating paper, Needham[1] argues the choice between LC and DC and plumps for the latter, largely on the grounds that it provides, however imperfectly, some principles and predictability. The present writer is not so sure that the choice would be necessarily right; there are many 'academic' subject areas where the order and collocation of LC, although dated, seem to give it the edge in scholarly libraries over the more 'popular' DC approach for book arrangement on the shelves – despite deficiencies in subject analysis and sometimes over-zealous use of A–Z order. That DC (not to mention BC and UDC) has a sounder theoretical basis is clear, but then some writers actually glory in what Richmond calls the LC 'illogical sprawl'. Dr Richmond herself praises LC as a unique system 'wide open (for adaptation, growth, expansion and change) in an age of logical dead ends and leaping cross-fertilization (of disciplines)'.

Is the system suspect and outdated because of a lack of sound theory or, on the contrary, is it strong because of its abiding aware-ness of the need to be constantly practical and utilitarian, the commitment of libraries to it and its unique place at the centre of the national library system of the United States? The answer to this question must be partly a matter of opinion, but before it *is* provided there remains the important matter of automation and mechaniza-tion, both within and without the Library of Congress, and their effect on the classification. This fact must influence the future of all our classifications and the MARC record will affect LC more than most. Certainly many MARC users are also users of this classification and we must ask if the scheme offered, whatever its detail and past success, is suitable for complex information retrieval problems, SDI profiles and similar tasks. It is there at the very heart of things and thus may well be accepted with good grace, although the

---

[1] This appears as an appendix to his *Organizing Knowledge in Libraries*, 2nd edition. Deutsch, 1971.

pressure for radical changes could be greater in the future than in the past. The Library of Congress staff and others may point to the distinctive features, sturdy independence and fine practical record of achievement offered by the LC classification, but the question at the beginning of the paragraph needs to be answered honestly, if partly subjectively. It does seem to the writer and to many others, especially British trained classifiers, that it is paradoxical and even ironic that the system at the hub of subject retrieval in the MARC record is one which is still reasonably sound for book arrangement in a large academic library, but which lacks the clear and predictable theoretical basis for subject analysis so badly needed in a complex and sophisticated retrieval situation, which is so demonstrably elephantine, and is now forced to resort more and more to mere pigeon-holing. Its history and position make its future assured, but it is hardly 'wide open', in the best sense of the expression, for the requirements of machine-searching. We close, in hope perhaps more than realistic anticipation, with a quotation from Jay E. Daily's introduction to Dr Immroth's work on the LC vocabularies: 'We can look forward to a time when the hit or miss methods of subject analysis so far used by the Library of Congress and all other libraries which depend upon it for this vital service to patrons will be supplanted by . . . controlled methods.' The publication of the alphabetical subject headings and class-marks in a systematic order[1] is possibly at least a tentative start towards the removal of internal inconsistencies within the Library of Congress subject retrieval apparatus *in toto.*

---

[1] Williams, James G., Martha L. Manheimer and Jay E. Daily (editors), *Classified Library of Congress Subject Headings.* 2 vols, Marcel Dekker, Inc. 1972.

CHAPTER TWELVE

The Colon Classification

Introduction. Each country in turn seems to produce a distinctive librarian who is the prototype of his profession. India would probably choose Shiyali Ramamrita Ranganathan (1892–1972), whose life indicated a fantastic capacity for sustained effort and a remarkable single-mindedness for the cause of librarianship. After graduation, he lectured in Mathematics in the Government College, Madras (1917–20), and then (1920–23) was assistant professor of mathematics in the Presidency College, Madras. Without prior library experience, he was then appointed Librarian of Madras University Library and was sent to England to study methods at the British Museum. There the Director suggested to him the advantages of the University of London School of Librarianship. At the school at that time he found the only subjects which really inspired him were library administration and classification. The original author of this *Manual* was lecturer in the latter field and gave Ranganathan the advice which he recalls in *Abgila* (March 1953), to read library economy, to work for a month in a public library and, with that experience, to visit different types of libraries. He proved to be a most alert, critical and enquiring student, knowing exactly what he wanted and travelling England for it, as he later travelled much of the world. He returned to Madras as one with a mission for the improvement and extension of libraries for his people in town and country. He was a founder of the Madras Library Association and in 1928 delivered a university extension course to nearly one thousand teachers on library science, which led to the founding in the following year of the first Madras Summer School of Library Science. Thereafter, for twenty years, he combined with his librarianship at the university his headship of the school. The next two years he spent as university librarian and professor of library science at Benares Hindu University; and from 1947–55 he was professor of library science at the University of Delhi, which bestowed its doctorate upon him as 'the father of librarianship in India'. In his retirement, he was honoured as National Research Professor of Library Science and continued to write with enthusiasm and vigour, ever developing his ideas on classification theory.

The need for the development of librarianship in India acted as a tremendous spur to Ranganathan in his younger days. The teacher in him was accompanied by an urge to write of his experiences, experiments and speculations; so much so that he set out apparently to rewrite the whole of librarianship, first in terms of Indian necessities and to instil the library idea into countrymen not well aware of them, and gradually to promulgate his theories on a world basis; he became in consequence the most prolific writer on the subject. He assured his British lecturer that he felt a specially constructed classification was necessary for India and was warned of the long and Herculean labour involved in the construction of a scheme and in the task of keeping it up-to-date, but Ranganathan was undeterred. He felt that the fact that so many libraries made alterations to DC indicated that the scheme was not altogether successful. His Colon scheme was soon in being, was tried out in his own university library, and was published in two slim volumes in 1933. His first substantial book, however, had been his *Five Laws of Library Science* (1931). Between the first and second editions of CC he read the theoretical writings of Bliss and enunciated his own theory in *Prolegomena to Library Classification* (1937), in which he expounded twenty-eight Canons of varying importance. In his *Library Classification: fundamentals and procedure* (1944), he produced an extensive body of classificatory exercises and a number of novel terms, most of which are now part of the standard vocabulary of modern classification theory. Of his other books, we would particularly commend the *Elements of Library Classification*; as a straightforward account of Ranganathan's work it is best read first by the student who wishes to consult these writings. *Classification and Communication* is a most readable and challenging work, and perhaps the most mature summary of Ranganathan's classificatory labours is given in his *Philosophy of Library Classification*. But there are numerous books and periodical articles from his pen which seek to explain his distinctive ideas on our subject. CC itself is now in its seventh edition.

Certain fundamental ideas and goals lie behind all Ranganathan's work in the classificatory field and these can be discerned in even the early editions of CC. They include his insistence that bibliographical classification should consistently obey the five laws of library science; the desire to fully express in a class-mark the subject of a book and then to add a distinctive book mark, thus individualizing each book in the library; the wish to create a classification which would adhere in uncompromising fashion to definite principles; and the idea that the individual classifier should be given the maximum opportunity to anticipate revision in the published tables of the scheme by constructing his own class-marks for new subjects as these arise. His zeal for the establishment of a helpful, filiatory, order is seen in his rejection of the earlier book classifications and his constant striving to improve his own.

Features and Principles. CC is not a series of tables setting out, in graded fashion, a conspectus of the whole universe of thought in a continuous sequence, with each subject developed from its broad outline to its most specific parts and with a notation for every subject so listed from the most general to the most minute; it is not, in other words, an enumerative scheme. As our preceding studies have shown, the other classifications have their main tables worked out largely enumeratively, although most of them provide for notational synthesis and extra detail through systematic and mnemonic schedules which develop and qualify all or some of the subjects in those main schedules. Apart from the enumeration of broad conventional subject areas which can be submitted to facet analysis, Ranganathan has produced an entirely synthetic system, in which it is clearly recognized that most topics are compounds that are best specified by the appropriate linkage of elements. Elements or isolates are arranged systematically as *foci* within categories or facets, each category consisting of concepts produced by a single characteristic of division.

The outline of the scheme is of traditional canonical character, a number of basic fields being identified and listed. Within each such area, facet analysis must take place before any compound topic can be classified. The scheme itself gives a good deal of practical advice for this procedure and there is, of course, an appropriate programmed text based on the sixth edition of CC. The fundamental idea to grasp is that the classificationist has related all facets to one or another of what he has described as five fundamental concepts – Personality, Matter, Energy, Space and Time. (Usually written merely as PMEST.) Time and Space are obviously applicable to all disciplines, so their divisions, or foci, are given once and for all at the beginning of the schedules; but the foci in P, M and E differ from class to class. The classifier selects the appropriate main class or basic discipline[1] and analyses a compound subject into its facets. The next step is to assemble the foci concerned from these facets, employing PMEST as a citation order – although it must be remembered that, in many cases, only one, two or, at the very most, three of the fundamental concepts will be represented. In a complete class-mark, we can quickly pick out the facets which are present, since each is introduced by a distinctive punctuation mark. Thus a comma (compulsory in the new edition, but optional before this) heralds Personality, Matter is prefixed by a semi-colon, Energy by the colon (originally the only punctuation mark used), Space by a full stop, and Time by an apostrophe.

Before providing a few examples, it is as well to consider briefly once again the use and validity of the PMEST formula as a citation order. Ranganathan's own conviction that the formula has imperfections is attested to by the necessary use of Rounds and Levels of facets (to be described) and by the transfer, in the current edition, of a vast range of foci, from the realm of Energy into the once largely idle Matter facet. It seems odd too, in a sense that Space and Time, those vast concepts which 'tease us out of thought' should be relegated to the end of the citation sequence, but it is obvious that the subject matter of an item is usually more important or, to use Ranganathan's term, more concrete than the geographical region or time period to which the subject is restricted. We do find instances where a geographical region is important, but it then becomes the Personality concept (in subjects like history and politics) for example, while in Literature it is clear that literary periods or movements must be regarded as significant – as Personality rather than Time. We might thus, when regarding the CC facet formula, almost use the words of Charles Lamb and say 'Nothing puzzles me more than time and space; and yet nothing troubles me less, as I never think about them.' The more important Personality, Matter and Energy divisions are found within the schedules for individual disciplines. We may ponder long on the theoretical niceties of the boundaries between them, although in practice they are always

[1] A distinction can be made between Main Classes and Basic subjects. Some main classes contain basic subjects and facet analysis is applied within each basic subject. Thus Philosophy as a Main Class contains Ethics and Metaphysics as basic subjects. Facet analysis is applied within each of the latter and not to the philosophy class as a whole.

fixed for us by the classificationist. Personality is a core or root concept present in most compound subjects and Energy an activity, process or operation. Matter now incorporates many 'Matter – Property' isolates and some 'Method' isolates formerly in the sphere of Energy, in addition to materials as such. While it is good to see this facet given more work and while we are assured that changes in the current edition arising out of this transfer are minimal (several colons to be altered to semi-colons), it is strange for trained eyes to see the class-mark in CC for our subject as 2;51. Apart from some common Energy isolates, the use of the category Energy is likely to decline.

In an earlier chapter, a practical example from the sixth edition was provided. We can practise facet analysis in CC by looking at other examples and by now employing the current edition. Let us consider four compound subjects:

a) '*Monetary economics in USA during the 1960s.*' In this instance the main class is x Economics and the facets represented are Personality (Money), Space (USA) and Time. After notational synthesis we would have as our class-mark:

x ,61 .73 'N6
Main
Class [P] [S] [T]

This means, of course, that Monetary Economics in the 1960s, for instance, would be x,61 'N6 and that Economics in the USA is x.73. (Many class-marks quoted here are of a rare length and complexity since several items at 'the book level' have only one or two facets.)

b) '*Hygiene of the eye.*' Here we have our main class L Medicine and the facets are Personality (Eye) and Energy or activity (Hygiene). Thus we achieve through gradual assembly of components:

L ,185 :5
Main
Class [P] [E]

From this we realize, for instance, that Hygiene as a subject is L:5.

c) '*Prevention of poverty.*' In this instance we go to Y Sociology as our main class. Poverty was once in the Energy facet as a 'problem', but is now in the Matter isolates. Energy is, however, represented by the activity of 'prevention'. So, as we have no Personality facet here, we obtain

Y   ;434 :5
Main
Class [M] [E]

d) '*The anxieties of the old.*' Main class s Psychology. Personality and Matter/Property are represented. So the class-mark in this final brief example is:

s   ,38 ;56
Main
Class [P] [M]

The facet formula is complicated by the fact that the classifier may be faced with examples which bring facets from all five categories into operation; more important, he may find that some of the five fundamental concepts occur more than once in the faceted pattern of any topic. Ranganathan has catered for such examples by the concept of *Rounds and Levels*. It is recognized that two foci relating to Personality may sometimes be required before the introduction of Energy. In such an instance there is said to be more than one *Level* of Personality. (See the Literature class for instance.) On the other hand, the energy facet may give rise to a recurrence of facets relating to Personality, Matter, Energy or all three concepts. When these arise after the first Energy facet, we are said to have a second manifestation or *Round* of facets. Energy is an important and pivotal category, since the reintroduction of Personality, or Matter facets *after* Energy represents a new Round. On the other hand, we may have two Levels of, say Personality *before* Energy is introduced or without Energy being present at all. Thus in the example '*The work of the British Prime Minister*' our class-mark reveals two personality facets, manifested as successive levels, with the 'State' and the 'officer' as the foci concerned:

e) V ,56 ,21
      [P1] [P2]

Rounds (in this case of Personality) can be shown by Ranganathan's own example:

f) '*X-ray therapy of tuberculosis of the lungs*', which is specified as L,45; 421: 6, 253. Here 'the lungs' represent the Personality concept in the first round and 'X-ray therapy' is Personality in a second round, this second manifestation *following* the application of the Energy idea which is :6 Therapeutics. The idea of Rounds and Levels soon becomes familiar and should be regarded as a variation on the PMEST theme, necessary because of problems arising from the endeavour to provide a citation order with only five categories which is valid for the whole field of knowledge. The distinction between Rounds and Levels is really simply to enable us to cope with certain specific documents – they are fortunately few – which offer more than one manifestation of a particular facet, and at the same time preserve the sought helpful citation order.

Another matter covered comprehensively by CC is that of the problem of complex document or multi-phased work which has a foot in each of two quite separate branches of knowledge. We have seen this problem already and examples of it, although relatively rare, have increasing literary warrant. *Colon* was the first system to distinguish this problem clearly, for although, as Ranganathan points out in some of his books, the traditional schemes sometimes enumerate multi-phased subjects or sometimes make a tentative effort to enable them to be specified through number-building, there is no real attempt there to lay down systematically a principle which will enable us to deal with *any* complex subject of this kind and to distinguish each *type of phase* in the notation. In CC such items must first be classed by the symbols denoting the facets in its primary phase; the secondary phase can then be introduced by means of an assigned lower-case letter introduced by an ampersand – the digit indicating a change of phase. Thus we have, to borrow an example from the influencing phase:

c & gU The influence of geography on physical science.

It should be perceived that it is most helpful to accommodate such documents in the scheme near to the beginning of the class represented by their primary phase. The above item, for instance, is obviously specialized in relation to items dealing solely with the physical sciences and should follow them in the classified sequence, but it deals with the influence of a subject on the physical sciences *as a whole* and, therefore, should precede the volumes which are restricted to special branches of this field. CC retains the various important types of phase – influencing, comparison, bias, which we mentioned earlier; it also recognizes a difference phase, which would be seen in such a subject as: '*the difference between the philosophical and religious notions of evil*'. Multi-phased subjects should be distinguished from similar complex documents which deal with the interaction of two subjects drawn from a *single* class of knowledge. These demonstrate an *Intra-facet relationship* or, in some cases, an *Intra-Array relationship*.

CC also contains various tools known as Devices and – as with the other features – their study at first-hand is recommended. They include the Classic Device (ClD) which is used for arranging the various editions of a 'classic' work and literature relating to it in helpful sequence within a class. There are also the Chronological device (CD) and the Geographical Device (GD), which enable us to use space and time divisions to form isolates in other facets on appropriate occasions. Thus in Class V History, for example, the Personality concepts are not enumerated, for they are geographical entities and can be culled from the common space facet by means of (GD). These devices are both used in class Q Religion, where (CD) provides dates for the start of religious movements and (GD) indicates appropriate regions where certain religions flourish. The rarely used Alphabetical Device (AD) provides for A–Z sequence within a class, if appropriate. There is also the important Subject Device (SD) which is always bracketed. Here we borrow the notation for an isolate in one class to specify the same isolate in another class. For instance, in class Q, the Hebrew Religion is specified by the number 5 in the Personality facet. If, however, we want to classify 'The sociology of the Jews with special reference to marriage customs', it must go into class Y. Here we have Y,73 Sociology of ethnological groups, the groups being specified by (SD). Marriage is specified by 317 in the Matter/Property isolates, so the final class-mark is Y,73(Q5);317.

All this apparatus of facet or phase analysis and use of devices is woven into a complex and yet extremely logical and comprehensive unity to form the schedules of CC. There is a constant insistence on helpful order of arrays of foci within facets as well as in the PMEST controlled citation order through which a chain of topics is gradually forged. The principle of inversion is strictly applied, so that individual facets appear in a vertical filing order in the sequence TSEMP. Thus we might have:

x Economics
x'N6 Economics in the 1960s
x.73 Economics in the USA
x.73'N6 Economics in the USA in the 1960s
x,61'N6 Monetary economics in the 1960s
x,61.73'N6 Monetary economics in the USA in the 1960s

In this way, scattering is restricted to the minor facets.

Notation. Ranganathan has distinguished between the Idea Plane and the Notational Plane, the latter being the servant of the former. So turning away now from these novel and intriguing ideas, we find that the notation of *Colon* is extremely mixed. It relies heavily on numbers, but when fully employed uses letters, brackets, Greek symbols, and punctuation marks also. It reveals Ranganathan's constant insistence on the necessity for an ultimate economy of 'co-extensiveness of subject and class-mark' and is most hospitable to new topics. It is expressive of the structure of the scheme to a greater degree than the notation of any other general bibliographical system and clearly shows each change of facet, demonstrating also (although a little less clearly) change of phase. Its indicators and punctuation marks are also sometimes convenient pauses or breaks in a class-mark. Opponents of the scheme often suggest that the notation is impossibly long; this may well be because they have seen a few very long notations from CC which denote highly specific documents. In other cases, the notation is as short as that of rival systems. Ranganathan has suggested[1] that long notations do not bother the reader. He argues that just as the passenger in an aeroplane is not concerned with the way in which the engine works, providing he reaches his destination safely and reasonably promptly, so the reader is not concerned with the notation if he can find the book or books he wants quickly. This particular analogy is rather misleading; although the notation is, as Ranganathan contends, primarily a tool for the librarian, the reader must use it to go from the catalogue to the shelves and he will need to follow the notational sequence to determine the order of material on those shelves. True, Ranganathan might say that the catalogue is a staff tool and that good plans of the library and shelf guides will be far more use to the reader than the notational symbols; nevertheless most librarians believe that the readers should use the catalogue and it seems desirable that, for both reader and librarian, the notation should be

---

[1] *Prolegomena to Library Classification*, 2nd edition, 1957, pp. 281–2.

concise in as many cases as possible. Ranganathan is surely on safer ground when he points out that the small library which wants simple classification and short notation will obtain it, as most of its books there will deal with simple, straightforward subjects; the larger library, coping with specialized material and employing classification in depth must, it seems, accept the longer class-marks for many of its documents. Ranganathan indeed sees in notation the possibility of an international language; in *Colon*, therefore, it is always used with great precision. It is succinct in the broad fields of macrothought, but it does not, to use the classificationist's own phrase, 'shirk the challenge' of the exact classification of more difficult material. Many changes in the current edition are basically notational ones, but the notation remains extremely hospitable, offering interpolation to a marvellous degree and thus preserving the chosen order of topics.

Synthesis and Mnemonics. CC is the one general scheme which is entirely synthetic; indeed we have inevitably considered this 'main feature' already. The older, conventional schemes, of course, are not entirely enumerative; DC perceives the value of number-building, SC had great possibilities in this direction, BC has elaborate tables for the task (although Bliss seems to have been slow to realize the necessity for the provision of such tables), and the new BC has tremendous synthetic potential, as has UDC. It might be said, for example, that the use of the colon sign in UDC was virtually the first clear recognition of a rudimentary form of phase analysis. But only Ranganathan has produced a fully faceted classification for the whole field of knowledge as yet. *Colon* is the one general scheme which clearly recognizes the need for the breaking down of subjects into their constituent parts, the listing of each of these parts once and for all by the classificationist in its appropriate category, and the provision of rules for the fitting together of the parts from the various facets. The enumeration of basic recurring concepts only, rather than of all known subjects, has greatly decreased the size of the schedules of CC. Thus we find that synthesis is achieved through facet analysis, phase analysis, intra-facet relations, and also through the use of a table of *Anteriorizing Common Isolates* (similar to common form divisions), and one of *Posteriorizing Common Isolates* (Personality and Energy foci applicable to many classes) listed with the common Space and Time Isolates at the front of the schedules. The Anteriorizing Common Isolates must now be introduced by an upwards arrow ↑. Thus 'A bibliography on physics' is C ↑ a.

The tremendous mnemonic value of such a formidable synthetic apparatus must be remarked upon. Each isolate is denoted by a distinctive symbol whenever it is used as part of a class-mark; thus, as far as systematic mnemonics are concerned, CC has a notation with more memory value than any other general classification scheme. The student should notice that CC has other mnemonic features. There are very few literal mnemonics as used by Bliss, but, in addition to the mnemonic effect obtained from the listing of basic isolates in the schedules, an attempt has been made to develop a new form of mnemonic. These unscheduled mnemonics, or *seminal* mnemonics as Palmer and Wells dubbed them, take the form of a list of entities associated with a particular digit. The introductory part of CC shows that Ranganathan has tried to gather together certain allied concepts into groups and to represent each grouping by one of the digits 1–9. The digit 1, for example, is associated amongst other things with unity, God, the world, and so forth. The method at present set out as a Mnemonic Device (MD) appears to be highly subjective, but the aim is to provide a guide to the classifier who is confronted with a new subject and who wishes to anticipate the incorporation of this subject into the tables of CC. Thus if a new subject cropped up and most of the isolates revealed by the facet analysis of this subject were listed in the schedules, the individual classifier, it is claimed, should be able to anticipate the number for the remaining isolates by reference to the table of seminal mnemonics. Therefore, if the new isolate dealt with unity or a related theme, the classifier would realize that 1 was the appropriate digit for it; he would be able to work out the decision of the classificationist in advance.

Ideally this method would result in various classifiers in different libraries being able to deal with newly created subjects without waiting for the next edition of the classification and yet achieving identical results. The *self-perpetuating classification* which would result from the complete development of such an idea is still some way from us, however. It would be extremely difficult in practice to obtain complete agreement with regard to the associations of ideas with digits; indeed *Colon* tells us that it is highly desirable that all foci formed by this device should be considered at meetings of users of the scheme. Even if agreement could be reached in this direction, it would seem unlikely that all classifiers would independently apply these seminal mnemonics perfectly or that all new subjects could be immediately correctly placed in the scheme by means of them. The cynical might even be inclined to dismiss this idea altogether as indeed Metcalfe, perhaps the severest critic of cc, tends to do. Yet the notion is a most ingenious and interesting one; it is significant to note how A. J. Wells was able to select suitable digits for the foci in the Energy facet of a classification for packaging through the use of this idea.[1] The careful reader of cc will observe for himself also how often in the tables of the scheme a concept is represented by the digit which we would anticipate if we were familiar with the seminal mnemonics. Thus, for example, in the Common Time Isolates, lower-case p represents a meteorological period and p5 the wet season; the list of seminal mnemonics shows liquid and water among the ideas associated with the digit 5, so this is obviously a logical choice for 'wet season'.

Index. This may be regarded as a Relative Index, but it differs from the normal type of index in that it merely shows where standard parts, or foci, can be found in the schedules; the class-marks obtained from the linking together of such parts are not given in the Index. We have entries such as:

Lending 2(M),62.   X(P),62
Partnership Z(P2),315

Our two random examples indicate that the concept 'lending' occurs in Class 2 Library Science, where it is denoted by 62 in the Matter facet; it also arises in Class x Economics where, in the Personality facet it is also denoted by 62. Partnership occurs only in Class z Law, where it belongs to the second level Personality facet and is represented by 315. The overall effect appears to be an economical and satisfactory one; the index can certainly not be used alone, but then no index should ever be so used. In cc it is a useful key to the various basic classes and their isolates and is truly complementary to the schedules of the classification.

Use and revision of the scheme. This classification has, like BC, suffered from the fact that it arrived in the world of librarianship at a time when most general collections were committed firmly to earlier systems. Indeed Dewey had done his utmost to convince both Bliss and Ranganathan of the futility of creating their own systems. *Colon* is, however, used in an increasing number of libraries in India, although its use elsewhere is slight. In Britain, it has been employed in the Library of Christ's College, Cambridge, where

---

[1] This is discussed in R. S. Parkhi, *Decimal Classification and Colon Classification in Perspective*, 1964, pp. 469–70.

several important oriental collections are housed. It appears to work quite well there and the staff comment favourably on the memory value of some schedules, although certain classes give rise to difficulties. Metcalfe suggests that many Indian librarians are indifferent to Ranganathan's theories or sceptical concerning them; yet it is certain that the increasing volume of library literature from that country testifies to the impact which the principles behind *Colon* have made on many of the younger generation of librarians, despite the fact that DC is the most popular scheme still in India. The use of CC's distinctive principles can, of course, also be seen in Britain and elsewhere in the number of special classifications, constructed on completely faceted lines, that are now becoming available.

The revision policy of CC has left much to be desired. Editions have been produced regularly and radical changes have sometimes been made to incorporate new theories and developments of older ones. Certain promised depth-classification schedules have not materialized, although several relevant articles have appeared in *Library Science with a slant to Documentation*, indicating how CC could be suitably developed and extended. The fact is that this has been very much a one-man classification and has owed a great deal, not only to Ranganathan's ingenuity but to his amazing fund of energy and enthusiasm also. The idea of a self-perpetuating classification has not been fully developed; indeed it is possibly unattainable. In this case, CC may suffer from its long lack of an editorial board to carry out systematic revision based on the needs of users and developments in the field of knowledge. There is no official bulletin announcing proposed changes or additions and, it must be confessed, any librarian using the scheme would be likely to disregard many of the changes made on account of their drastic nature; no well-established library can easily incorporate wholesale changes into its classification system. It may be noted, in this respect, that at Christ's College, Cambridge the fourth edition of CC is used and no attempt is made to recognize ideas introduced in later versions unless these can be acknowledged without undue difficulty. It can be observed that the recognition of the five fundamental categories, for instance, was not introduced until the third edition; also, as we have already observed, the *Colon* was originally the only punctuation mark used to separate facets, but there are now several others. These changes are commendable in the sense that they represent strenuous efforts to maximize achievement; they do, however, make things more difficult for a library which has adopted

an early edition of the scheme. It might even be argued, one supposes, that CC has the advantage over DC in changing and keeping
up-to-date because it is not so widely used. For it is the generally
accepted scheme that cannot afford to introduce significant alterations or structural changes.

Conclusion. One is conscious that the methods behind CC are so
different from those of the conventional schemes and that the
terminology in some ways is so complex that it is difficult for a
writer to do the scheme justice or explain it to his satisfaction in a
single chapter. Ranganathan's own books (read, apart from the
Elements, chronologically) do much to familiarize us with his distinctive ideas and terms and the overlap or repetition that occurs
inevitably to some extent in these volumes also helps to drive home
the essence of the more important theories. CC offers the enormous
advantage of the completely faceted approach; the clear rules for the
formation of subjects from the constituent elements represented by
the foci in these categories enables the classifier to specify many modern subjects which are difficult to fit into the less plastic enumerative
framework of older systems. CC is a slim volume also in comparison
with the older schemes, as unit parts rather than composite subjects
are enumerated. This lack of bulk should facilitate the use of the
scheme once the basic principles have been grasped. The system
now has many capable advocates, but Dr Ranganathan himself was
long the most active of these, urging us seriously to consider the
advantages offered by a faceted general scheme and indicating that
reclassification can be achieved in established libraries by the
method of using the new scheme for new accessions and much used
older volumes and leaving the little wanted stock arranged in a
parallel sequence by the superseded classification. Despite this
insistence upon the value of the osmotic method of reclassification
as he calls it, CC is having the same difficulties in gaining recognition
in practice that are met by other comparatively new general
classifications.

Bliss, although he appreciated some of Ranganathan's ideas, was
a rather harsh critic. He questioned the need, even in documentation, for such lengthy and formidable symbolizing as CC's complete
specifications carry; they are certainly unlikely to be used in ordinary
libraries. The importance of the *Colon* system lay, he felt, in what
Ranganathan would describe as its wholehearted recognition of the
synthetic principle and its provision (through phase analysis) for
the specification of complex subjects. He considered, however, that

'its systematic devices and its complicated pseudo-mnemonic notation are too much of a burden for any bibliographic classification'. Nevertheless, he concluded, 'the erudition, insight and ingenuity of the author are truly admirable'. The general order and collocation in CC are good through the rigorous application of the PMEST citation order, Rounds and Levels, the use of Devices, the meticulous attempt at suitable arrangement of foci in an array within each facet, the recognition of phase relations, and the use of the inversion principle. However, notational complications impede speedy filing in a manual system and certainly the layout and display of facets and their hierarchies within the schedules has often left much to be desired and impedes speedy classification. Moreover PMEST, ignoring its quasi-metaphysical overtones, is not always satisfactory in practice. The use of Rounds and Levels, the problem of defining 'Personality' and the increasingly demonstrable doubt and overlap between Matter and Energy all suggest to some observers of the scheme that, whatever the merit of fundamental categories as the basis for a valid facet citation order, there are more things in heaven and earth than can satisfactorily be explained by the PMEST formula.

Other critics draw our attention chiefly to the difficulty of the terminology, the very uneven development in classes, the emphasis on the East and on Indian library requirements, the problems arising out of the considerable changes made from edition to edition, and the failure of Ranganathan to acknowledge his debt to the older systems – UDC in particular. There is more than a grain of truth in at least some of these complaints. The Eastern emphasis of the scheme is understandable; it is perhaps, as Foskett suggests, based on a recognition of the 'literary warrant' of India. This does not, of course, prevent us from applying the same principles to classifications designed for the Western civilization. The difficulty of the scheme and its terminology are, in part, acknowledged by its classificationist, who insists that nevertheless the extra effort made to master it will bring more than adequate rewards to the classifier and that part of the difficulty lies in breaking free from the shackles imposed upon our thinking by the older enumerative approach to classification. The debt to UDC is certainly evident but, as De Grolier[1] says, 'In relation to UDC a certain number of improvements are noted, probably greater flexibility, more hospitality'. The UDC use of

[1] *A study of general categories applicable to classification and coding for documentation*, 1962.

synthesis is not as thorough as that of *Colon*; the older scheme is tied to an enumerative framework and does not clearly recognize a facet formula. De Grolier justly adds that *Colon* 'presents also some great gaps, especially in the classes relating to the physical and natural sciences and to their applications'. This hinders its adoption in appropriate special libraries. But perhaps the very greatest objection to the use of the scheme lies not in this, frustrating though the gaps and omissions are, nor in the notation employed (which is sometimes long and awkward), nor again in the fact that CC appeared long after other schemes had been generally accepted, important though all these factors may be; it lies rather in the difficulty encountered in coping with any classification which, chameleon-like, alters considerably as the need rises. The constant deletion of unsatisfactory features and grafting on of new ideas make CC essentially a vehicle for experiment rather than a working classification.

Bliss once suggested that 'the system is well worthy of study by those who contemplate constructive developments in bibliographic classification'.[1] This appears, in retrospect, to be a colossal understatement, for CC, and particularly the analytico-synthetic methods associated with it, have influenced recent classification study greatly, even to fascination. Even the perceptive and eminently practical American writer, J. H. Shera,[2] thinks Ranganathan's the most fertile mind that has addressed itself to the problems of library classification, but he points out that CC's severest critics are prepared to dismiss the system in the words used by Carlyle of seventeenth-century England – 'grand unintelligibility'. If we ignore the prejudice, one way or the other, of some writers and review the scheme objectively, we find that it has given enormous impetus to classificatory research and that the methods expounded, or some of them, may prove to be of great seminal consequence and possibly more important than the scheme itself. The enormous sifting of ideas and minute and uncompromising examination of the field of knowledge which underlies all of CC (and which is still taking place at the Documentation Centre at Bangalore in such tasks as the measurement of the growth of isolates in individual facets) testifies to this continuing impetus and seminal influence. CC will never be a widely used scheme, however. Its relatively late appearance, serious

[1] *Organization of Knowledge in Libraries*, p. 304.
[2] *Classification: current functions ...* In *The Subject Analysis of Library Materials*, edited by M. F. Tauber, 1953.

gaps in coverage, and uncertain revision policy disqualify it as a widely usable shelf classification, although at the book level it is not unduly complicated. But it has, in its detail, influenced and can continue to influence classification for mechanized retrieval systems. Ranganathan himself always argued that one scheme could do both jobs, but perhaps sub-consciously he was, in his quest for precision and perfection, steering CC towards the realm of mechanized information retrieval where logical efficiency is all important and complexity is of little consequence. Certainly it is in the latter sphere that *Colon* helps to open up new vistas. Finally it must be said that it is clear that CC has provided a refreshingly stimulating contribution to our subject. It is not itself the information retrieval system of tomorrow, but the classifications which jostle for that privilege are likely to owe a most significant debt to Ranganathan's pioneering work.

CHAPTER THIRTEEN

The Bibliographic Classification

Henry Evelyn Bliss devoted a large part of his life to the study of classification. His original thoughts and plans are expressed in an article in Library Journal for 1910 and yet BC was not completed until 1953, just two years before Bliss's death. His earliest articles and the substantial books which followed them all pointed, however, to a new scheme of classification that he must always have had in mind, which would be based upon a theory of knowledge deduced from long and precise studies of all the methods of organization, as far as they were available to him, that man has used in the ordering of his activities and mental processes. Bliss was born in New York in 1870 and completed his education in the College of the City of New York, in which he became a librarian in 1891. He served there until his retirement in 1940, and during the latter part of the time had been allowed facilities by the College authorities to pursue the studies which have had so important an influence upon librarianship. The record of the life of such a man cannot have been dramatic; indeed Dr Campbell has made us aware of the lonely dedication of Bliss's later years.[1]

The major writings of Bliss and the details of editions of BC need to be stated at the outset. His first book, *The Organisation of Knowledge and the system of the sciences* (1929) was the result of his long and arduous study of all methods of organization – in nature, in society, and in intellectual occupations. It examines the work of philosophers and other scholars in arranging subject fields and explores the underlying structure of the universe of knowledge. *The Organization of Knowledge in Libraries* (1933; 2nd edition, 1939) relates this structure and Bliss's findings more specifically to bibliographical organization. It criticizes existing book classifications in some detail and discusses the role of classification and notation.

[1] Library Association Record, November, 1955, p. 461.

BC in outline is found in *A System of Bibliographic Classification* (1935; 2nd edition, 1936) and the first full edition of the scheme appeared in four volumes over the period 1940–53. This is the Bliss classification that many librarians know, but a second edition was prepared under the aegis of the Bliss Classification Association and is due to appear in 1975; much of the detail and examples in this chapter come from this current edition.[1] There is also a very useful abridged *Bliss Classification* published in Britain by the School Library Association at the end of 1967.

Features and Principles. The second edition of the full BC is largely the work of J. Mills, at the Polytechnic of North London, with the help of Valerie Lang and Vanda Broughton as successive research assistants. Jack Mills had advised and aided in the compilation of some classes in the final volume of the original BC schedules and is a staunch advocate of the scheme, as well as an acknowledged expert on classification, while Miss Lang came to the task of revising BC with experience gained in helping to formulate an important special faceted scheme – the business classification devised at the London Graduate Business School. The new edition of BC is radical, as one would expect in the case of a classification that has not been fully revised for twenty years or more, and full use has been made of modern classification theory. The original principles and features of BC which were acclaimed have nevertheless been carefully maintained. These are to seek out and reflect the consensus of expert opinion in all areas; to collocate related subjects, and to subordinate each special topic very carefully to the appropriate general one; to provide alternatives in cases where the consensus (or majority viewpoint) is difficult to determine; and to employ a concise notation. These principles, aimed at combining scholarship and practical utility with economy and adaptability are considered below in more detail.

1) *Consensus.* 'The scientific and educational consensus', as Bliss usually called it, is simply a way of acknowledging that an effective classification must be based upon the way in which the majority of subject specialists expect their material to be organized and the way in which subjects are taught in universities and colleges. Bliss claimed that the classificationist could find, in each subject field, this consensus and act accordingly. He also stated that the con-

[1] The current edition had not been published when the *Manual* went to press: examples are drawn from the advance circulation of certain draft schedules.

sensus is relatively stable and tends to become more so. The notion of consensus as a fundamental idea in striving for helpful order in *any* classification has been discussed earlier in the *Manual*, but it must in fairness be said that some librarians have either doubted the existence of a clear-cut consensus viewpoint among experts in some subject fields or else have questioned Bliss's success in finding it. Others have queried the stability of any consensus, especially in this age of newly forged interdisciplinary studies, because extensive research often upsets settled opinion. There is some justice in such arguments and it may be added that BC is occasionally prone also to an understandable fault in a basically 'one-man' scheme – the intrusion of personal opinion or idiosyncrasy. Yet there is a great deal of evidence that Bliss did, for the most part, find a useful and durable order and the quest for the consensus has resulted in a very sound basic structure. In the new edition, this is enhanced by the application of facet analysis and a clear citation order within each class.

2) *Collocation and subordination.* The first of these simply involves the bringing together of closely allied subjects. Bliss's deep study of the earlier schemes of book classification had provided him with many examples of faulty grouping, or collocation, and he was determined to avoid such faults in his own system. Thus in BC we find a careful attempt to bring disciplines which have strong relationships into close proximity. The best example, although certainly not the only one, is seen in Bliss's efforts to collocate certain pure sciences with the appropriate technology. Brown of course, had thought of this, but had over-worked the idea; usually, it is better to separate pure and applied sciences – there are only a few which merit collocation. Bliss realized this and he links together only those pure and applied sciences which are really likely to be required together by the majority of readers. His efforts to achieve subordination in BC can be seen in the way in which he carefully ensures that each specific theme is subordinated to the appropriate general one (which is, in turn, subordinated to a more general one still), and, in a rather more specialized sense, in the idea of gradation by speciality, or as it is sometimes called, serial dependence. This means that certain subjects draw upon the findings of others and are, in this sense, more specialized than the disciplines from which they borrow ideas. It is thus argued that, in a classification, the dependent subjects should follow the (often co-ordinated) topics on the findings of which they

rely. It is an idea which Bliss derived from his wide reading of the philosophers, especially the great French writer, Auguste Comte. The theory of Comte determined that such sciences as were simple, self-contained, and complete, preceded and influenced those which were more complex, derivative and dependent; thus astronomy, mathematics and the physical sciences went before the biological and sociological and led finally to his terminus science, morals. The British philosopher, Herbert Spencer, declared Comte's order to be impossible, yet his own ideas represent it closely. The notion can also be glimpsed in these words of Bertrand Russell:

> 'We may divide the sciences into three groups: physical, bio-logical and anthropological . . . In the anthropologic group I include all studies concerned with man: human physiology and psychology (between which no sharp line can be drawn), anthropology, history, sociology and economics. All these studies can be illuminated by considerations drawn from biology . . .'[1]

In book classification, and in BC especially, this notion provides us with a principle for determining helpful order, particularly helpful order in array. If two subjects are, roughly speaking, of the same status or rank, the one which borrows from the work of specialists in the other subject field should come after the other in the array.

3) *Alternative location.* It may be stressed once again, that this is not the same as alternative treatment or arrangement. The latter idea occurs in nearly all schemes for certain topics such as biography; it is recognized in BC in the literature class (where four alternative arrangements are provided in the original edition) and for biography, of course, and elsewhere. But alternative location is a different matter and is virtually a unique feature of BC. Bliss was anxious to accommodate his scheme to meet the needs of large minority viewpoints within the consensus; he recognized that, for certain subjects, there were two or more possible locations in the sequence of classes that were almost equally acceptable. For these the alternative location idea is provided. Photography, for instance, can in BC, be with technology or with the arts; Economic History can be subordinated to general history, but can also go under Economics. Religion is preferred by Bliss at P, where its associations with History and Ethics are stressed by contiguity; but another legitimate mode of thought stresses rather the associations with Metaphysics; so AJ is

[1] *Icarus: or the Future of Science*, 1926, pp. 8–9.

reserved as an alternative place, where Religion may be expanded like class P as given in the schedules. Bibliography and Librarianship may go in class Z, in class J as a branch of education, or may be placed along with generalia material. Another important group of alternatives is concerned with Applied Science and Technology. Bliss gives a preferred arrangement by which the more specialized technologies are subsumed under their parent sciences while the more general are grouped together in class U. However, alternative places are provided for all major technologies; the library applying the scheme can adopt whatever collocation is considered to be best.

It will be seen that these alternative locations are for variant placings sanctioned by scholarly authority, but differing from the classificationist's own recommendations. They recognize what Bliss would call the 'relativity of consensus'. L. A. Burgess, a British admirer of BC, has described the idea as playing a prominent role, 'not only in the broad outline, but in detail throughout the schedules'. Clearly a library would need to choose, in each case, one alternative and adhere to this; so that the rejected place(s) would be left blank as far as that library was concerned. Otherwise a form of cross-division would occur; some books on say, photography, would be at one place, others at the alternative location. This must not happen, for the scattering of books which deal with the same subject defeats the whole purpose of classification; what is needed is for each library to select the placings it wants and to ignore alternatives. In practical use, it will only be necessary for the classifier to record decisions; for guiding is so carefully provided throughout the schedules of BC that there is very little danger of confusion. Professor Dunkin has argued that if there is a consensus there should be no need for alternatives,[1] but this viewpoint confuses majority needs and acceptance with unanimity. Consensus embraces the former, but can never achieve the latter. Indeed, by and large, this novel BC feature of alternative locations, although it means that different libraries using the scheme will not enjoy complete uniformity of practice, is to be commended as a handsome concession to rival, but equally legitimate, schools of thought embraced within the folds of the scientific and educational consensus. It is probably overworked at times, but it does allow the nature and needs of a particular library to be catered for to a great extent and some of the alternative locations given, together with the alternative treatments supplied in certain classes, give the flexibility needed

[1] Dunkin, Paul S. *Cataloguing USA*. American Library Association, 1969, p. 128.

to solve dilemmas that face all classifiers, whatever scheme they adopt.

Notation. If we exclude – for simplicity – opportunities for synthesis to begin with and also ignore Bliss's equivalent of the Generalia Class, where numerals are employed, the basic notation of BC is composed of capital letters. Bliss defended letter notation on grounds of its great capacity and shows that, despite a certain amount of wastage arising from the avoidance of odd or awkward combinations of letters or from unused alternative locations, a letter notation can accommodate major topics with brief distinctive class-marks. All methods to achieve notational brevity were employed. Bliss selected an alphabetical notation and allocated or apportioned it with very great care. He frequently used non-hierarchical notation, an idea that has been developed further in the second edition because of the gain in both brevity and hospitality. He also sacrificed detail, where necessary, in the interests of notational economy. Examples of concise notation for even quite specific topics – which in other schemes are either not provided or are burdened with long or relatively long class-marks – include:

AYAN   Index numbers (in class AY Probability and statistics)
QEH   Depressed areas and twilight zones (in class Q Applied
        Social Science)
SFJ   Admissibility of evidence (in class S Law)
VWYUF   Creole jazz music (in class V Music)

These are from the revised BC, while the original full schedules offer examples such as:

ZHH   Simplified cataloguing (in class Z Librarianship)
CNL   Iridium (in class C Chemistry)

It can thus be seen that the idea of founding this classification on clear and definite principles is continued into the notational sphere. The second edition does *not* sacrifice detail in the interests of concise notation, however, for it rightly believes that precision in classifying should be there for those libraries that want it and indeed the detail of the new BC fully matches DC and even LC. But the detail is not compulsory and the carefully allocated and often non-expressive letter notation remains, on the whole, extremely economical as far as class-marks for topics enumerated in the schedules are concerned. It is also, partly because of its deliberately erratic habit with regard to expression of hierarchical structure and partly because it is faceted, now very hospitable to new topics. The notation from the main schedules reveals the chosen order very clearly, but ordinal significance becomes a little blurred if extensive synthesis is used.

Synthesis and mnemonics. In the original BC, notational synthesis, for the exact classification demanded by documentation is provided by twenty-two principal Systematic Schedules. Many of these have sub-schedules appended for more detailed expansion, making in all forty-six in the revised list in Table 4 in Volume 3. As in the use of similar tables incorporated into other schemes, symbols from these schedules are added to those denoting the subject of the book; the added symbols give precision to the original placing by introducing some such consideration as external forms or locality. They can be added without confusion at any stage of sub-division by topic. Actually, only the first four Schedules are of general application; and even these are not equally applicable throughout the main schedules; the remainder are applicable to groups of classes, to single classes, or to sub-classes; but all are mnemonic and consistent throughout their field of use. Bliss indeed claims that these tables for synthesis (his own term is 'composite specification') are 'more special, more mnemonic, and more economical' than DC's ideas of number-building.

There are too many of these schedules, as many were grafted on to the basically enumerative BC at a comparatively late stage in its development, with resulting notational complexities. The idea in the revised BC is to replace the schedules of specialized application, whenever possible, with scope for retroactive number-building accompanied by suitable guidance. In class J Education, for example, Bliss offered Systematic Schedule 14, which was not entirely satis-factory in that its sequence did not blend with the order of class J as a whole. Now it is replaced by the retroactive notation idea and a particular type of school can be quite simply qualified by other facets:

JN Secondary schools
    Subject divisions here begin at JNM to allow for the use of earlier letters in the employment of the retroactive principle, eg,
JNJS Use of radio in secondary schools (taken from JJS Radio)
JNKO Chemistry in the secondary school (Chemistry is JKO within the curriculum facet JK)

This new idea, a characteristic Mills' innovation, is now a fundamental feature, but there is still a need for special schedules to take care of common facets. Bliss's Schedule 1, the equivalent of the DC standard sub-divisions, has been extensively recast in the recently revised BC and offers great detail for those who want it in that an amazing number of recurring entities and forms can be specified and place, time and phase relations are also introduced through its numbers. (The BNB influence via its own development of common sub-divisions is strong here.) Form divisions are introduced by the number 1; common recurring concepts or subject sub-divisions are introduced by the numbers 2–75; the numbers 76–79 introduce the secondary phase in a complex subject; 8 introduces place and time (hitherto embraced by Schedules 2 and 4). The lower-case letters of the place divisions distinguish them from time divisions.

Thus, in applying the new Schedule 1 we might have:

NI871   *Films on the history of America*
(Where 1871 stands for the form of presentation 'films'.)

ZNPGD 117 *Chain indexing: a programmed text*
(Where 117 conveys the form of presentation 'programmed text'.)

UE2   *A bibliography on engineering*
(Where 2 represents the recurring concept 'bibliography'.)

YUM79PRA *The Roman Catholic Church and censorship*
(Where 79 shows that a phase relationship – influencing phase is involved.)

FH8jt   *The Flora of the Netherlands*
(Where jt represents Holland in the common place facet introduced by the digit 8.)

The place schedule has been revised to bring the order of the old Schedule 2 into line with the geographical sequence of main classes M–O; Bliss's vision frequently exceeded his powers of execution in matters such as this.

Examples of compound class-marks could be multiplied, but it need only be said that by rationalizing and reducing in number the proliferation of Systematic Schedules and by building into the faceted structure of individual classes the possibility for synthetic classification which needs no special facet indicators and preserves helpful order – the provision for synthesis is enormously increased in the new BC. Indeed, like UDC, it should now be thought of as primarily a faceted rather than an enumerative scheme.

Such synthesis provides, as a natural by-product, rich dividends in systematic mnemonics. The letter notation also affords literal mnemonic opportunities, as the original edition showed:

CD Chemical dynamics
HB Human body
HH Human hygiene
NA North America

Sometimes these take a different form from that shown above. Thus class B is physics and C is Chemistry, so that Physical chemistry has a borderline position and the mnemonic class-mark CB. But, if over-employed, literal mnemonics would lead to the alphabetical scattering of several related themes. The new edition, like the original BC uses them only when order permits; they are thus employed casually and indeed Bliss sometimes called them *casual* mnemonics.

Index. A full relative index is provided as the third volume of the new edition. Its predecessor, although not seriously inadequate, could be faulted in various ways. Despite its size, it had minor inconsistencies and omissions; in addition some topics were indexed but not enumerated in the scheme itself. This was not an oversight by Bliss, but apparently an attempt to cater, via the index, for some specific topics not shown in the schedules (perhaps because of the quest for notational brevity) but which the classifier might seek. Above all, this index was not clearly based on the idea that an A–Z key should act as a location device and concentrate on displaying subject associations *not* shown by the classification. There is thus some repetition of the work of the classification itself. The second edition has taken these factors into account and offers a relative index which complements the schedules to form an essential and integral part of a consistent and predictable system. It thus concentrates on locating topics and showing the 'distributed relatives' which are inevitable in any fixed citation order of facets within classes.

Use and revision. BC is used by about 100 libraries, although it is – as with other schemes – difficult to carry out an accurate census since not all members of the Bliss Classification Association are users and some users (alas) are not members of the BCA. Its popularity is confined to academic and special libraries which are mostly within Britain and the British Commonwealth. Several users are colleges or institutes of education. This is hardly surprising, as Education was a subject which especially interested Bliss and class J is acknowledged as possibly the best in the scheme. There has been little or no enthusiasm for BC in North America. This is due in part to interest there, over many decades, in classification practice – as displayed in LC and DC – rather than in theory and innovation, plus the conviction that these twin giants are with us to stay for shelf arrangement and that alphabetical indexing systems offer the best hope for information retrieval and the arrangement of large subject catalogues. But it is also due in part to a failure to recognize the merits of Bliss's work, or if one prefers to think of it in another light, to the failure of Bliss and his supporters to build up a large sub-stantial market for his scheme. Bliss had been encouraged by several British writers, by De Grolier, and by Martel and Richardson; yet from the first he met with apathy and even hostility, especially from certain DC supporters. This opposition in the United States was in fact never overcome. BC is used there in the City College, New York, of course, and in at least one special library, but the general lack of enthusiasm is only too clearly apparent. Bliss, more than any other great classificationist, is the prophet without honour in his own country.

Bliss could be criticized for failing to initiate a satisfactory revision programme for his scheme. For ten years or so after his death in 1955, the American bibliographical services company, H. W. Wilson, together with a number of British enthusiasts, such as D. J. Campbell, J. Mills, and C. B. Freeman, did sterling work in pro-ducing and distributing a bulletin. The BC bulletin later became a regular annual and when the Bliss Classification Association was formed in 1967, this new organization took over from Wilson's the work of distributing the bulletin and became a body which could link BC users, and advocate and seek to perpetuate the scheme. The original BC was most out of date in the sciences, since the volume containing these classes appeared in 1940. Thus several recent BC bulletins have concentrated on providing new schedules in scientific fields, in accordance with contemporary literary warrant, by utilizing certain supplementary schedules of the *British National Bibliography*. Many BC users had, in the meantime, made their own departures from the original classification with individual extensions and adaptations. This is understandable in view of the uncertainty which once existed about the perpetuation of the scheme. But there is now much to woo them back to orthodoxy, where possible. The School Library Association *Abridged* BC (1967), which owes much to the little-publicized efforts of a small group including C. A. Stott and C. B. Freeman, is a fine and well-balanced scheme for those smaller libraries wanting a sound and simple classification with brief notation. Jack Mills has been the driving force behind the BC bulletins for some years and a grant to his institution, the Polytechnic of North London, plus generous financial help from some subscribers to the Bliss Classification Association, enabled the preparation of the new full edition to take place under Mills's direction.

This second edition of the full BC retains all the outstanding features of the original, but has some distinctive merits of its own. Chief among these is undoubtedly the rigorous and consistent application of facet analysis which should ease future revision and has provided a welcome degree of clarity in the schedules (not always a feature of the first edition) and predictability[1] which the individual classifier will welcome. Others include the wise decision to draw on the detail and order of several existing special classifications of acknowledged merit in fields such as business, engineering, medicine and physics, and on BNB supplementary schedules and incorporate these into BC whenever they are helpful and can be profitably woven (with notational change) into the texture of the original. There is, in all this, a constant regard for literary warrant. In notation, the reliance on non-hierarchical or non-expressive class-marks has increased and the retroactive principle is now very frequently used in notational synthesis. The Bliss equivalent of Generalia Class (Anterior Numeral Classes) has been partly remodelled so that, in addition to the expected subjects, it incorporates places for works on *all aspects* of concretes such as 'iron', 'gold', 'water', or 'the moon'. Works dealing with single aspects of these and similar concrete themes are still, of course, to be classified within the appropriate subject discipline.

This revision is radical, rational, far-seeing and impressive, although individual users of BC may be slow to accept the new edition *in toto* or to retreat from personal adaptations and extensions cultivated over the period when BC was stagnant or almost so. The policy for future revision seems reasonably well based, although the financial backing is in no way comparable to that enjoyed by DC, UDC, and LC. It is likely that future BC revision will not need to be as frequent as that of DC. The impetus for such revision as is wanted

[1] A standard citation order has been devised and is used wherever possible.

may well depend on the reception given to the current edition and the extent to which it can win for Bliss's classification new admirers at a time when the trend is very much towards the increased acceptance of schemes which can be viewed as international standards linked to national centralized cataloguing services.

Conclusion. When judged by theoretical canons, BC has many merits and very few faults. It combines erudition, helpful order and adaptability with a clear and predictable facet structure and a generally concise and hospitable notation. The revision policy, notwithstanding the comparative dearth of monetary resources, is now more satisfactory. But there remain factors, several of them in the realm of administration and cataloguing economics, which may be crucial. Although BC is a fine general scheme, perhaps particularly sound still in the social sciences and humanities (although the new edition offers much additional detail in the sciences, too), it could be argued that few new libraries will adopt the second edition. Apart from the queries on the grounds of standardization, likely non-inclusion of BC in MARC tapes, the geographical limitations of a largely alphabetical notation and the time and cost of reclassifying, there is a simple chronological factor to face. In the library world generally, but perhaps in North America in particular, DC and LC came first and had a firm grip on the arrangement of most libraries before BC was initiated. What they had and still have, they will be determined to hold. Indeed, the title of a collection of Bliss's poems, *Better late than never*, leads inevitably to speculation of what might have happened had Bliss committed himself and launched BC say twenty years earlier.

BC users now have both an excellent second edition of the full schedules and a valuable abridgement for small libraries. Both are up to date and it will be a pity indeed if there is not some increase, however small, in the use of these tools. They will certainly remain popular in a number of libraries, but it is somewhat ironic that the scheme which in scope, emphasis and fundamental *raison d'être*, most invites comparison with DC and incorporates such a judicious blending of traditional and modern classification theory is – on account of economics and the entrenched position of rivals – unlikely ever to emerge as a really widely used classification. Mills once wrote of a scheme being partly, at least, a test bench on which ideas and theories could be hammered out rather than a widely used system; he was speaking of CC, but – whatever its reception – these words would seem to fit the revised *Bibliographic Classification* admirably. BC is now practically a new and British scheme, but it staunchly retains the best of Bliss's considerable accomplishment. It deserves both careful study and greatly increased application; it will certainly have the one, but receipt of the other is more dubious and problematical and will not come without an appropriate 'advertising' and marketing campaign.

Appendix to Chapters 9–13

Practical Classification by the various schemes: a suggested exercise

A manual of this kind cannot lay much stress on the classification of actual documents; the emphasis is very much on principles and, to a lesser extent, on classification policy. Practical classification work is, however, important. Thus, although there are programmed texts on some individual schemes, it has been thought worthwhile to include an exercise which can be applied with all or any of the general schemes and – in the case of some examples – with appropriate special schemes, too. Although a relatively short exercise, it is capable of variation, by any interested individual, in a host of ways.

The simulation of a real working 'classification' situation in a textbook is most difficult and the exercise relies on titles, with annotation where necessary, which is a rather poor substitute for seeing the items themselves. Nevertheless, the examples represent a wide subject 'spread' and are all drawn from literature published in the last twenty years. Selection has not been entirely at random and, by and large, these examples will give *more* difficulty in classification than would a random sample of the same size. In short, some examples are easily placed but several are not. Those who attempt some or all of the examples – which are arranged alphabetically by author but can be tackled in any order – and employ more than one scheme, might examine their results in the light of the following criteria:

Does the scheme permit specific classification?
Is the notation satisfactory? (eg, is it unduly long or cumbersome?)
Can compound and complex topics be specified adequately?
Is the order of the scheme helpful? (ie, is each item placed in what seems to be a suitable environment?)
Are the schedules, especially in technical fields, up-to-date and complete?
Might my decision need to be recorded in a library's authority file for future reference?
How long did the classifying take me?

(The last question assumes that a number of items are classified by one scheme as a timed operation and that the classifying of the same items by a different scheme is timed. Prior experience with the schedules of any one scheme and consequent familiarity with them may, in some cases, affect results.)

Note: The construction of an A–Z subject key, using chain procedure, may also be attempted (and the results assessed) for each example classified.

Examples

Bailey, L. C. *Youth to the Rescue: an important study of youth's response to the challenge of human problems.*
Young people's opportunity to help, through voluntary service, the deaf, dumb or blind and those in hospitals or homes.

Beach, J. W. *The Concept of Nature in Nineteenth-century English Poetry.*

Bloomhill, G. *The Sacred Drum.*
A survey of African folklore and mentality. The social system of the native, including such subjects as magic, witchcraft and superstition, is described.

Bravmann, R. A. *Open Frontiers.*
Catalogue for an exhibition on West African sculpture.

Christophersen, P. *Second-language Learning: myth and reality.*

Christopherson, D. G. *The Engineer in the University.*
Engineering in the modern university curriculum.

Dekker, J. *Business and Television.*
Concerns TV reporting of business and commerce.

Dolinger, J. *The Head with the Long Yellow Hair.*
A descriptive account of Ecuador, based on the author's travels among head-shrinking Jinaro and Aushiri Indians.

Edgar, A. D. *Experimental Petrology: basic principles and techniques.*

Gillispie, C. C. *Genesis and Geology.*
Surveys the relationship between theology and scientific thought in the first half of the 19th-century, giving the opinions of British geologists of that period.

Hanson, R. C. P. *Allegory and Event: Origen's interpretation of scripture.*
Origen was one of the greatest theologians in the early (third-century) Christian Church. He held that, in addition to the literal meaning of scripture, there was often a deeper significance revealed by allegory. Thus he tended to regard certain Biblical incidents as symbolical of a moral message.

Hart, F. *Understand your (Association Football) Pools and Win.*

Hayward, C. H. *Woodwork Joints: kinds of joints: how they are cut and where used.*

Hellyer, A. G. L. *Picture Dictionary of Popular Flowering Plants.*

Helpis (Higher Education Learning Programmes Information Service).
A catalogue of some audio-visual materials made by institutions of higher and further education.

Hutchinson, Sir J. *Essays on Crop Plant Evolution.*

Jackson, H. *The Anatomy of Bibliomania.*
A study of the pleasure and influence offered by books. The author agrees with Aldous Huxley that 'the proper study of mankind is books' and he demonstrates the ways in which they can captivate a reader to the point of obsession.

King Edward's Hospital Fund for London. Voluntary Service Information Office. *Voluntary help in the field of mental illness.*

Lighthill, M. J. *Waves in Liquids and Gases: the seventh Selig Brodetsky Memorial Lecture.*

Macmillan, H. P., *Baron Macmillan. Local Government Law and Administration in England and Wales.*

Melville, R. *Erotic Art of the West, with a short history of Western erotic art* by Simon Wilson.

Patrick, J. *A Glasgow Gang Observed.*
The sociology of the 'gang' in juvenile delinquency is considered in the light of an actual example.

Perkins, D. *Buying a House.*

Pike, E. R. *Finding out About the Etruscans.*

Ponasse, D. *Mathematical Logic.*

Roueche, J. E. *Catching up.*
Remedial education for slow-learning adolescents in the United States.

Shannon, C. E. and Weaver, W. *The Mathematical Theory of Communication.*

Spencer, K. G. *The Status and Distribution of Birds in Lancashire.*

Stryker, P. *The Men from the Boys.*
A collection of imaginary dialogues which seek to illustrate the attributes of a good executive in industry. It analyses subtle differences that distinguish 'ordinary' managers from those who have reached full executive stature.

Symons, L. J. *Russian Agriculture: a geographic survey.*

Smirnov, A. A. *Problems of the Psychology of Memory.*

Taylor, H. O. *The Classical Heritage of the Middle Ages.*
Deals with the transition from the Classical to the Mediaeval during the 4th–7th centuries; and shows the historical development from the pagan to Christian world in art, literature, ethics and ideals.

Thompson, J. *Introduction to University Library Administration.*
Concerned mainly with British university library situations.

United States. Agricultural Marketing Service. *Analytical tools for studying demand and price structure*, by R. J. Foote.

Wakefield, D. ed. *Stendhal and the Arts.*

Weikowitz, J. and others. *Introductory Statistics for the Behavioral Sciences.*

Wright, A. F. ed. *Studies in Chinese Thought.*
A series of essays that pays especial attention to harmony and conflict in Chinese philosophy and considers the difficulty of the adequate translation of Chinese philosophic notions into other languages.

CHAPTER FOURTEEN

The Task of Constructing a New General System

In addition to the five classifications just considered in some detail, there are various other general schemes which, although now rarely or never used, offer many points of interest to the student of classification – Cutter's *Expansive Classification* (EC), Rider's *International Classification* (IC), and Brown's *Subject Classification* (SC) all come to mind. There are also many special classifications well worthy of attention, most of these now adopting a fully faceted structure. Various claims and counter claims are made for different systems and it is clearly desirable to attempt an evaluation of each scheme on theoretical and practical grounds. But without returning to this evaluative process, it is necessary to state baldly a fundamental fact which has become very clear in recent years. It is that we must make a clear distinction between the classification of physical items in shelf location and classification for information retrieval. The full and vigorous application of classification theory to shelf arrangement would (alas) increasingly produce many notations of unacceptable complexity. What is more, although, even at the book level, we now have many subjects with two or three distinct facets, our citation order will only bring *one* concept to the fore for arrangement purposes in the linear sequence of material on the shelves and thus the value of revealing all the facets in the class-mark, although not wiped out, is drastically reduced. The picture changes considerably, however, if we look at classification within a mechanized retrieval system, where concept co-ordination can take place in a way which enables each significant concept to be brought to the forefront in turn; here the analytico-synthetic approach offers enormous advantages. Somewhere between these two functions is the classified catalogue or information file, on cards or in some other conventional form, which deals with descriptions rather than the physical documents themselves and can thus provide a number of subject approaches to each single document if necessary, but which shares with shelf arrangement some limitations of linear display. It has become abundantly clear that a system aimed at shelf arrangement might not suit a classified catalogue and certainly will have great difficulty in serving a large-scale and perhaps mechanized information retrieval system at all well, while a scheme drawn up with computerization specifically in mind could hardly be expected to satisfy the needs of shelf arrangement.

Ranganathan often argued that, because the subjects of yesterday's periodical articles are often those of tomorrow's books, a single multi-purpose classification should exist to tackle both large and small packets of subject information – in the way that an elephant's trunk can pick up, with equal facility, both big and minute objects. The analogy no longer seems to hold good, if indeed this particular analogy ever did. It is not the size of the packets that confounds the attempt at providing an all-purpose system, but rather the difference – for both classification and notation – between the arrangement of physical objects in a predetermined general to special, unidimensional sequence and the amassing of concepts in fluid fashion within a computer store. There are those who believe, in fact, that the prevalent view of classification as a shelving device has impeded its acceptance in many minds as a tool for organizing sophisticated retrieval systems.

For the shelves we have DC and – for many academic libraries – LC. BC may, if its 'marketing' programme can match its potential on the 'production' side, still provide a modest challenge here. For information retrieval we have UDC which is now undergoing reconstruction and being subjected to close scrutiny with regard to future international co-operation and standardization in documentation. All these schemes have aspirations in varying degrees with regard to mechanization, but unfortunately the ones which offer the best structural potential (UDC, CC, and revised BC) are at a disadvantage in terms of administration and economics, especially within the context of the United States or United Kingdom MARC record. But perhaps none of these pre-computer age systems is *really* suitable for the arrangement of a mechanized information store? Many enthusiasts believe that a new general classification is urgently needed in this sphere and it is interesting to examine the long and still uncompleted evolution of such a system.

Because that evolution has been necessarily gradual, it is worthwhile to consider first of all the development of research into classification theory. In Britain, a Classification Research Group (CRG) has existed since 1952. The links which the foundation of this organization had with the recommendations of the Royal Society Scientific Information Conference of 1948 are often rightly stressed, but it must also be emphasized that the group came into being essentially because of the enthusiasm of individuals, plus the growing realization that special classifications were needed and that the development and co-ordination of a new corpus of principles might have far-reaching effects for general classifications. CRG members have been closely associated with the making of special faceted schemes, for although they have no commitment to any one scheme, their early *credo* expressed their conviction that faceted classification is advantageous, indeed essential, for information retrieval purposes. They have also carried out advisory work and re-examined the foundations of notation, and their cumulative achievement – when we consider that the work of the Group has been largely based on spare-time activity – is impressive. Many leading names in our subject field – B. I. Palmer, B. C. Vickery, E. J. Coates, B. Kyle, J. Mills, and D. J. Foskett – have been prominent in the work of the Group in the two decades of its existence; much of this work is reported in occasional bulletins which appear in *Journal of Documentation*, but there is a considerable and growing bibliography apart from these.

The success of the CRG has led to the formation of other organizations of this kind, the best known being the Classification Research Study Group in the United States. Certainly there are many areas of our subject field which offer both a mental challenge and a practical task for the subject approach to the organization of knowledge presents, notwithstanding the very genuine intellectual problems of author-title cataloguing and description of documents, the most formidable difficulties – witness the difficulty of achieving standardization of practice. There is thus scope for a variety of research into classification with different groups in various countries or regions perhaps undertaking complementary tasks and there is still plenty of opportunity for newly-recruited enthusiasts for classification and indexing to show their intellectual paces. The explorations of the (British) Classification Research Group members, as partly sketched above, would probably be viewed by most objective interested critics as pre-eminent, in terms of significance and seminal influence, despite the work and enthusiasm – to select but a few names – of De Grolier or Gardin in France, Pauline Atherton or Phyllis Richmond in the United States and Ranganathan's successors at Bangalore. (The CRG, it must be said, although often disciples of Ranganathan, have been increasingly prepared to create their own original paths – paths which sometimes diverge from his.) Their research has also involved the quest for a new general classification, which is the central theme of the present chapter and increasing emphasis has been placed upon this in recent years. Finance for the construction of such a scheme came from a NATO grant and later from OSTI. Considerable progress has been made, especially by Derek Austin who, as a CRG researcher based at the *British National Bibliography*, has been able to test his investigations against the needs of a wide variety of published documents.

It is highly noteworthy that the new scheme to be created was originally envisaged as a multi-purpose system suitable for the shelves, for classified catalogues and for information retrieval. It is now to be aimed solely at the field of mechanized information retrieval, a fact which further emphasizes the necessity of a distinction between various aims and philosophies in library classification. A cynic might think that the change in viewpoint is a reflection of the fact that librarians are conservative creatures, that no new scheme for the shelves could justify the trouble or cost of change and a consequent recognition of the futility involved in creating any new shelf arrangement system. However, it is true to say that there is a greater need, in the sphere of mechanized retrieval, for a new classification. Richard Coward, in his work with UK MARC, sums the matter up so succinctly that he is frequently quoted, as he deserves to be: 'One thing can be said with certainty about Dewey and the Library of Congress Classifications. They are totally unsuitable for machine systems . . . The field is open for a general classification designed for use in computer systems.' Such a system could utilize many aspects of modern classification theory and exploration because it would, of necessity, be called upon to carry out a much more complex and sophisticated range of duties. The advances made in the work by Austin show the influence of many other researchers and have involved, among other things, the deep analysis of semantics in a quest for a citation order and pattern of concept linkage that can be applied effectively over the whole spectrum of knowledge. Two very strong influences, both stemming from the CRG members, deserve consideration in their own right. They are the study of the theory of integrative levels (perhaps associated in a librarianship context chiefly with D. J. Foskett) and the relational analysis and distinctive operators employed by J. Farradane.

Integrative level theory tries to discover a logical and durable 'progressive' or 'developmental' order in the evolving structure of nature itself. It recalls the ideas of Richardson and Cutter; an attempt to find 'out there' in the vast universe of entities, a structured pattern of change and progress which a sufficiently sensitive, intricate and orderly classification can capture and reflect. It is not, however, a theory exclusive to, or originating with, librarians. It was put forward with vigour in Britain nearly forty years ago by the biochemist, Joseph Needham, and later developed and expounded by such writers as J. K. Feibleman and – in France L. Glangeaud. The essence of the idea can be explained in a few words of Needham's.[1] We must accept 'the existence of levels of organization in the universe, successive forms of order in a scale of complexity'.

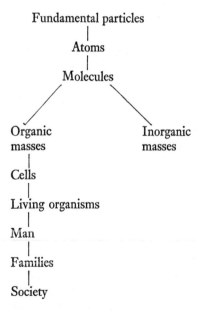

A vast and continuous evolutionary process is believed to take place and, within this evolving structure, successive levels can be identified – what is seen as merely a 'part' on one level, might itself be a

[1] Needham, J. *Time, the Refreshing River (a collection of addresses and essays)*, 1943, p. 234.

'whole' at a lower level. Each level possesses unique features and properties which serve to identify it, but a continuous relationship between the various levels can be discerned. It is, Needham tells us, 'a sharp change in the organizational level' which 'often means that what were wholes on the lower level become parts on the new, eg, protein crystals in cells, cells in metazoan organisms and metazoan organisms in social units'. One might, therefore, construct an outline primitive sketch of the progression from 'low' to 'high' levels according to the theory. (The diagram on the preceding page is merely a simplified illustration, but even in it there would in practice be other forks in the developmental road.)

Feibleman has put forward laws governing the levels and the theory has support and respect among several modern scientific philosophers, although it is not itself altogether modern, for it can be found, in essence, in the ideas of several nineteenth-century writers. Some would regard the theory with scepticism, arguing that it has inconsistencies and gaps or that it is unproven and liable to different personal interpretations; others claim that, in an age of fragmentation, it shows us how hidden developmental links can unify the field of knowledge. The real value of integrative level theory for our subject, however, lies in the extent to which it can usefully be applied to the making of a new general classification. Douglas Foskett argues that some classificationists have already, independently and largely unconsciously, used this theory or closely associated principles in parts of their scheme (Bliss and his idea of gradation by speciality spring at once to mind) and certainly Austin has been influenced by it; indeed, in 1967 he reported to the CRG on its value and problems as the basis for a general classification. The point is that the theory may shed light on the problem of determining a simple to complex sequence of entities and it should, of course, be employed with caution and as and where it is appropriate – it can, for instance, probably be applied more easily in some disciplines than in others.

Another very different body of theory is seen in the work of Jason Farradane. The original and somewhat subjective ideas of this author were first expounded at length in the *Journal of Documentation* in the 1950s and the present writer, with a then solely public library and 'classification-is-for-the-shelves' background and attitude found them difficult to place within the framework of classification *in toto*. This was because they relate again chiefly to a mechanized retrieval context and part of the genuine intellectual difficulty presented by the articles is due to the fact that librarians and even information scientists (Farradane, alas, would insist on the distinction) were not ready to receive their ideas. Farradane examined the structure of knowledge and the learning process in children who form mental patterns in a gradual fashion by relating what they perceive in day to day experience. He concludes that subject relationships should be expressed by the inductive method – we start with individual concepts and assemble them. This idea that there is a universe of concepts to be synthesized rather than a universe of knowledge to be divided is akin to Ranganathan's methods, but the latter postulated main classes and carried out his facet analysis within these. Farradane has no main classes; to use his own distinctive terminology, 'Isolates' (individual concepts) are linked to form relationships. 'Operators', in this system of relational analysis, are the special symbols which link the isolates to show how they are related and each operator has a unique meaning.

Two or more isolates, linked by operators as a subject statement, form an analet. Some care is needed in the selection of vocabulary, but the chief control is achieved by the operators, which convey the kind of meaning or link that exists between the isolates. Farradane declares that there can be nine operators[1] only and each has a distinctive symbol:

Concurrent	Concurrence /θ	Comparison and Self-activity /*	Association /;
Non-Distinct	Equivalence /=	Dimensional and State /+	Appurtenance /(
Distinct	Distinctness /)	Reaction /-	Causation or Functional Dependence /:

[1] In his paper, cited at the end of this chapter, Farradane explains the use of each.

So, if we wish to specify, for example, three imaginary subjects such as:

'Bonemeal contains nitrogen'
'The revision of scientific encyclopaedias'
'Tiredness brought about by over-study',

then we have three distinct analets which might read as follows:

Bonemeal /(Nitrogen
Science /θ Encyclopaedias /– Revising
Study + Excess /: Weariness

and filing can take place under selected isolates or under all of them. An operator used in a negative sense has a bar above it; thus Milk /(Vitamin C is another analet to indicate that Vitamin C is not present in milk.

The whole aim of the system is to draw on mental processes, as revealed through psychology, to develop an alphabetical index which will reveal information reliably by showing not only that concepts are related, but also *how* they are related. In this latter aim the operators are essential and they carry out a classificatory function. They are necessary to combat the vagaries of natural language because, to quote Farradane, 'language is at best a poor tool for exact expression and is subject to endless misuse, misinterpretation and change'. Thus it is through the operators that we see the way to interpret the linking of concepts, although it may be objected that one needs to know the meaning of each operator to make sense of any given analet. Another possible objection is that too much stress is placed on 'syntax' via the operators and not enough on vocabulary selection. True, the equivalence sign can control synonym problems, but it is perhaps partly due to the relative freedom of vocabulary that hidden intermediate terms must be sought and specified for the accurate composition of some analets to be achieved. The operators, it may be noted in passing, are in a sense themselves 'classified' by Farradane. Such categorization, and indeed the whole system, could be deemed to be highly individualistic; Farradane has applied it to thousands of cases, but it does bear the unmistakable stamp of his own powerful intellect and personality. Others have met with difficulty in both the selection and linkage of terms. Although it *can* be communicated and was one of the methods examined in the Information Science

Indexing Languages Text (ISILT) at College of Librarianship, Wales a few years ago, the system does give an indexer problems and consistency is difficult to achieve. As it stands, it does not provide us with suitably structured concept strings for machine searching. Yet Farradane's work is an important venture which has preferred scientific method to philosophic method; although rarely used, except by Farradane himself, it has greatly influenced Austin's research, as also has the concept of evolutionary aggregation of parts into wholes and the recognition that the whole is rather greater than the sum of those parts – the theory of integrative levels. They are by no means the only influences, although among the most significant ones; another striking influence, for example, is Chomsky's work in the sphere of semantics and comparative linguistics.

In reviewing the progress made with the CRG scheme itself, there is no way in which a commentator's exposition can equal the excellent and easily accessible writings on this subject by Austin. But if we remember that a summary is not a substitute for these, the following enumeration and explanation of key points may help to explain the problems and objectives for the still developing new general system.

1) The idea of a series of main classes which can be subjected to an extensive process of sub-division is completely abandoned. Progression is from the specialized to the more general, through the gradual assembly of concepts.

2) For mechanized retrieval, notational coding need not be short. What is essential is that it should clearly identify and label each part of a compound topic. The various concepts must have a unique and distinctive notation which can and will identify them whenever they appear. Thus if 'the moon' was notated at, say, 874, that coding would represent it in any and every context where it might be needed. (In a scheme like DC, 'the moon' rightly appears in several disciplines or contexts – but is given a different notation each time.)

3) No existing scheme offers a valid citation order which is truly the same for all disciplines and can be neutrally, confidently and consistently applied in diverse areas such as mathematics, ethics, sociology, geology, and literature. Such an order is needed for a computer store.

4) In classifying books on shelves, scattering unfortunately arises in all facets save the principal one. This is not so in mechanized searching, since after concept strings have been made according to the chosen citation order, strings can be rearranged and each significant concept can come to the fore in turn. As the limitations of linear order are removed in such searching and concept strings are reassembled there are no 'distributed relatives' because there is no scatter. A citation order might thus seem a classic case of a superfluous idea that could be cut away. It is not. A planned and acceptable citation order gives a rational pattern for organizing the concept file and the putting of enquiries to it. It also helps considerably in distinguishing between various subjects formed by combinations of the same concepts and clears up laxity of phrasing or ambiguous word combinations by showing *how* the concepts are related and linked. This rigorous control may be especially helpful in areas within the social sciences or humanities where we have innumerable 'soft' subjects and a consequent imprecision in terminology. To use somewhat frivolous examples by way of plain illustration, 'the philosophy of literature' is not the same as 'the literature of philosophy', 'the state accumulation of wealth through tax' is not quite identical to 'state taxation of accumulated wealth', nor – except perhaps in the case of a famous dormouse – is 'I sleep when I breathe' the same thing as 'I breathe when I sleep'. The point is that a machine cannot recognize false or misleading verbal relationships; thus in any compound topic the right expression of relationships through their assembly via a correct and consistent citation order is of paramount value.

5) A search has thus been made for such a suitable citation order. (Here we see the influence of Ranganathan, Vickery, Farradane's operators, integrative-level theory, and semantics, together with comparative linguistics. Of great interest too – despite basic differences in the approach to the problem – is the use of prepositional phrases in the articulated subject indexing system developed and advocated by Dr M. F. Lynch and his co-workers at Sheffield University.) The evolving citation order must apply to all subject fields and be, if possible, independent of language. Experience to date shows that it is based not on a notion of decreasing concreteness, to use Ranganathan's phrase, but rather on the minute examination of the use of words and their assembly in natural language sentence structures. This is because its object is to provide a sequence of

concepts which is sensitive to linguistic meaning and can eliminate verbal ambiguity rather than to decide which relationships, among many possible ones, shall be selected for linear display. The CRG/BNB quest has led to the establishment of a thesaurus of concepts as is found in post-co-ordinate indexing (and computer adjustment of concept strings gives the advantages of that technique while the citation order for the primary statement offers the necessary control to eliminate 'false sorts' and the retrieval of unwanted data). Related terms within the thesaurus are linked by means of conventional, 'see also' references. A distinction has been made, following general CRG research lines, between *Entities*, which may be physical objects (artefacts) or mental conceptions (mentefacts) and *Attributes*. Attributes may be properties or activities of various kinds; some of them have proved elusive as far as strict categorization is concerned.

6) A series of operators or relators has been made. These serve as the grammar of the system and act as concept role codes and linking devices to ensure that the citation order is achieved. These too are still evolving, and are examined in the section which follows and concerns PRECIS – the indexing technique which has proved such a useful and important early by-product of the research. These relators show the way in which concepts are joined and the part played by each concept in the subject as a whole. (It may be added that in mechanized retrieval they are replaced by special tags which convert the notated relationships into a number of coded instructions for the computer's manipulation string.)

The system as a whole is obviously a vast and still developing package; there is still much to be done in finalizing the citation order and relators and in notating the concepts. The eventual end-product may be viewed as a complex, but efficient and sensitive meta-language or as a notated international thesaurus rather than strictly as a classification – a switching language with a vengeance. Neutral and independent in terms of subjects, cultures and language, it will have a fully predictable citation order which is unique in two separate and important ways. These are firstly its 'common' application to all disciplines and secondly its avoidance, thanks to the power of the computer to manipulate speedily a logical concept string, of what has traditionally been the root problem of any settled order of citation – the distribution of related material from minor facets.

That the system is complicated there is no doubt – and perhaps some of the theories involved in it or those which preface it are 'mind-benders' on first acquaintance – but Austin rightly points out that the complexity need not bother the enquirer, for it is only the concern of those who operate the system. The final pattern of the scheme will be indebted to many thinkers, but will owe most to the intellectual energy, perseverance and clear thinking of Derek Austin himself. It should certainly fully meet the criteria which he enumerates[1] for the satisfactory interrogation and searching of machine-based information stores.

The predetermined and consistent citation order and the operators show the links between concepts and the part played by each concept in the subject as a whole. They reveal themselves in PRECIS, the preserved context subject indexing that has been used by the *British National Bibliography* since January 1971, a date which coincides with that publication's switch to computer-production methods. This indexing system represents the first major practical outlet for the research. It provides, for an A–Z subject index, a series of specific entries for compound topics with each significant part of the compound being brought to the fore in turn. This is also true of chain indexing, but an important difference is that, in the new system, the full context in which a concept is found is revealed in each and every index entry – hence the name PREserved Context Indexing System. For each example, a primary PRECIS statement is generated, using, across the whole subject spectrum, the analysis, operators, and citation order which have evolved from Austin's research programme. This gives us a lead term with the context displayed as a string of concepts below it, thus:

| Lead | (Term under which index entry is filed) |

| Display | (A series of terms showing the 'environment' in which the single lead term is found) |

The system is so designed that secondary statements can be achieved simply by computer manipulation of this concept string which arose from the all-important primary statement. The first part of the display becomes the new lead term, the former lead moves to the

---

[1] In Palmer, B. I. and Austin, D. *Itself an Education*, 2nd edition. Library Association, 1971, p. 78; and again in Maltby, A. (editor). *Classification in the 1970s*. Bingley, 1972, p. 217.

right to qualify it and the rest of the display stands. Thus we have, in our secondary statements:

| Lead | | Qualifier |

| Display |

and the process is completed until each significant concept from the display has taken the lead position. When the final concept comes to the fore, there is no 'Display', but all the other concepts appear as Qualifiers.

Before demonstrating the procedure with actual examples, the operators themselves should be introduced. They have recently been revised, in the light of working experience and – as used in BNB indexing since January 1974 – they stand as follows:

MAIN LINE OPERATORS

Environment of observed system	o	Location
Observed system (Core operators)	1	Key system: *object of transitive action; agent of intransitive action*
	2	Action/Effect
	3	Agent of transitive action; Aspects; Factors

A ————————————————————————

Data relating to observer	4	Viewpoint-as-form
Selected instance	5	Sample population/Study region
Presentation of data	6	Target (or bias)/Physical form

INTERPOSED OPERATORS

Dependent elements	p	Part/Property
	q	Member of quasi-generic group
	r	Aggregate
Concept interlinks	s	Role definer
	t	Author attributed association
Coordinate concepts	g	Coordinate concept

Continued overleaf

B ──────────────────────────────

DIFFERENCING OPERATORS *(prefixed by S)*	h	Non-lead direct difference
	i	Lead direct difference
	j	Salient difference
	k	Non-lead indirect difference
	m	Lead indirect difference
	n	Non-lead parenthetical difference
	o	Lead parenthetical difference
	d	Date as a difference

CONNECTIVES

| *(Components of linking phrases; prefixed by S)* | v | Downward reading component |
| | w | Upward reading component |

C ──────────────────────────────

THEME INTERLINKS	x	First element in coordinate theme
	y	Subsequent element in co-ordinate theme
	z	Element of common theme

The first experience of these may well be one of bewilderment, but a study of the evolving classification, as revealed in Austin's writings, and the observation of a few fundamental rules will help to explain the purpose of these relational operators, or role codes, and to facilitate their application. The rules mentioned insist that the concepts denoted by numerical codes are always assembled in their ordinal sequence. (In the original version of PRECIS, coding was different and combination was in reverse numerical order!) Each concept string must contain at least one concept coded (1) or (2). The sense of the string virtually depends on the presence of such for, whatever the syntactic purpose of the other concepts as revealed by the codings, these two categories are basic main line operators. (5) Study Region, may sometimes be needed as an alternative to (0) Location for a geographical concept (for instance if we are dealing with a study of the plants of Scotland and not merely a study of plants that happens to be carried out there.) The letter operators, although an essential part of the system, are in a sense subordinate as they act as links or bonding devices, when and where necessary, between numerically coded concepts. The operators cannot all be demonstrated here, but two examples – one simple the other much more complicated – which have literary warrant, may help to illustrate them and appear below. (They are linked with DC here, as in BNB.)

Example (a) R. J. Lukens. Chemistry of fungicidal action 632.952
Subject analysis for the primary PRECIS concept string gives:

(1) Fungicides   (Key system)
(2) Chemical reactions   (Action)

Thus the primary statement is

Fungicides
Chemical reactions.   632.952

Computer rotation provides one secondary statement only, with 'Chemical reactions' coming out of the display to take the lead position and 'Fungicides' becoming a qualifying term to show the context:

Chemical reactions.   Fungicides 632.952

The two statements are, of course, filed alphabetically in the subject index.

Example (b) M. Walker. Poor man, beggar man, thief: the story
            of the New Horizon Youth Centre.   362.293

This demands more intricate analysis, as follows:

(0) London   (Environment)
(1) Young people   (Key system)
(q) Drug addicts   (Quasi-generic subclass)
(1) Young drug addicts   (Substitute phrase)
(2) Rehabilitation   (Action)
(3) New Horizon Youth Centre (Agent)

This leads to the entries:

PRIMARY   *London*
STATEMENT   Young people. Drug Addicts. Rehabilitation.
             New Horizon Youth Centre.   362.293

FOUR   1. *Young People.* London.
SECONDARY   Drug Addicts. Rehabilitation. New Horizon Youth
STATEMENTS   Centre.   362.293
             2. *Drug Addicts.* Young People. London.
             Rehabilitation. New Horizon Youth Centre. 362.293
             3. *Rehabilitation.* Young Drug Addicts. London.
             New Horizon Youth Centre.   362.293

STATEMENTS 4. *New Horizon Youth Centre*. London.
(*continued*)   Rehabilitation of young drug addicts.   362.293

and these five entries in the A–Z sequence ensure a full context entry under each key concept.

In addition to primary entries and the secondary entries which are generated by machine manipulation, through the operators being 'translated' into suitable computer coding, PRECIS has a thesaurus of terms to deal with the problem of synonyms and to provide cross-references to and from related terms from various hierarchies. This is also an integral part of the system and so, if we turn to BNB, we find numerous signposts which have been found to be necessary in the building up of the system and for working consultation. These do not necessarily proceed solely in a general to special direction, but often do so. We find, for instance, signposts such as:

Children's literature	Dead
see also	see also
Comics	Body snatching
Equines	Food
see also	see also Biscuits
Horses	Catering
	Cookery
	Drinks
	Health Foods
	Nutrition etc.

PRECIS has developed much in its short life, but it has been tried and tested extensively and with great success in the cauldron of the national literary warrant. It should thus be viewed with confidence, despite the misgivings of Mineur[1]; indeed its achievement augers well for the new general scheme. PRECIS indexing is applicable whatever classification is used and is thus independent of any one system. It is also neutral with regard to discipline and – while in its revised form its increased logic may make it definitive 'as far as English is concerned'[2] – the deep syntactic analysis on which it is based possibly makes it applicable to several languages. One accepts that many manual cataloguing systems will use the rival chain procedure for several years to come, but with the increasing use of

[1] Mineur, B. W. *Relations in chains*. Journal of Librarianship, July 1973, pp. 175–202.
[2] Austin, D. Personal communication. 21. 12. 1973.

mechanization and increased participation in the U.S. and U.K. MARC projects, an indexer's knowledge or awareness of PRECIS principles will be of growing significance. PRECIS is virtually certain to take a firm place in the creative work of the new British Library and is making some impact overseas, notably in Canada and Australia. In time perhaps several organizations which do their own cataloguing in full or in part will employ it: this depends on its continuing success within national bibliographies. As a tool which shows the full subject context in each entry for an A–Z index, is freely faceted bringing each sought term to the fore, has adequate supporting cross-references, and is based upon a citation order which is, in turn, founded upon deep and sound analysis of sentence structure, it holds excellent promise as an information retrieval language for MARC. Its appreciation and eventual greater use in A–Z subject indexing outside the British Library might depend upon a more widely available thesaurus.

Bibliography on Section Three

The schemes themselves must be studied, for there is no substitute for a first-hand acquaintance with them. A special scheme may also be selected for study with great profit. Where a scheme has an editorial introduction (eg, DC, UDC), this should be read carefully.

Apart from some relevant works already cited, a book which has chapters on each scheme is:

Maltby, A. (editor). *Classification in the 1970s*. Bingley, 1972.
  (Sarah K. Vann writes on DC, and W. E. Matthews supplies an appendix,
   G. A. Lloyd writes on UDC;
   J. P. Immroth writes on LC;
   M. A. Gopinath writes on CC;
   J. Mills writes on BC;
   D. Austin writes on the creation of a new compatible general system.)

Other readings on the individual schemes appear below.
Dewey Decimal Classification
A programmed text for practical work is

Batty C. D. *Introduction to the eighteenth edition of the Dewey Decimal Classification*. Bingley, 1971.

Vann, S. K. *Dewey abroad: the field survey of 1964*. Library Resources and Technical Services. Winter, 1967, pp. 61–71.

Young, H. H. *The enduring qualities of Dewey*. In Allerton Park Institute. *The role of classification in the modern American library*, edited by T. Eaton and D. E. Strout, 1960.

Custer, B. A. *Dewey 17: a preview and a report to the profession*. Library Association Record, March, 1965, pp. 79–83.

Still valuable. Winton Matthews' equivalent paper on the 18th edition is appended to Vann's chapter in the work edited by Maltby and cited above.

Reviews of the 18th edition should be sought and read. There is, for instance:

Chan, Lois Mai. *Dewey 18: another step in an evolutionary process*. Library Resources and Technical Services. Summer, 1972, pp. 383–99.

Sweeney, R. *Dewey 18*. Catalogue and Index, Summer, 1972, pp. 1, 10–12.

Universal Decimal Classification
A recent book, of high merit, is:

Foskett, A. C. *The Universal Decimal Classification: history, present status and future prospects of a large general classification scheme*. Bingley, 1973.

Bakewell, K. G. B. (editor). *Classification for information retrieval.* Bingley, 1968.

Contains a good basic account of UDC by Bakewell.

There is also:

Lloyd, G. A. UDC *as an international switching language.*

Rigby, M. UDC *in mechanized subject information retrieval.*

Both papers are in Wellisch and Wilson (editors), *Subject retrieval in the Seventies* (already cited).

A useful source of information, although older is

BS 1000c Guide to the use of the UDC (by J. Mills) 1963.

More difficult reading, but stimulating at times are the papers in

Perreault, J. M. *Towards a Theory for* UDC. Bingley, 1969.

A sound programmed text for practical work is

Wellisch, H. *The U.D.C.: a programmed instruction course.* University of Maryland, 1970.

Library of Congress Classification

This is the most difficult of the general schemes to appraise according to strict theoretical canons. Among useful readings, we have, apart from texts already cited:

Immroth, J. P. *A Guide to Library of Congress Classification.* Libraries Unlimited, 1968.

Immroth, J. P. *Analysis of Vocabulary Control in LC Classification and Subject Headings.* Libraries Unlimited, 1971.

Angell, R. *On the Future of the LC Classification.* In Proceedings of the International Study Conference on Classification Research, Elsinore, 1964.

Schimmelpfeng, R. H. and Cook, C. D. *The Use of the Library of Congress Classification.* American Library Association, 1968.

Includes a list of users, compiled by M. F. Tauber.

Colon Classification

Ranganathan's own books are important, especially his *The Colon Classification.* Rutgers University, 1965. See also his *Colon Classification, edition 7: a preview.* Library science with a slant to documentation. September, 1969, pp. 193–242.

At the time of writing, it seems that the 7th edition is likely to appear in parts within this journal rather than as a separate publication.

A programmed text for practical work is:

Batty, C. D. *Introduction to Colon Classification.* Bingley, 1966.

Bibliographic Classification

Bliss' own writings, although monumental, provide the only really valid historical background. They are:

The Organization of Knowledge and the System of the Sciences, H. W. Wilson, 1929, and *The Organization of Knowledge in Libraries*, 2nd edition, 1939.

The latter includes a critique of the other general classifications.

Mills' splendid paper (already cited in the volume edited by Maltby) is the best account of the new edition, but his editorial comments and schedule examples in recent annual *Bliss Classification Bulletins* should also be examined.

Research towards a new system

On Farradane's work see his own paper – *Some fundamental fallacies and new needs in classification*. In Sayers Memorial volume, edited by D. J. Foskett and B. I. Palmer. Library Association, 1961.

On integrative levels one could read D. J. Foskett's paper in the Sayers Memorial volume just cited, or the more recent critical article,

Huckaby, S. A. S. *An enquiry into the theory of integrative levels as the basis for a generalized classification scheme.* Journal of Documentation, June, 1972, pp. 97–106.

On recent work of the (British) Classification Research Group, there is:

Foskett, D. J. *Classification for a General Index Language.* Library Association, 1970.

Austin's papers on his own work include those in Palmer, B. I. *Itself an Education*, Maltby, A. (editor), *Classification in the 1970s*, and – on PRECIS and its use in BNB – the paper in the volume edited by Wellisch and Wilson. (All three works have already been fully cited.)

There is also:

Austin, D. and Butcher, P. PRECIS: *a rotated subject index system.* Council of the British National Bibliography, 1969.

On the evolution of PRECIS there is Austin's important article in *Journal of Documentation*, March 1974, pp. 47–102.

Classification Policy and Practice

CHAPTER FIFTEEN

The Classified Catalogue

Classification, or systematic arrangement has, quite apart from its considerable utility in organizing material on the shelves, various other functions in librarianship and information work. It has, as we shall see later, considerable potential as a controlling device in information retrieval languages. There is, too, very great scope for classificatory practice in library catalogues and in published catalogues and bibliographies. In the latter sphere, there are many examples of the use of the well-known general systems and several which exhibit individualistic classifications of varying merit. Interesting examples of classifications in published bibliographies include that designed for the American Economic Association's *Index of Economic Articles*, developed in consultation with experts. This has twenty-three main classes and nearly seven hundred sub-classes. It is said to be 'a compromise between principles and practice', but its groupings are eminently sensible and reflect literary warrant to a commendably high degree. There are several other bibliographies which exhibit systematic arrangement of varying degrees of detail and in some cases that arrangement is suitably notated. Some classifications of this kind are certainly worthy of scrutiny and appraisal, but it is classification within a library catalogue that concerns us primarily here.

An effective catalogue is an indispensable key to the stock in libraries of any size. Whatever type or form it may take, it should provide some means of showing what books are available in the library on each subject and by each author. Some librarians have argued that the subject approach via the catalogue is superfluous, since the personal knowledge of his subject field and its literature which the enquirer possesses, plus the use of appropriate bibliographies, will suffice. But, in a large research library, bibliographies and the subject catalogue both have their merits and are largely complementary; to neglect the provision of a subject catalogue in such an environment is to place a real impediment in the path of the investigator who wishes to pursue a detailed subject search of the library's own resources. One realizes that catalogues can sometimes be a hindrance rather than a help. In modern public branch libraries, for instance, the catalogue that is limited to the stock of the branch may inhibit readers and discourage requests for items which could be provided quickly from other branches. A union catalogue at every branch is now possible, but if this solution is rejected it may even be best to do without branch library catalogues. But, in libraries which do need and have catalogues (and they are many) the subject approach as such can never be redundant. The two major types of catalogue – dictionary and classified – really only differ with regard to this *subject* approach to knowledge. Both provide an alphabetical sequence of author, entries and references with, where necessary, entries under titles, series, editors, translators and so forth. The one type of catalogue employs alphabetical subject headings as 'labels' on its subject entries with references to deal with synonyms and to connect related subject headings, whereas the other accepts a classified order.

The merits and defects of both types of catalogue have been discussed by several writers; they are ventilated again here because it is necessary to stress that the use of classification within the catalogue is potentially a fundamental role for any scheme. Any writer who discusses the alternative types of catalogue will have his preference and perhaps his prejudices; these often depend upon his library background and 'first impressions'. The choice of the present writer is doubtless obvious – this despite the fact that his first professional years were spent in a library with a dictionary catalogue. A discussion of the advantages of the rival types has been postponed so that the structure of the classified catalogue can first be explained, but the reader should not accept the author's own arguments uncritically when that discussion is reached – its object is to provoke thought as well as to put a personal viewpoint.

No apology is made for considering, as a preliminary step, the ways in which the catalogue and the classification in use are complementary tools for the organization of knowledge in a library. Although some of the points made may seem self-evident, it is certain that students often overlook several of them; they should be constantly borne in mind in our studies. The shelf classification is concerned with the arrangement of items themselves – tangible objects which can only go in one place on the shelves; the catalogue, however, deals with entries representing these books. Thus if a book deals with, say, three subjects, it can only have one place (under the dominant subject) in the shelf arrangement; in the catalogue, three subject entries can be made. The catalogue will also clearly reveal works which the reader may not find on the shelves because they are out on loan, or away at the binders, or shelved in an over-size sequence, or forming part of a special book display. It may well help to draw attention to non-book material on a subject. The catalogue is also more varied than the classification in that the latter caters only for the subject approach to knowledge; the catalogue does this also but, in addition, it provides author, title, and other entries to aid its users. It can thus be seen that, although com-paratively few readers in most general libraries use the catalogue, it has great merit and certain advantages over the classification scheme; this is equally true of both classified and dictionary or other alphabetical subject catalogues. Of course, it must be stated that the shelf classification has, in some respects, advantages over the catalogue. It deals with books and not with mere entries and most readers prefer to get to the books as quickly as possible; they do not wish to consult a catalogue, but rather to browse at the shelves. If neatly arranged and well guided, the classified sequence on the shelves can be of inestimable value to the reader. Those readers seeking a book by a particular author, however, or those wishing to find all the books which the library has on a particular subject, may well find that they need to consult the catalogue. But then, of course, these are not rival tools; they are intended to assist each other in the arrangement and retrieval of knowledge and the wise and well-instructed reader will make good use of both classification and catalogue.

The nature of the classified catalogue, in its full and orthodox form, is such that it consists of three sequences:

1) The classified sequence in notational order.
2) The A–Z author/title sequence.
3) The A–Z subject index.

The classified file, sometimes thought of as the principal sequence of the three, contains at least one full entry for each item in the library. A typical example is shown below:

> LC 4015
> Passow, Aaron Harry.
>   Education of the disadvantaged; a book of
> readings, by A. H. Passow, Miriam Goldberg
> and Abraham J. Tannerbaum.
> New York: Holt, Rinehart and Winston, 1967.
>   503p.   22cm.

The alphabetical subject index serves simply as a key to this classified sequence; it does not refer directly to individual items, but lists
topics along with their relevant class-marks. Thus, as Congress is
the classification in use in our example, the subject index entry
reads:

> Disadvantaged persons: Education   LC 4015

The phrase *alphabetical author index*, sometimes used to denote the
third sequence of the classified catalogue, is really a misnomer. This
is not a mere index in the sense that the subject index is; it is rather
an author/title catalogue, for – unlike the alphabetical subject key –
it gives details of individual items. The enquirer who seeks for a
known item can use this alphabetical catalogue and then, having
obtained the required class-mark, can go to the shelves. It is the
enquirer who makes a subject search without a known item in mind
who must use the classified sequence and its A–Z key. The author/
title catalogue contains entries such as:

> Passow, Aaron Harry
>   Education of the disadvantaged: a book of
> readings, by A. H. Passow . . . etc.
>   LC 4015

and – if a title entry is thought to be justified –

> Education of the disadvantaged: a book of
> readings, by A. H. Passow . . . etc.
>   LC 4015

These entries are supported by appropriate references, for instance
in the case of an author who sometimes uses a pseudonym and
sometimes uses his real name.
  While author cataloguing has become increasingly standardized

through the acceptance of the *Anglo-American Cataloguing Rules*, it is true to say that there are still many barriers in the way of standardization in subject cataloguing; indeed, while recognizing that the author/title approach has its own intellectual problems, it is probably correct to say that – in all types of catalogue – the subject approach presents most of the real headaches. What are the problems concerned and how does a systematically arranged catalogue endeavour to deal with them?

Every cataloguer sometimes handles a book, report, film or other item which covers more than one subject. Unless it is truly polytopical, the classified catalogue will endeavour to show, in its principal sequence, added subject entries for themes that have been ignored in the shelf classification. Thus, if a book dealt with English Local and Central Government and was shelved in DC at 352.042, then the main catalogue entry would be made under this class-mark. But the classified sequence would also have an entry for central government, the secondary subject in this case, arranged as follows:

354.42
(shelved at
352.042)   Author
Title and date

It will be noted that these secondary entries *must* make it quite clear to the catalogue user that the class-mark under which they are filed differs from that which represents the chief subject of the book and at which the book is actually shelved.

The cataloguer may go further than this and analyse the contents of composite works in his catalogue. The case against analytical entries, which deal with some part of a book as distinct from the book as a whole, has always been that they consume time and catalogue space, may rarely be helpful, and may even confuse the reader who employs the library catalogue. On the other hand, the subject analytic especially may help to fully reveal the resources of the classified library. Analytical entries fit quite readily into the classified catalogue; author and title analytics for parts of composite works will go in the alphabetical author sequence, while the subject analytic will be placed in the principal section of the catalogue in a similar manner to the added subject entry. An example will, once again, serve to make this clearer:

Subject Analytical Entry

> 332.642
> (shelved at
> 650) WARSON, Ronald
>   The Stock Exchange.
>   (In Modern Business Training. 1965.
>   pp. 239–255).

Subject Index Entry for above

> STOCK EXCHANGE   332.642

Thus if the reader wants books on this theme, he consults the alphabetical subject index to obtain the appropriate class number. He then searches at that number in the classified sequence where he will find, in addition to entries for whole books, entries for significant *sections* of volumes – such as the one in our example.

Analytical subject entries should be distinguished in our minds from an added or secondary subject entry which deals with a book or other item in its entirety. However, the classified sequence itself which incorporates all subject entries is supported by an alphabetical subject key and the construction of this key, or index, is also of interest to us. The A–Z subject index is valuable as a signpost to the library's own subject resources, which is easily comprehended and employs familiar terminology. There is really little excuse for merely providing the index to the classification scheme as a substitute, although some libraries do this. A subject index of one's own can be made fairly rapidly and it is not very space consuming for, once an entry has been made for a topic, it will stand in the index for *all* the items on that specific theme in the stock of the library. To rely instead on the published index to the classification in use may have three disadvantages: it will confuse readers by listing subjects and class-marks not represented in the stock of that particular library; it will not recognize any modifications to the scheme in use, whether authorized or not, that have been made by that library; and, from the British librarian's viewpoint, if the scheme emanates from, say, America or India, it will employ terms in its index that may seem rather strange or ambiguous to readers in this country.

It is important that the A–Z subject index be compiled in the most useful way possible. It should locate topics for us without fail, should be able to display subject groupings (one would hope usually relatively minor associations) which the classification ignores, should endeavour to minimize the effort of searching, and should be as economical as possible. With regard to the point about reduced searching effort, it is customary to index synonyms directly thus

POISONS	RA 1195–
	RA 1270

and

TOXICOLOGY	RA 1195–
	RA 1270

rather than to make a 'see' reference from one to the other. Since this is an index rather than a catalogue of actual subject entries, it is just as economical and more effective to allow the reader to obtain the required class-mark (an LC one is assumed here) at once whether, in this case, he searches under toxicology or under the more 'popular' equivalent.

In order to show in the index the distribution of associated topics within the classification in use and at the same time to seek economy by ignoring in the index those relationships which the classification does demonstrate, it is now customary, in manual indexing, to use Ranganathan's chain procedure. This provides us with a conscious and rational technique in place of 'hit or miss' methods of subject indexing. It is probably easier to apply the procedure with a fully faceted scheme, but it is independent of any one scheme and can be used in conjunction with any system. Chain indexing links the process of verbal subject analysis very closely with the general to specific chain of progression exhibited by the classification's hierarchy. (An hierarchical notation expresses this most clearly but is not *essential* to chain indexing.) The indexer begins with the most specific step in the notational chain and works his way back to more general terms, indexing each step in context. Thus if we consider the specific topic in DC –

Wedding Etiquette 395.22

we find that the chain of classification leading to it is:

390 Customs
  395 Etiquette
    395.2 Etiquette for special occasions
      395.22 Wedding etiquette

Our index entries will be four in number if the chain procedure is used here:

Weddings: Etiquette 395.22
Marriages: Etiquette 395.22
Etiquette   395
Customs   390

The index entries always work from specific terms back to general ones, that is upwards rather than down the classification hierarchy. The following points should be noted:

(*a*) The indexer may sometimes find that the classification is not sufficiently specific and that he needs to add some steps of division in order to cater for the precise subject with which he is dealing. This does not occur in our previous example but, in DC for instance, one sometimes finds it necessary to show the *same* class number alongside the last two or three links in the verbal chain because of lack of specificity in the classification. Thus we may have a chain that ends, for instance:

Engineering mechanics   620.1
Masonry materials   620.13
Natural Stones   620.132
Sandstone   620.132

(*b*) The indexer must watch for synonyms. If these occur, it will be necessary to make two or more entries to correspond with the appropriate step of the notational chain; thus, above, we have indexed both marriages and weddings against the class number 395.22.

(*c*) There may be steps in the notational hierarchy which are unwanted for indexing purposes, either because no enquirier is likely to search under the appropriate verbal terms or, more probably, because of faulty *subordination* in the classification scheme in question. Such steps are known as *unsought links*.

(*d*) These should be distinguished from *false links*, which arise when the notational chain is lengthened without an appropriate verbal term being supplied. In DC, for instance, if a zero is needed to introduce a standard sub-division or geographical table number, it is clear that this zero represents a notational extension for which there is no verbal equivalent. It is merely an indicator that form or geographical divivision is about to be employed. False links also refer to virtually 'nameless' concepts – in our example above 395.2 *Special occasions* might be so regarded.

It can be seen that some of the entries in our example contain a qualifying term after the word or phrase indexed; this is an essential part of chain indexing since it helps the completed index to take due account of any weaknesses in the basically excellent notion of classification by discipline. Even more significantly, it makes the index complement the classified order by showing that some topics can crop up in more than one context, for it distinguishes, for example, between –

Marriages: etiquette   395.22

and

Marriages: statistics   312.5

The provision of several entries per item which chain indexing demands is not excessive, for it must be remembered that each entry will stand for all the resources a library has on the specific subject concerned and will not need to be repeated. Thus, as a library first grows, the index will grow rapidly; once most subjects to be covered are represented in the stock, index growth is very slight.

The advantages claimed for chain indexing are that it offers a logical technique which supports rather than repeats the work of the classification and is reasonably frugal with regard to the bulk of the index. Its use and achievements are both considerable and it will doubtless remain popular in many general libraries with classified catalogues, although now challenged by PRECIS – the mechanized system of 'total context' index entries which has supplanted it in the BNB. Apart from the problems of searching out false and unsought links and the possibility of extra work in the indexing procedure due to lack of detail in a classification, other difficulties have arisen, especially in an information science context. If a highly specific subject package contains, say, four, five, or six distinct elements, it may be necessary – although scarcely economic – to cite them in many more combinations in the index than the strict application of chain procedure allows. J. R. Sharp's SLIC indexing (Selective Listing in Combination) provides an interesting manual alternative which can in such circumstances produce a fuller index without being too uneconomic in terms of bulk, or production costs. This is achieved by considering all possible combinations of terms and by then excluding groupings which form a part of a larger combination. Thus with four elements, cited in a classification as ABCD and indexed in reverse order, we would have with SLIC indexing an entry for DCBA but not for DCB or DC. There would be an entry for DBA but not for DB. In this way, with four elements, fifteen possible entries are reduced to eight; with five elements, thirty-one possible entries would be reduced to sixteen. The method commands attention, particularly in special libraries, and we mention it again in that context; it shows useful entries which chain indexing ignores, but it may not be feasible in terms of time and costs.

Sweeney[1] has shrewdly shown some problems which face chain indexing even in a more general context. He argues that as the reader is unaware of the link between the A–Z index and the classified sequence of the catalogue, the strict rules of chain indexing should sometimes be broken and some entries could be allowed which *repeat* the classification's own citation sequence of elements, especially when dealing with the final specific steps in the hierarchical chains of progression.

Whatever our views on this, it is clear that chain indexing has challengers and has problems as well as benefits. It is also evident that some intellectual effort must go into the making of a complete classified catalogue. In any comparison between the two chief types of subject catalogue, however, it must be recognized that the dictionary catalogue also has problems and demands effort. Indeed, because of the problem of selecting and linking, via cross-references, appropriate specific alphabetical headings, the dictionary catalogue is acknowledged as more difficult to construct than its classified rival. Its success in North American libraries and elsewhere is partly indicative of Cutter's great and lasting influence, but also partly of a prevalent viewpoint which restricts classification to the role of a 'browsing booster' at the bookshelves and is suspicious of specific classification and its more refined applications in the more complex spheres of catalogues and information retrieval. The classified catalogue is independent of language and certainly verbal ambiguities and other terminological problems can wreak havoc with alphabetical subject catalogues; in turn, of course, it may be countered that the classified catalogue depends, in no small measure, on the efficiency or otherwise of the classification system employed. It is sometimes said that a dictionary catalogue can complement

[1] Sweeney, R. *The index to the classified catalogue.* Catalogue and Index, July, 1970, pp. 10–12.

shelf order by stressing other possible groupings, but the A–Z index, which should be regarded as an integral and indispensable part of a classed catalogue, also does this. Any classification must separate *some* related material; the language, customs, politics, history and literature of a country, for example, are distributed by subject. But, whatever the nature of the distribution, an index based on chain procedure or one of the alternatives based on rational principles will at least reveal the scattering. For example, under the heading of the Nigerian Yoruba we might find:

	Class marks (imaginary)
Yoruba: Nigeria: Anthropology	HRJ
Yoruba: Nigeria: Folk Songs	HLMX
Yoruba: Nigeria: History	GBL
Yoruba: Nigeria: Language	TGE
Yoruba: Nigeria: Social Problems	DRS
Yoruba: Nigeria: Wood carving, etc.	KVHP

In the dictionary catalogue, 'see also' references endeavour to carry out the same basic task – that of revealing the whereabouts of 'distributed relatives'. One of the great problems with a dictionary catalogue, or any alphabetical subject catalogue, is the comparative dearth of rational and communicable principles to guide the indexer. The large subject headings lists work on the assumption that each item should receive the alphabetical heading (or headings) which precisely describes its subject and that related headings should be linked by 'see also' references – these going from broad to specific headings, but not vice-versa. This, in effect, presupposes an agreed, although invisible, classificatory structure of headings; yet in practice the rules are followed in very imperfect fashion as the lists demonstrate. The immediate pressures of new accessions in daily cataloguing practice seem to have led to a slow but continual erosion of these admittedly somewhat tenuous and elementary principles, followed by traditional dictionary cataloguing and the substitution of some *ad hoc* decisions. Thus anomalies and inconsistencies arise, especially in large alphabetical subject catalogues, owing to the lack of an adequate theoretical superstructure for full dictionary cataloguing.

Many enquirers seek information on a single, clearly defined specific subject and in such cases both types of catalogue should be helpful. Indeed, the dictionary catalogue, although more time-consuming for the librarian to compile, is rather more direct in providing such information; presumably, in the classified catalogue, the enquirer goes first to the A–Z subject index and then to the appropriate part of the classified sequence. But several subject enquiries are rather vague and a search thus needs to be readily broadened or narrowed. Others want information on a group of allied themes rather than a single topic. It is in such cases that any classified catalogue should be much more effective than its rival, since its structure facilitates the expansion or contraction of queries and browsing over a wide range of allied subject entries. What is more, the principle of specific entry in alphabetical subject catalogues handicaps the enquirer seeking *all* available information on a broad general topic. A search by the writer in a leading British public library's large dictionary catalogue in 1973 under two such broad topics – WATER AND WATER SUPPLY and PAINTING – revealed that, in addition to the information under these headings, numerous 'see also' references to allied headings in other parts of the catalogue existed. In the case of WATER AND WATER SUPPLY there were twenty-five such references; in the other instance there were twenty-six, plus the instruction 'and see also under the names of individual painters'. This is not a criticism of the catalogue concerned and such references are important and necessary, but they do show the great problems and the tortuous methods imposed upon a subject researcher by the alphabetical distribution of related headings in any large dictionary catalogue. It would be misleading to suggest that a classified catalogue would collect all entries on such subjects, but certainly the scattering – and thus the searching time – would be far less.

It is sometimes suggested that, despite the collocative advantages of classified cataloguing, readers reject them on the grounds of complexity. Such objective evidence as exists on this point, chiefly from catalogue use studies, shows that many readers largely reject any catalogue. For those who do not, however, the initial approach in both cases is the alphabetical one and it must be recalled that library staff often use catalogues on behalf of the reader and need the most effective tool available. It would be most interesting to have a 'use study' that would contrast the rival catalogues by examining them both in the same working situation. In the meantime, it can be confidently said that guiding is the answer to any complexities in the catalogue. Indeed whatever the type of catalogue, the varieties of physical form now becoming customary make good guiding and instruction vital if the catalogue is to be effectively used.

The nature of that guiding is, in part, determined by the method of presentation, but it is imperative that it should be thorough and be based on the attitude and viewpoints of readers.

Finally, in comparing and choosing between the dictionary and classified catalogues, there is the viewpoint that, for a small public library at least, the purely alphabetical catalogue is best. Several public librarians might concede the superiority of a classified catalogue for scholarly collections or for detailed subject enquiries, but would press the merits of alphabetical simplicity for the small catalogues of their lending libraries. This viewpoint probably had much to commend it until recently. We have already stated, however, that many such libraries – if they have a catalogue at all – need a union catalogue and this is, thanks to new physical forms offered by mechanization, now a possibility. But a large subject union catalogue, displaying the full resources of a library system within each of its branches, needs the benefits of classificatory grouping as much as does the catalogue of a research collection – thus the conventional argument is no longer a valid one. In Britain at least, the advance of computerized cataloguing and the use of MARC tapes for the production of some local catalogues are changes which should strengthen rather than diminish the appeal of the classified catalogue.

Before leaving this subject, it may be pointed out that the dictionary catalogue, consciously or otherwise, itself contains classificatory features. General to special 'see also' references or the making of such references between co-ordinate terms implies an invisible but very real hierarchical structure. What is more, advances in knowledge (and the consequent need for subject headings in alphabetical catalogues to be highly specific) have led to the use of many compound headings and here the old 'classification' problem of citation rears its head. Do we enter 'Temperature transients in thin films' under –

Superconducting: Temperature transients: Films

or

Films: Superconducting: Temperature transients?

And should we face the possibility of rotating the elements in such specific compound headings for instance? Cutter's pioneer work in this area, although valuable, is insufficient for modern needs and we are faced with the problem of how specific is 'specific' in the advice he gives. We are then called upon to consider the ideas for the sequence of concepts in compound verbal headings as presented, for example, by Coates[1] and by the writings of D. W. Austin.

[1] Coates, E. J. *Subject catalogues: headings and structure.* Library Association, 1960.

CHAPTER SIXTEEN

Classification Policy and Library Administration – I

'The meaning of efficiency must have something to do with the optimal use of resources to attain a goal, but what is optimal frequently involves policies of a given organization.'

R. R. FREEMAN AND P. ATHERTON

Introduction. There are times when the needs of classification and the requirements of library management differ. It must not be thought that the classifier and the library administrator are perpetually at war with regard to their wishes and plans. Very often they are one and the same person. But, if the latter state exists, the librarian as administrator has to make many decisions which affect, or may even alter his decisions as a classifier. It is thus now necessary to review many aspects of classification policy and practice and some of the practical considerations which inevitably influence it. In doing so, we may note, even if we do not entirely support it, Professor Raymond Irwin's wry statement[1] that the truest remark ever made about library classification is that it depends for its success far more on the goodwill and reasonableness of those who have to work it than upon its own logical perfection.

The first aspect for review concerns the design of the library itself. Classification can be affected by the size and nature of the building, the number of floors, and the number of departments that exist. It certainly is affected by (and in turn affects) the amount of space available, for, at the risk of stating the obvious, it can be said that a classified library needs more space than an unclassified collection. If books are merely arranged in order of accession or in some random sequence, the space for new additions can be left at the end of the sequence; such adding cannot alter the significance of a

[1] Irwin, R. *Librarianship: essays in applied bibliography.* Grafton, 1949, p. 89.

useful order which does not exist. In the classified library, however, it is usual to leave spaces at numerous places, so that material can be freely added at any point in the existing sequence. The effect is that more shelves must be provided than would be necessary in an un-classified library. It may be added that the shape or individual features of a building can influence the communication of a systematic arrangement to readers (a staircase can intervene in a most inappropriate part of a classification sequence, for instance) and appropriate guiding must combat such problems. Such apparently mundane matters as the height at which books are shelved can also influence the impact of classification and indeed the whole pattern of reading habits can partly depend on such artificial and accidental factors.

A further complication is that classification is not confined to is books. Apart from its use in catalogues, there is the problem posed by pamphlets, periodicals, films, records and other media.[1] Allied to these is the simple factor that the shelving or filing of items is affected by their size and format. It is obvious, for instance, that book and pamphlet quartos or folios cannot stand side by side with ocatavo books and pamphlets without a loss of vertical space that few libraries can bear. Over-size items thus go in separate classified sequences. Such separate sequences may also arise when older items are kept in stacks, or when a classified sequence in a public lending library is mirrored by one in the reference department.

At this point, it is useful to distinguish between the librarian's use of the terms broken order and parallel arrangement or parallel classification. The former expression indicates some disturbance of the strict classified sequence; thus if the library uses DC and the large classes Language and Literature are brought together for convenience, broken order is employed. This is the obvious example; the student who has been observant when visiting libraries will find many more, but, perhaps none that occurs more frequently than this. Broken order, then, occurs when adaptations are made to the scheme in use. It also arises when special displays are created and material is drawn for these from many parts of the classification scheme. The whole object of broken order is to arrange the book-stock more effectively and to promote the use of books; it should be applied wisely, for often the order selected by one of the great classificationists, although imperfect, is more useful than many of the rearrangements produced by librarians, apart from those

[1] This problem is considered further in the next chapter.

exhibited in temporary and attractively presented book displays. One occasionally sees examples of so many unjustified 'breaks' in the classified sequence that 'shattered order' is the phrase that leaps to mind. The normal and over-size sequence that we were previously considering affords examples, not of broken order, but rather of parallel classification – two or more 'complete' sequences are involved. Likewise, we see parallel arrangements in the different departments of a library with their various sequences. It is best, within each department, to shelve over-size volumes in an entirely separate sequence, although some libraries like to reserve the bottom shelf in each bookcase for such 'parallel' material. However, the main point to be stressed is that the existence of many separate sequences in a classified library does not invalidate classification. There is a vast difference between searching two or three collections of material on a subject (because the books concerned are of different sizes, or because a distinction has been made between reference and lending material), and searching hopefully, but almost endlessly, though a huge unclassified collection or series of collections.

The selection of a classification scheme is also an important matter, especially with regard to the variety of ways in which the system chosen will affect the library service. In choosing, we should look well ahead and ensure that immediate or short-term needs do not deflect us from the right choice. There are probably distinct advantages to readers when many libraries are arranged in similar fashion. Of course, this will only be approximate; no two libraries are likely to make identical decisions perpetually. But, in the British public library scene, for example, changes in local government areas have served to underline the benefits of neighbouring authorities using the same system; there may be much re-classification otherwise when amalgamations take place. There are also advantages in the reader finding, say, in the Birmingham Public Library the system to which he has become accustomed in Manchester. It seems, therefore, right to some to accept the widely used DC, simply in order that the library may form, as it were, one more branch of the great national library of which every library in every town may be considered to be a section. Of course, there are counter-arguments. Uniformity in this respect tends to disregard the character and the 'literary warrant' of individual collections. It has been suggested also that the adoption of a uniform system of classification throughout all libraries would be quite unsuitable to the special librarian and would generally eradicate or stultify initiative. There is, nevertheless, a very strong case nowadays for as much uniformity as possible in general libraries; the administrative advantages of this are overwhelming and the librarian whose initiative is circumscribed by his classification must have very little initiative.

In most situations the work of selecting a classification has been done long ago and the present task is to apply it consistently and to maximum effect. This means that the system must be carefully examined, root and branch; its outline, hierarchy, method of subdivision, notation, index and mnemonic features should be thoroughly grasped. In spite of all our preparatory study, this is no easy task; the newcomer to classification is apt, in the traditional schemes especially, to place a book without checking back from the sub-division to the main heading under which it appears. Another prevalent mistake is to crowd books on subjects for which there are headings in the sub-divisions into the main class. One also sees even worse elementary mistakes. Notations are copied incorrectly or are confused, historical numbers being mistaken for geographical ones, for example. A study of the scheme in its entirety would prevent many errors of this kind; what is more important, it would suggest the full possibilities of a scheme, which are often greater than appear on the surface. Classificationists will often plead that such a thorough study will convince us that their scheme offers as good an arrangement as we are likely to get and that unauthorized adaptations are thus to be shunned; be that as it may, the classifier should certainly take pains to fully comprehend the scope and character of the system which he elects to apply.

A centralized classification service. Many large libraries or library systems centre their cataloguing activities in a single specializing department, and the concept of cataloguing or indexing being provided centrally at a national or even an international level is but an extension of this idea. Such a service may save staff time and reduce costs, but it has other solid arguments to recommend it also, for it promotes high and consistent standards of classification and cataloguing. The father of such services is that offered by the Library of Congress, which has carried out this kind of work since the beginning of the century. Many countries have been regrettably slow to emulate it; in Britain, it was the foundation of the *British National Bibliography* in 1950 that eventually provided the stable basis for such a service. In the classification sphere DC has been used, originally with quite extensive modifications based on the longᴸerm needs of a detailed classified national bibliography, but more recently in strict accordance with the orthodox provisions of its current edition. The arrival of Library of Congress and BNB MARC tapes in the bibliographic arena also has implications for classification. There are now many compelling reasons why libraries should use the classification as provided by the national bibliographic service, or at least keep sufficiently close to its practice to be able to integrate with it, if required. The whole concept of such a service provides a very powerful impetus for standardization in all the indexing processes. Now, it may be advanced by the British librarian, as counter-arguments, that standardization has not been achieved, or that much material that comes before the classifier is not within the scope of BNB and its MARC record. A library using a classification other than DC might also maintain that a machine-readable bibliographic record needs a more detailed and sophisticated system of classification than Dewey's. Such arguments cannot be ignored, but they can be answered. That standardization has not yet been achieved on a sufficient scale is true enough, but there is bound to be increasing pressure to conform to accepted standards in the future. Those who do not will not be able to reap the full economies offered by a national central bibliographic service. Much material is outside the scope of such a service, but more and more items are likely to be pulled into the national and international bibliographical net in future and it is best to be prepared. What is more it is clear that MARC can or could accommodate three or four classifications as subject coding for documents, if necessary, although this may affect the time and cost of preparing the record. DC, LC and sometimes UDC will be represented. If there is sufficient demand, perhaps BC or a new scheme aimed at machine-retrieval system needs could be accommodated. The remaining themes in this chapter and those of the next will always be valid in a consideration of classification policy in an individual library, but it is worthwhile to state, with some emphasis, that most libraries ought at least to be in a position to participate in the benefits of national centralized classification and the information retrieval facilities of MARC. To be too much out of step could be very costly in the long term.

Broad versus close classification. There arises the question in general libraries: should the chosen scheme be used as it stands or only in part? If our library is not a large one, is it necessary to go further than a thousand places – the three-figure position of DC?

Would not further sub-division mean unnecessary minuteness, with the attendant disadvantages of long call-marks? Further, even if there is a real advantage in minute classification, is this not neutralized for the reader because he cannot understand or remember a long class-mark or call-mark? One recollects the view of one writer from the United States who argues that 'classification, like the mathematical symbol π, is never perfect no matter how far extended'.[1] However, many librarians who advocate a limited use of a classification scheme, do so on grounds which should now be negligible. The constant growth of libraries makes reasonably specific placings inevitable in all collections except extremely small ones or, perhaps, in an old cathedral or similar library, which is complete and will never increase in size. The reader is not so unintelligent as some librarians appear to think; he can usually understand numerical or alphabetical notations unless these are extremely long. When he is unable to follow the sequence, it is usually because the guides and other aids with which the library should be furnished, are lacking or inadequate. The practical point to bear in mind is that classification should be carried as far as is necessary to define and segregate the subject matter of the books; otherwise specific themes will be intermingled and hidden in a broad containing class. Sooner or later, in nearly every growing library, the full classification will be needed and alterations to class-marks on older stock and records involve a great deal of work. Thus to classify closely, if not an immediate practical necessity, may well be an ultimate economy, provided that the library adheres to the classification originally selected; no librarian enjoys retracing his steps to extend classification symbols allocated, say, ten years ago, which are now discovered to be too general for his collections. Cutter's Expansive Classification was an interesting experiment in both broad and close classing, but his advice 'be minute . . . be not too minute' is not altogether conclusive, because it is difficult to say what being too minute means. The more positive rule, 'Classify a book in the most specific heading that will contain it' is preferable; because, if this is observed, it must bring the whole classification into play. Ranganathan, with much justice, speaks with contempt of 'the regression to broad classification, even to the abandonment of classification . . . as if saving shelf space is the *summum bonum* of library service'.

[1] R. B. Downs in his paper *The administrator looks at classification.* In Allerton Park Institute: *The Role of Classification in the Modern American Library*, 1960.

There are those who would challenge such arguments. Raymond Moss,[1] for instance, in a typically provocative paper, argued 'we should cease to regard classification as a method of placing documents in the most "specific" place for all time, but rather as a continuing process of revision resulting in further division of a class only when the number of documents in that class is becoming too great for convenient administration or location'. The advice is understandable, but should be treated with caution. Certainly, the librarian of a small collection may group his material only broadly, provided that he considers the *potential growth* of his stock. Broad arrangement is often found in school libraries and in children's departments within the public library service, where it is adequate to provide the younger reader with a simplified plan of the system in use and enables him to comprehend, without undue effort, the elements of the methods librarians use to organize material. DC and BC, chiefly through their abridgements are quite adaptable for service in such small units. (To help in the meaningful cutting of classmarks, DC numbers now appear in appropriate segments on centralized cataloguing records.)

Broad classification is encountered elsewhere in practice; sometimes in circumstances where it can scarcely be condoned. One expects the author approach to be a dominant one in university or other large academic libraries; in fact, one sometimes still finds that a subject catalogue is not even supplied. Yet, although the undergraduate is concerned largely with authors or with specific references supplied by his lecturers, he surely seeks other material about his subject on occasions and a reasonably specific arrangement is thus necessary lest he spends more time searching for suitable material than reading it. The needs of the post-graduate research worker in university libraries are also important in this context. If close classification is evaded because it leads to impossible notations or because it consumes staff time which might otherwise be released for direct reader service, then the motive is laudable. If, however, its neglect is the product of lack of concern for the information needs of the student and researcher and represents a simple desire possibly to save the librarian some brain-wear, it cannot be supported. Many academic libraries would, in fact, benefit from a more closely classified and well-guided arrangement, especially in their catalogue.

---

[1] Moss, R. *How do we classify?* Aslib Proceedings, February, 1962, pp. 33–42.

Mentioning the catalogue serves as a reminder that broad arrangement on the shelves has inevitable repercussions for cataloguing. We can have a detailed classified catalogue, for instance, and a cruder form of classification on the shelves. This seems to work well in certain cases, but would often prove impractical. Alternatively, we can classify broadly on the shelves and have an alphabetical subject catalogue. Broad classification often, in fact, does imply a dictionary catalogue – but the latter has enough work to do without taking on much of the essential subject analysis of material which could be performed by classification. In conclusion, then, we think of specific subject arrangement as the norm for the catalogue and, whenever practical, for the shelves also. It is the only true way, in both spheres, to be faithful to literary warrant, to pin-point material, and to achieve a really helpful sequence. Some libraries depart from this norm and are justified in so doing, but others which classify broadly should not do so, for they would be better served either by close arrangement or a different type of order altogether (presumably one of the 'reader interest' variety) than by a classification which is merely a skeleton of an accepted system.

Use of alphabetical order. When broad classification is adopted, it may be worthwhile to sub-arrange items in each broad category by alphabetical order of topic; alternatively, A–Z author order may be employed. The first of these two methods is, of course, extensively used in LC, which certainly does not make use of broad classification; it is, however, also a process which could be adopted in a small library, alphabetical subject order within a broad class being preferred to further systematic sub-division. We observed in Chapter I that alphabetical order of one sort or another is useful for the arrangement of certain categories of material and that, at times, it is a helpful method of sub-arrangement within the classification. The essential thing is that a library must not use A–Z order merely because it is simple or easy to apply; the alphabetical arrangement can only justifiably replace a classified one if we are sure that no loss of efficiency results. When the detail of the systematic order is unwanted, when there is no obvious systematic method of arrangement to apply, or when it does not seem necessary to show closely the relationships between specific topics; these are the occasions which call for the use of alphabetical arrangement. Alphabetical author order for fiction, and as a means for the final arrangement of a number of books on the same specific topic within a class, is common; if a large biography class is maintained, the great lives may be arranged in alphabetical rather than systematic order. The smaller public library may also apply the notion of broad classification, categories of a popular kind such as motor cars, gardening, outdoor sports, etc., being sub-divided at an early stage by the A–Z sequence of topics. And, of course, A–Z order may be used for some 'non-book' material also; it will inevitably take some part in the organization of knowledge, as an alphabetical catalogue of some kind is indispensable. Yet usually, particularly in our larger libraries, the role of A–Z order in shelf arrangement for non-fiction is a comparatively small one. The National Lending Library at Boston Spa (now, of course, an integral part of the British Library) has afforded an excellent example of the extensive use of alphabetical order in arrangement. This is, however, to be regarded as a special case; a library which consists chiefly of long runs of scientific journals can scarcely be considered as a typical example of the stock and needs of most collections. We repeat once again that the A–Z order, whether by author, title, or topic, is only to be used in most general libraries when the specific classified order is obviously unsuitable. The fast-growing library should be classified closely; the task takes no longer than broad classification and the job is done once and for all. Therefore, the various general schemes of classification must supply the necessary detail for such an arrangement. Those libraries not needing all this detail can easily ignore such sub-divisions or provision for synthesis which they consider to be superfluous. It is significant that DC offers instances, at 658.9, for example, where A–Z order may be preferred to systematic order, but it also gives good reasons for usually choosing the classified order rather than the alphabetical.

Adaptation. The student must take care to distinguish between broad classification and the alphabetical method of sub-arrangement. They may indeed be used together, but there is no reason why a scheme should not, in fact, classify in some detail before resorting to alphabetical sub-arrangement by topic or by author within its classes. However, we may leave this theme here and consider another administrative problem which the librarian faces when he applies a scheme. Should he apply it as it stands? Or will he be well advised to adapt it to his own library's needs and adjust classes which he considers to be awkward or inadequate? As modifications are often made in schemes, this question deserves thought. It is curious that the librarian mind is so constructed that it likes 'nibbling at classification schemes' – to use a phrase of J. D. Brown. In part, this is due to the weakness of one kind or another that a librarian can see in the scheme he has chosen; few schemes, indeed, do not seem capable of improvement in some way when we have tested them. Yet a distinction should be made between adaptation recognized by the classificationist, or by the editors of a scheme, as reasonable adjustments and those modifications which are unauthorized as far as the classification's editorial body is concerned. A former editor of DC, D. J. Haykin, once asserted that many of the complaints about that system arose because librarians were not prepared to take it as it stood, but insisted upon making their own adjustments; one can see Haykin's point of view when he suggests that, if this is done, it is not fair to blame DC for the unhappy results. Thus most librarians will be well advised to make only those modifications which are suggested in the introduction to the scheme as possibilities (BC, with its alternative locations, is especially generous in this respect); other adaptions are likely to prove misleading and, if the classification is widely used, much of the commendable uniformity of practice between libraries will be lost as a result of these novel alterations. As the editor of a leading American journal on our subject wrote not too long ago, 'We would never recommend wholesale or impetuous revision or "adaptation" of classification schemes. Too many libraries have faced or are facing expensive reclassification because of past improvisation. Once tampering with numbers has begun, the movement accelerates and the innovator finds himself (and his successors) committed to moving farther and farther away from the source.'[1]

The modifications which are usually made involve the bringing together of such subjects as Language and Literature in DC and the association, in the same system, of the History and Geography of the same country. There are various ways of achieving the latter; they mostly result in an arrangement such as –

942.21 History of Surrey
T42.21 Travel in Surrey

Here the divisions 914–919 have been abandoned and travel books go into the History section, being distinguished from history books by the replacement of the digit 9 by the letter T. It is also customary to remove fiction from the classified sequence, whatever the scheme used, and to shelve modern fiction in an alphabetical arrangement by author. In some public lending libraries there is a small collection

---

[1] Piercy, Esther J. *Library Resources and Technical Services.* Fall, 1965, p. 413.

of quick-reference books, separated from the rest of the stock, without regard to the place of each reference work in the classified sequence as a whole. Thus adaptations often lead to the state of affairs which librarians describe as broken order.

One finds occasionally that adaptations of a more ambitious and sometimes ingenious kind are made. The danger always lies in the fact that being out of step may jeopardize acceptance of a sound new edition or participation in centralized classification and a computer tape service. By and large, we must incline to the view that if a system is, like DC, widely used and acknowledged, it is best used as it stands for the arrangement of general material; adaptations should not go beyond those permitted by the scheme's introduction. Indeed, to write a full history of all the modifications of this or that system which have been made to answer the convenience of librarians would occupy an inordinate space and would not serve any purpose, except usually to show the futility of the work; in short, adaptation is to be shunned unless the reasons for the modifications are very powerful indeed. The only reasonable exception to this advice is the local collection or other special material in the general library.

Re-classifying a library. Perhaps an even greater issue than that of adaptation is the possibility of re-classification. If our stock is arranged according to a system which is rapidly becoming obsolete and a better method is readily available, should the change be made? This question does not admit of a ready answer. Some would offer the rather glib reply that a library should always be prepared to change the classification system and should face up to the challenge of employing the best methods available, discounting temporary inconvenience; others will offer the equally unsatisfactory retort that re-classification of an established library can never be economically justified, or cannot even be contemplated by a busy librarian. Tennyson once wrote

Our little systems have their day
They have their day and cease to be;

but bibliographical classifications, once rooted, are harder to drive out than his words suggest. The answer lies somewhere between the extreme views. A librarian faced with the possibility of accepting a new system must carefully consider its long-term advantages with regard to the scholarly and satisfactory arrangement of material on the shelves and of entries in catalogues. In some cases, impending mechanization may provide the needed spur. He must also weigh up the cost of a change in terms of time, labour, the problem of altering many records, and the task of maintaining a service to readers while the re-classification process is being carried out. The actual financial cost of the operation is also important; it is most unfortunate that, despite some discussion[1] on the subject, we have no fully reliable published estimates of either the cost of classification itself or the expenditure involved in re-classifying a substantial collection. In Britain, certain public libraries have changed from SC to DC in recent years and some academic libraries have abandoned obsolete systems for more flexible ones of their own devising. In the United States, several have switched to LC. Librarians in many countries face this kind of problem and are inevitably reluctant to embark upon such a programme of work because of the number of volumes which have to be re-examined and reallocated by the classifiers and because – and several librarians consider this to be the key factor – no established general scheme has yet a clear-cut advantage over the well-entrenched DC for public libraries and indeed for many academic libraries. The latter, it is true – and especially university libraries – do often prefer an adapted form of LC or a good 'home-made' system; one of the best examples of the latter is the scheme made in the nineteen-fifties by Kenneth Garside for University College, London, and based on faculty reader interest there.

If the problem of changing over hundreds of classified volumes to the new scheme is considered the major difficulty and the librarian is otherwise convinced that re-classification is a necessity, the answer may lie in adopting a fresh scheme for new accessions and regularly-used older material only, while adhering to the older system for the arrangement of most of the material already in stock. This would avoid allowing the methods of the past to prevail over and dictate to the needs of the present and future, without giving rise to so much reorganization. It is a notion which Ranganathan has called the osmosis method of re-classification and it has been adopted in some libraries. It results in an arrangement where there are two parallel sequences for a time representing different classifications (apart from any parallel arrangements which may exist within each of the two schemes). Gradually, however, the older

[1] L. R. Morris, for instance, argues that established classifications differ but little in efficiency and reclassification is the silliest of all ways to spend money. *Library Journal*, September 15, 1966.

system will be driven out by the preferred classification and will eventually only be found in stack-rooms where the reserve stock and rarely used material is arranged. This method is surely the most painless way of injecting a new method of arrangement into a well-established library service. It is not ideal, but it does tend to abolish the argument that re-classification is unthinkable because thousands of volumes will need to be changed over to the new system. On the other hand, many librarians will, it must be confessed, be very reluctant to re-classify even if this method is contemplated. There are obvious disadvantages in employing two different schemes side by side for a number of years and these cannot be lightly disregarded. Dr D. J. Campbell has suggested that the osmosis method is unsuitable for special libraries and can best be practised in collections which retain much obsolescent material.[1]

Naturally *some* re-classification is taking place continually in many libraries, for when a scheme is revised and re-locates a few topics, it is well worthwhile to re-classify any portion of the stock which is still in use and which has a location that *seriously* conflicts with the new recommended placing. But writers on our subject have been quick to see how uneconomical the entire re-classification of a medium-sized or large library usually is. In such an instance, the work involved in changing the scheme can be justified only if the subsequent advantages are truly enormous. As Professor Maurice Tauber has pointed out on several occasions, the onus in this matter really lies with the makers of a new system, who must prove that re-classification by it will yield durable advantages in the medium or long term.

Let us imagine, for a moment, that a long-established library does decide to re-classify. How could this operation be accomplished with the least possible disruption of its service? One may start with the sections most in use or the sections most in need of re-classification, for instance. As for procedure, this may well depend on the library and the two systems concerned. One can only sketch an outline method which might be followed, but this may be sufficient to indicate how the task *could* be approached. First of all, a space must be cleared to house some re-classified volumes in their fresh arrangement. Next, the classifiers must attack the older system class by class, transferring material from each class in turn to the appropriate part of the new arrangement. The latter will grow slowly

[1] *Making your own indexing system in science and technology*, Aslib Proceedings, October 1963, pp. 282–303.

in the space provided and fresh space will soon become available as large gaps arise in the older sequence. As material is transferred, the appropriate records in the catalogue must be altered and the book stock in the older arrangement must be gradually contracted, so that space is available where it is most urgently needed. Eventually, all the stock, or all that the librarian decides to re-classify, will have been removed to the new sequence which will soon grow with extraordinary rapidity. This 'gigantic game of chess', as C. D. Batty once described it, will certainly involve a great deal of effort. If the task is pursued too rapidly, there is a risk that errors will be made and old class-marks left undeleted in the catalogue; it must, therefore, progress steadily, but relatively slowly. At all times books must be available for the reader. Thus all staff must be kept informed of the state of the huge task and must know which class has been removed from its old sequence for re-classification at any particular time in the operation; they must know also which subjects have already been re-classified. The staff will obviously be burdened with extra work at such a time and the library should certainly display a notice informing readers of what is happening and inviting them to seek help if they cannot find any item which they may require during the transitional period. One sometimes finds at times like this that the reader appreciated the old system more than one suspected!

CHAPTER SEVENTEEN

Classification Policy and Library Administration – II

At the risk of some repetition, it is worthwhile to stress in any consideration of the day-to-day administration of the classifying process, certain practicalities which must go hand in hand with a sound knowledge of classification theory. The classifier should get to know well the scheme he applies – its merits, faults, and alternatives, and must not classify by its index alone. He should be careful to ascertain the true subject of each item he classifies and should record 'decisions' on difficult examples for future reference. Items should be placed at the most useful specific location offered by a scheme; in many cases this is obvious, but in some it is not and the contents and preface should be scanned closely. Equally important is the matter of consistency, and this is facilitated by the building up of an authority file. One does not accept, because it derides every real purpose of classification, Dewey's uncharacteristic view that it does not matter much where a book or other item is placed as long as that place is clearly indexed; one must accept the view that it is extremely confusing – because of the possibly independent views of different classifiers and a lack of guidance as to decisions previously taken – to have several places for items on the *same* subject.

Guiding. A very important matter of an administrative kind is that of adequate provision of guiding as a simple key to the chosen arrangement for an open-access library. The classified arrangement is unfamiliar to the library user; to ensure that material is quickly located and the collection fully exploited, the librarian must provide a series of guides to act as the link between the familiar but unhelpful alphabetical approach and the little known but far more helpful classified arrangement. There is a real danger that, unless the systematically arranged sequence is well guided, the reader in public and even in academic libraries will fail to find his way quickly to the particular book or section of the library that he needs. There are still libraries which provide insufficient guidance to their classified arrangement or which offer notices which are amateurish, vague, or inadequate. The reader need not know much about the classification in order to reap the benefits which it offers; good guidance can enable him to grasp the elements of the arrangement and find his way about the library quickly and easily. We find nowadays that retailers are forced to study consumer requirements closely if they are to sell their products; likewise librarians must study the users' problems and requirements if a first-class service is to be offered. There can be no doubt that one of these requirements is a good standard of guiding, especially with regard to larger collections. The reader needs a number of clues to and indications of the classified arrangement. These are:

1) A good catalogue.
2) A plan of the classified library.
3) Class guides.
4) Bay and shelf guides.
5) Individual book guides.
6) A printed pamphlet.
7) Personal assistance whenever possible.

Ignoring the description of the catalogue as a guide, for this received separate treatment in an earlier chapter, we may consider the function of each in turn.

One of the best guides to the shelf arrangement as a whole is a plan, showing the positions of the bookcases and giving the numbers and names of the main classes contained in them. Ideally, a large plan of this kind will be placed in the entrance foyer, or be given some other prominent location in the library. The reader will be given a broad, overall picture of the classified arrangement through this plan and he will ascertain from it the approximate location of any topic. Small reproductions of such plans, say, of postcard size, can be published, so that readers may possess their own copies. But we are more concerned here with the large bold plan which the library exhibits near to its entrance. There are many possibilities for a plan of this kind; one of the most interesting innovations along these lines has been at Luton Public Library, where a large plan of the push-button type has been provided. The reader selects the subject he requires and presses the appropriate button. The area of shelving in which books on this topic can be found then lights up on the plan.

Many of our other guides are affixed to the shelves or bays and are, as we have indicated, an alphabetical key to the systematic arrangement. A class guide is one which is placed at the top centre of a bookcase, or at the beginning of a large class on the shelves. Sometimes it is merely a bold statement of the class number and subject, such as –

300 SOCIOLOGY

or it may set out the main divisions of the class, possibly with reference to parallel classifications, as –

300 SOCIAL SCIENCES	
301 Sociology	360 Social services
310 Statistics	370 Education
320 Political science	380 Commerce, Communications
330 Economics	390 Customs, Folklore
340 Law	
350 Public administration	
See also the 'over-size' collection for books too large to be shelved here.	

These class guides may take various forms, but they should always be colourful and attractive to encourage readers to take notice of them. Obviously much artistic taste and ingenuity can be given to such bold signs; it is well worth-while to have such detail as perfect as possible.

Large classes which occupy several bays of shelving require closer guiding; and the most convenient units to guide are the bay, or tier and the individual shelf. Much experiment and ingenuity has been expended on such guides and many forms are in use. The idea behind these guides is that they shall reveal exactly what a bay of shelves contains and what is on each particular shelf. They may be placed at the end of the bay in the form of a framed notice, on the shelves in the form of blocks, or they may be provided in the form of a series of narrow strips which can be attached to the edge of the appropriate shelves. It may be noted that the 'block' idea consumes a great deal of shelf space and thus the other methods are usually to be preferred. It is possible also that the large bay guide can make the reader aware of allied subjects that, unfortunately, are housed in some other part of the classification system. Great care must be taken to ensure that all such bay and shelf guides are moved as the stock in each section expands, as it always will in a living classified library. There is no point in guides which are misleading because a class has extended its boundaries and left the guide badly positioned. Yet, alas, this situation is still encountered in a few libraries.

After each bay has been clearly guided and shelf or topic guides have been liberally provided, further assistance is provided by guiding the individual through the notation of the classification in use. Every book must clearly bear its class-mark on the back of the cover. This class-mark reveals its position in the classified arrangement and is the link between the entries in the catalogue and the shelf classification. Some controversy has arisen about the position of the notation and, while such controversies as 'up or down the spine' or 'the top versus the bottom of the spine' may appear reminiscent of certain portions of the novels of Jonathan Swift, there is a good case for uniformity of practice, in that the library looks neater if all notations appear, say, two inches from the bottom of the book. Occasionally, however, exceptions will need to be made. All we really wish to demonstrate here, however, is that notation is itself a guide to the classified sequence; provided it is not too long and that the symbols which it employs have ordinal value, the reader should be able to follow it fairly well.

A most useful guide to the modern library, especially one with several departments is the printed pamphlet or brochure. This may give a general conspectus of the library's services and can give a simple explanation of the method of arranging material on the shelves coupled with notes on how to find a book through the catalogue. The catalogue should also be separately guided, but the advice given in a printed pamphlet of this kind can be most useful nevertheless. There are many examples nowadays, in both public and academic libraries, of introductory guides in pamphlet form. They are usually to be found by the entrance or near to the catalogue and the reader is invited to take one away with him. Here again the librarian must consider carefully the most effective wording of the advice given in such a pamphlet and must ensure that it is attractively presented and that the reader is encouraged to take it and read it through.

The best form of guidance that the reader can possibly receive is that given directly by the staff. In these days of mass advertisement we find that printed guidance is sometimes ignored (although that is no reason for not providing it, for it will often prove helpful). No amount of guidance in the form of notices and pamphlets, however, can be regarded as a substitute for direct assistance from members of the staff. If possible new readers should always be given a brief description of the library services and its method of arrangement. The Reader's Adviser or other members of the staff should always be willing to explain to the users of the library how to find a book in the catalogue or on the shelves. The extent to which this advisory service can be given will depend, of course, on the number of staff available for professional work: it is because, in many libraries, there are not enough staff available that we have to rely so heavily on the other forms of guidance. But direct personal assistance is the best type of guidance of all and should be given whenever possible, although the other methods cannot be neglected. Personal help can make a world of difference to the impression of the library services which the reader receives and to the way in which he understands how to use these services intelligently.

The good librarian will select appropriate guides for his library judiciously. There is no point in overburdening the reader with notices, but there is likewise no excuse for failing to provide a reasonable standard of printed guides. The size of the library and the type of reader concerned with its services must be taken into account and as much direct help must be given as possible. After this personal aid has been given, the reader's ability to find his way about the large classified library will depend largely upon the other guides described here. R. L. Collison once suggested that effective guiding results from a common-sense policy plus an ability to see things from the reader's viewpoint. We would agree with this, but would stress most strongly the need for librarians to put themselves in the reader's position and test the efficiency of their printed guides by imagining themselves coming to the library for the first time in search of a book. Better still, for it is always difficult for the professional librarian to pretend that he is new to his library, some regular readers could be asked for their views on the quality of the guiding; they may well provide helpful suggestions which will enable us to demonstrate the classified groupings more powerfully and effectively and thus to offer a better service to our customers.

Costs of classification. As long ago as 1937, Grace Kelley raised the idea of a study of the cost of classification as a task of great practical utility. There have since been several investigations and surveys, but really next to nothing of solid worth for general application has emerged. If excess time *is* spent on classifying, this is clearly a waste of money and there is also the opportunity cost – the sacrificed alternative use of the time – to be considered. The difficulties in costing classification processes include the variety of libraries and the distinctive features of some, the lack of standardization both in the use of schemes and in classification procedures, and the fact that it is often difficult to separate classification time and costs *per se* from those of the total cataloguing process. Maurice Line's brief comments[1] on the findings at Bath University are interesting, but the results are too slight to act as a prescription for other situations. Many other surveys seem to be, although sincerely meant, little more than an advertisement for LC made by the converted and pre-committed. Some writers argue that broad classification cuts costs, but there is no hard evidence for this. One would certainly expect the use of centralized classification to reduce time and costs and the application of a system which is 'predictable' in its method and structure could also help. But conclusions must be vague in the absence of facts which can be applied to many situations. The profession needs sound cost-benefits analysis and the time/cost comparison of different schemes by people with no axe to grind. Indeed, for general libraries, the costing of classification is, along with an attempt to estimate its benefits to the consumer, now almost certainly the problem most urgently requiring examination. The growing application of modern management techniques to librarianship may help to provide more reliable evidence on this important topic.

Display work. Any open access library in which the stock is well presented and guided is a book display in the widest sense of the term: our best advertisement of our capabilities as librarians is reflected there. It has been rightly said that shelf classification is a backroom technique devoid of all value unless completed by a positive endeavour to advertise and circulate the book stocks on which it has been employed. We usually employ the word *display* in a more restricted sense than this, however. It is adopted for a special exhibition of books and other material on some particular topic or theme. This may well be a theme of current or local interest; in many cases, however, the display has been formed to gather together related material that the classification has scattered. No scheme can collect in one place (and this should by now be obvious to our reader) all the material relating to a subject; nor can it reveal all subject relationships, although the good scheme will

[1] *The cost of classification: A note.* Catalogue and Index, October, 1969, p. 4.

demonstrate the most important ones. Occasionally, the library may wish to exhibit together the 'distributed relatives' of the classification and a book display offers an excellent opportunity for doing this. If DC is the scheme in use, for example, an exhibition of material on *Psychology* could bring together books from many parts of the classification. In addition to the obvious material from various sectors of the 100 class we might have relevant books on religious, industrial, criminal, art, social, educational, and sales psychology, scattered in various divisions of the classification. The display will gather together this kindred material, for a short time, and indicate its presence and the relationship between the different aspects of this topic. Likewise, a display can be created on a particular country, the object in this case being to collect, from various classes, books on its history, geography, language and literature, political and economic life, religion, science, art, and culture. Lives of some of the great men from the country can also be included in the special temporary display. Thus displays are an outstanding example of the wise use of *broken order*. These displays may be maintained for a week, a month, or longer. Much will depend upon the popularity of the exhibition of books and, if the department concerned is a public lending library, on how easily the display can be replenished as material is borrowed. Sooner or later the books must be returned to their correct place in the classified sequence, for it is here that the most permanently useful sequence of topics is, or ought to be, revealed. Our displays are designed as short exhibitions which show other possible groupings from time to time. If made with vigour and imagination – with the help of specialists if necessary – they can support the classification well. What is more they can, in public libraries, do much to promote reading and to publicize the service.

Special materials. The role of classification and classificatory techniques for information retrieval in special libraries is considered in a later chapter, but the modern general library increasingly collects many varieties of material which can be regarded as *special* (including perhaps much fugitive material which is utterly lost without adequate indexing). These types of material sometimes demand a rather different treatment from the rest of the stock, but it may often be possible to cope by means of parallel classification or by modification and adaptation of the system in use. Some important 'special' categories are considered, below.

Periodicals. Such items may hardly be thought of as special, since they are found in nearly every library. From the point of view of arrangement, however, there can be no doubt that certain problems are raised. In many libraries the classification of such items is practised, yet would seem to be scarcely necessary. Current journals can be filed in alphabetical title order; bound volumes of back numbers are nearly always too bulky to be shelved with books, unless a great deal of space is to be wasted. They can be classified and arranged in a parallel sequence, or can be arranged in title order within such a separate sequence. The diversity of content of many bound journals is the factor which suggests that classification may be rather futile. If libraries are split into departments there may be some value in keeping, say, technical journals separate from general ones, and classification will achieve this; but in many libraries it is an unnecessary procedure. It is the content of the journal that is of value and, if a reader has the exact reference for the article he wishes to consult, the alphabetical sequence of bound volumes will suffice; if he wants to know what has been published in periodical form on a particular subject, the librarian must consult published indexes to journals or indexes of his own creation. It is here that classification can play a part. Despite the undoubted preference for the alphabetical subject heading approach in published indexing services, it must be evident that a *good* classification can be most helpful in arranging an index to periodical literature. The success of UDC in many special libraries in carrying out exactly this type of work testifies to this. We would strongly urge, therefore, that it is not the classification of journals that is important, but rather the classification of the articles which they contain. In an article in the *Wilson Library Bulletin* many years ago, Marie Prevost stated: 'The remedy for an unindexed periodical is not classifying but getting it indexed.' One agrees wholeheartedly, except that in many cases a classified index would be more useful for gathering together references to related articles than an alphabetical one, despite the latter's use of 'see also' references.

Classification of fiction. One very important category of material in public libraries, which is 'special' perhaps when the question of the efficient arrangement of the stock is considered, is fiction. By far the most popular method of organizing such material is the alphabetical sequence by author's name; this despite the fact that it results in a very long unbroken sequence of books in many libraries. While fiction may seem to provide the most obvious opportunity for the use of a straightforward alphabetical order, it should be noted

that attempts have been made to introduce a more helpful organization of large fiction stocks by means of a form of classification. To
arrange fiction according to DC or any other classification employed
for the remainder of the stock would definitely seem to be unhelpful
to readers. In the general library, it can be argued that while specific
requests may be received for a work by Jane Austen, Thomas Hardy,
D. H. Lawrence, or Virginia Woolf, most people merely want 'something to read'. Moreover, how many of our general readers know if
William Faulkner and Henry James – to use names at random – are
English or American authors; and how many have any notion of
their dates? Most libraries, therefore, remove all fiction from the
Literature class, although some may favour the classification of the
older novels of recognized literary merit and importance and the
alphabetical arrangement of all fiction published after, say, 1920.
In his *Primer of Book Classification*, W. H. Phillips argues for the
division of the fiction stock into three distinct sequences: fiction
published before the First World War, translated fiction, and
modern fiction. Within each grouping the arrangement would be
alphabetical by author. There would certainly seem to be some
advantages in such an arrangement in the large and busy public
lending library.

More involved ideas for the grouping of fiction have been advanced. Some libraries have employed broad groupings with regard
to the theme of the novel, arranging alphabetically by author within
each grouping. The systems suggested by L. A. Burgess and R. S.
Walker some years ago for the systematic arrangement of fiction
have not met with a great deal of response from librarians. The
problem is that, while it is certainly possible that the adoption of a
special scheme for fiction with its own notation might offer certain
advantages in grouping items in an interesting and useful way, it is
obvious that in many libraries the traditional methods are sufficiently
helpful and involve far less work. It seems likely, therefore, that the
employment of classification for the organization of novels will be
confined, when indeed it is used at all, to attempts to break up a long
alphabetical sequence of authors through the use of chronological
divisions of the kind suggested by Phillips or through the employment of a few broad and easily recognizable subject categories.

Classification of non-book items including non-print media. Non-
book materials and their organization are rapidly becoming of great
importance to many librarians. From the point of view of arrangement, the basic problems relate to the individuality of the many

categories and the variety of physical forms involved. Slides, records, manuscripts, microforms, films and filmstrips, pictures, maps and music scores are all important material and in some libraries one or more of these groupings may be of paramount concern. Arguments have been made for the use of a recognized standard general scheme, usually LC or DC, whenever possible. Certainly the general systems can be used and Croghan[1] has provided us with a guide which is at once a key to the wise choice of media terminology and a notational coding which, when added to the class-marks of a general system, specifies the medium or physical form of material. Thus, for example, 382. 9142 71 could represent a poster on the EEC (the Croghan number for posters and prints being added directly to the DC number). A standard scheme may be used with such specialized additions or as it stands. Either way, parallel classification will arise. The Media Resources Centre of the Inner London Education Authority, for example, uses DC 18 and has some ten parallel sequences, accepting that – in the words of Malcolm Shifrin, the librarian, 'the integrated subject approach should be through the [classified] catalogue'. But one writer on the subject, D. L. Foster,[2] argues that apart from the LC provision for music scores and maps, the general schemes make little attempt to cope with the growing variety of media. He suggests various alternatives, including A–Z author or title order, accession number order and a home-made classification and warns us that – if such material cannot be fused into a single sequence or system – we may need 'several collections held together by an array of classification systems and bibliographic tools'. The growing necessity of interest in these matters may well prove the mother of invention and already attempts are being made to devise systems and standards for non-print materials. In the short-term, at least, another of the alternatives mentioned by Foster, that of adaptation of a general classification, may prove acceptable. Modification and adjustment of a systematic order, with the acceptance that here is an outstanding case for parallel arrangement, seems infinitely preferable to a despairing turn towards an arbitrary sequence, although post-co-ordinate indexing cannot be altogether ruled out. Any librarian with one or more of the non-book or even non-print categories heavily represented in his stock

[1] Croghan, A. *A Thesaurus – classification for the physical forms of non-book media* Coburgh Publications, 1970.
[2] *Classification of non-book materials in academic libraries: a commentary and bibliography.* University of Illinois Graduate School of Library Science. Occasional Paper 104, September, 1972.

must, however, consider the long-term view also and keep in touch with ideas and new literature – there is already much in the sphere of cataloguing and appropriate code rules – on the storage and retrieval of the various media.

Local collections. This is a category which, in both acquisition and arrangement, has long held the attention of public librarians and contains its fair share of non-book items, with a consequent need for parallel arrangements. Special schemes exist for British local history materials; they include that worked out for *Aston Manor* by R. K. Dent, R. Austin's system for the county of *Gloucestershire*, the later (1953) scheme of more wide application prepared by A. J. Philip, and the much praised classification devised at *Derby* by J. Ormerod. The late J. L. Hobbs suggested that a faceted classification might well be devised and applied; others might even favour post-co-ordinate indexing for parts of the local collection. The usual solution, however, for any local collection is adaptation. Of all public library departments this one perhaps justifies a special arrangement most, and yet there are powerful administrative arguments for adapting DC or LC. Local history is thus one of the few outstanding cases where modification and adjustment to a scheme to make it conform to local needs can be clearly vindicated. The modifications made are legion and of varying efficiency, but then it *is* so very difficult to lay down a uniform pattern which can be applied as a standard to local collections of various scope within areas of different size and character.

In applying a special scheme or adapting a general one there are various problems to be faced. Is a topographical or subject arrangement best as the primary step; that is to say, will the greater number of readers enquire, for example, for all material on the churches of Sussex, or for items on Chichester, including those on its churches and cathedral? If topographical arrangement is preferred, the selection of the topographical unit may also be a thorny problem. Whatever classification decisions are made, we can be sure that a special collection of such variety of material and with such potential riches will need supporting indexes to specialized information which the staff can use on the reader's behalf. George Carter, in a revision of Hobbs's book which is cited in our bibliography, argues with perception that, in these days of increasing standardization in classifying, the local collection gives the public librarian a real chance to use his own initiative, ingenuity and knowledge of classification principles. Carter himself (surprisingly) favours basically chronological order for the shelves because of the variety of physical forms of material and (correctly) stresses the value of the classified catalogue for the comprehensive subject view.

It can be seen in summary, from this chapter and its predecessor, that there are many factors to be borne in mind in the implementation of a classification scheme and several 'special situations' to examine. The problems which arise as a result certainly do not invalidate classification, but they remind us that the study of its application and ecology can, in their own way, be just as interesting and significant as the examination of basic theoretical principles.

CHAPTER EIGHTEEN

The Limits and Problems of Classification

In the opening chapter of this book and elsewhere the case *for* classification in libraries and information services is stated with a good deal of vigour and conviction. No apology is made for such a statement, for the efficiency of classification is evident in many situations and in some is indisputable. The restrictions and weaknesses of classification need, however, to be kept in mind, partly because they deserve attention and study in their own right and partly because it is only through a recognition and awareness of classification's problems as well as its achievements, that the latter can be maximized. One critic of classification, whose sustained attack of detailed arrangement is well marshalled and still deserves scrutiny almost forty years later, is Grace Osgood Kelley, of the Queen's Borough Public Library in the United States. Dr Kelley's contention, based on long and varied experience, is that close arrangement defeats its own ends and that a sensible reduction of the classification detail used for organizing items on the shelves of a library is necessary. Her work, *The Classification of Books* (1938) suggests that minute subject analysis must be left to the catalogue which – to most librarians in the United States – meant and means the dictionary catalogue. The general argument along these lines is reinforced by a list of thirteen 'elements' which affect the value of classification in libraries. Some of these objections are possibly less valid now than when first put forward; but many will always be significant in any inventory of classification's limits. Grace Kelley modified her views somewhat a year or so later; the contribution from her pen to the quotations which follow our title page represents a sentiment with which we wholeheartedly agree.

Dr Kelley argues for broad classification rather than for the abolition of the process and makes an interesting distinction between difficulties which are inherent in classification and those that are not, but arise from its practical application to a library situation. This dichotomy is a legitimate one, but other distinctions could usefully be made nowadays, for the problems facing a shelf classification are (as we have seen) not altogether the same as those which exist in the systematic arrangement of a detailed catalogue or bibliography, while the emphasis and character of classification may change again in the case of information retrieval vocabularies within thesauri. A listing of some ten significant problems, as is done here, is a worthwhile and necessary task, always provided that it is remembered that some of these may be rather more acute with regard to information retrieval or catalogue order than they are for shelf arrangement and vice-versa.

One basic problem concerning order on the shelves is that a classified library consumes more shelf space than an unclassified one of the same size. This arises from the fact that, in the chronologically arranged library, new accessions can be simply added to the end of the existing sequences, whereas when subject classification is adopted, space must be left at the end of each class and sub-class for new material on each theme to be inserted at the appropriate point in the classified arrangement. The factor will always be with us, but no librarian now considers it to be an insuperable objection to classification; if we are sure we can be frugal with shelf space without detriment to reader service, well and good. But Ranganathan has remarked that the conservation of space on the shelves is by no means the primary purpose of librarianship; the extra room taken by a classified collection is generally very small in relation to the benefits offered. In older libraries, or others where readers do not go to the shelves, there is usually no close classification, although this is not always the case, and some of them possess classified catalogues. Usually such libraries have been arranged in the simple chronological order of accession. It may be thought too, that if there is a classified catalogue the purpose of classification on the shelves has been achieved by this means and shelf classification is superfluous if only the staff have access to the shelves. It must be emphatically confessed that some closed-access libraries seem to do well without classing that demands any real subject analysis or with a rudimentary arrangement by some factor other than subject content. Consider, however, even in libraries of the closed-access type, the daily quest of readers for a number of books on a given subject; and consider, too, the time that is wasted if the librarian is suddenly required to assemble all the books he has on, say, the French

Revolution, or Radium, on the Einstein theory or on Maritime law. He must classify his books to the extent of the subject every time he has to answer such a requirement. Would it not be better to do it once and for all by the simple act of classifying thoroughly the whole library?

A difficulty which must be recognized at the outset is that the classifiers themselves may be poor, or badly trained, workers; the enormous advances made in education for librarianship have done much to banish this limitation, but Jast's very long-standing remark, that it is one thing to have a satisfactory classification and another to have a satisfactory classifier, must be remembered and care should be taken to ensure that the system in use is properly understood and applied. The senior member of the staff responsible for classification and for the overall supervision of this work can do much to ensure that classification is being carried out in a correct and consistent manner. In addition, each classifier should be encouraged to consult reference works or look for advice in dealing with the infrequent really difficult example, especially if the subject field is a relatively unfamiliar one.

The layout of a library building can influence the impact of a classification by causing arbitrary breaks in its sequence. Guiding can combat this to a large extent.[1] A further problem or inconvenience which arises and must be remembered is that broken order and parallel classification affect the application of our shelf classifications. The impact of the former is best seen in the creation of temporary exhibitions and in groups of 'quick-reference' material. With regard to the latter, it must be said that there is no such thing as a library which is able to get all its material on a given subject together at one place, unless that library has a stock so small and so much accommodation that space does not matter. The first principle in the division of books is necessarily by size; it is clearly pointless to attempt to place folio and duodecimo volumes in the same sequence – thus parallel arrangements are essential. Such parallel classifications also arise through the existence of many branches and departments in a single library system and, perhaps more significantly in modern librarianship, due to the fact that we deal with maps, films, pamphlets, periodicals, gramophone records and other material as well as with books. Yet who would deny that several parallel classified sequences are much more satisfactory for

[1] It could be pointed out that, in the display of books or other printed documents, even the height at which an item is shelved affects its chances of notice or use.

the location of volumes and the juxtaposition of related material than no classification at all?

The two-subject work or multi-topical document is another topic for reconsideration here. It can obviously only go in one place in a classified shelf sequence, however precise the subject specification, unless several copies are purchased and distributed to different class locations. The latter procedure is not unknown, but cannot be commended. It is simpler to recognize that while a book or document as a physical entity can have but one location, classified catalogues and bibliographies can have more than one subject entry per item. Many multi-topical documents can be dealt with satisfactorily by selecting the dominant subject for shelf location or – if the work considers several related specific topics – by choosing a general heading that covers all the subjects concerned. Some libraries with many pamphlets and reports may, of course, use post-co-ordinate indexing and come to grips with the problem in this way. Even in the classification of books, however, these examples do arise and the most useful placing must be sought out, remembering that only if a work spans almost the whole breadth of knowledge should it be considered for the Generalia class. (It may be added that, even in the application of an enumerative classification, the understanding of the technique of phase analysis should assist greatly in selecting the most useful placing for some 'two-subject' books.) There remain a few genuinely stubborn items. To select but a single example, it could be argued that *The Shell Country Book* deals with many subjects within a rural setting – place names, village habits, folklore and mythology, astronomy, law, food, botany and zoology, geography, country writers and painters. No single location embraces all of these, but the work *can* nevertheless be classed according to dominant appeal. Likewise a work on 'The aged in society' could deal with numerous aspects and contexts of the lives of the elderly. Where difficult cases do arise, decisions taken should be recorded for future reference, since consistency is important both in stabilizing practice and revealing policy to future classifiers.

A basic difficulty in nearly all classification to date lies in the fact that concepts are co-ordinated at the input or indexing stage rather than postponing co-ordination until the store of documents is searched for an actual piece of subject information. Even a detailed, fully faceted scheme with a helpful sequence inherits the problem of a fixed citation order in each class. Information relating to primary facets will be collected, but this very act essentially distributes information on concepts from the minor facets – or indeed from any facet, minor or otherwise, which is not cited early in the number building process. Now this is an undoubted problem, especially in areas where a single 'consensus' viewpoint cannot be identified or where there are large minority opinions to be served. Post-co-ordinate indexing may sometimes provide the answer, yet this does not lend itself to organization on shelves or indeed to several other library situations. But before this inevitability of scatter promotes despair, it should be reiterated that classification is not a sole instrument in the organization of knowledge. It is supported by a relative A–Z index based, we would hope, on principles which complement the chosen order of the scheme. It is aided by cata-logues, by bibliographies, by displays, by personal assistance to readers. Because no single order satisfies all users, some critics would have us abandon the quest for helpful order. Rather than exhibit a sequence helpful to many but not to all, it seems we should offer an order equally unhelpful to everyone! Such super-egalitarianism does not stand up to close scrutiny. In virtually all walks of life an order, even with some flaws, is infinitely preferable to chaos. Consider as an example, the sequence of ideas in a film or even in a textbook such as this one. There are often several possible orders. The choice of any one, even the best, leads to some separation of related themes – but who would advocate a random sequence of events or ideas for the effective promotion of communication? Nor should we accept the view that 'any order will do'; the most useful citation sequence should be sought. It may be added that in computer-held files the idea of a primary facet under which a document is shelved is irrelevant and this objection may well fade into oblivion in future mechanized information retrieval, since the sequence of elements can be changed with each coming to the fore in turn, along with its full context.

Another weakness or problem that deserves to be spotlighted once again is the perpetual tug of war between the stability of structure which we look for in a classification scheme and the need for the schedules to change and progress in the light of research, new emphases and the evidence of recently published literature. New topics arise, old subjects expand or contract in importance, new relationships are formed and some older ones severed. The problem is perhaps most acute where the rate of change in knowledge is most pronounced – in the field of classification for information retrieval. For instance, the pleas for the retention of the basic UDC structure are understandable, as thousands of documents are already classified by it, but equally understandable are the cries for a change which will give UDC a chance to determine its future with regard to the best modern theory and practice, and in the light of the present and anticipated future structure of knowledge rather than the past. This problem of change versus stability is a serious one. Refusal to move with the times can have serious results; the longer revision is postponed the more radical and painful it becomes. Yet it is not mere inertia that makes some librarians reluctant to accept sweeping changes. One is not simply scrapping an obsolete piece of machinery, if one abandons a particular classification for a more modern alternative or drastically reorganizes a major class, the work of fellow classifiers, perhaps over many years, is at stake. This is why DC, for instance, looks for evolutionary rather than revolutionary change. If we adapt a famous Cutter quotation to fit the problem of speed of revision it might read 'Be bold, be bold, be not too bold'. For the shelves and for conventional classified catalogues the road of compromise is best, with schemes receiving continuous attention and new editions appearing at intervals not exceeding ten years. But in classifying for an information retrieval context, a higher rate of change is demanded.

Grace Kelley and many others have recognized this problem and its implications. Dr Arundell Esdaile[1] argued many years ago that to keep up with knowledge faithfully 'it is realized that the re-arrangement [of libraries using subject classifications] would have to be repeated at intervals of at least half a century, which in the life of a library represents indecent frequency. Yet such is the truth. The divisions of science are as impermanent as the shades in a kaleidoscope.' If by 'divisions' Dr Esdaile meant the greater classes, it is not the truth; nor is it the truth of the major divisions of these classes; the reliable classification will therefore need only to change in its specific points, in its minutiae. This is not, as a cynic might claim, a mere rearranging of our prejudices, but the incorporation of new data and appropriate adjustment. Continual editorial attention, thorough but gentle revision, and attention to users' needs and pleas can all ease the problem of change. So can the use of synthesis and a clear predictable citation order within the scheme. Some critics will not accept this. Raymond Moss, who has assailed the classifying process on various occasions, declares[2] that 'the few

[1] Library Association Record, August, 1933, pp. 242–3.
[2] *An Leabharlann* (The Irish Library), December, 1971.

well-known general schemes all suffer from the assumption that the pattern of knowledge was fixed for all time at just about the time they were created, a piece of nineteenth-century self-satisfaction which contrasts unfavourably with our own warring century of uncertainty'. The statement evokes some sympathy, but those classifications are not as inflexible as it suggests; indeed, in this computer age their rate of change, despite the arguments of the conservatives, is likely to increase.

This same basic problem once evoked a proposal for a sweeping solution from Lund and Taube, who introduced a scheme for a 'non-expansive classification system'. This defies all our traditions on classification; but is a thought-provoking paper still worth reading. It suggests that no classification can provide adequately for future knowledge and argues that the best system would be one divided into chronological groupings. Each of these 'periods', according to its standard of learning and the type of literature produced in it, would have a separate classification based on the order of knowledge as developed in that period. Each of the period classifications would be sealed, so that it cannot be expanded and nothing can be inserted into it except, we presume, the newly discovered books and documents of that period. The authors suggest nine parallel classifications of this kind for a great general library, each one carefully based on a close, retrospective study of the period which it covers. The result should be that the relationships between topics within these periods can be accurately expressed, or so it is claimed. Once again the reader is invited to consult our bibliography and to read this highly original article for himself. Much, very well balanced, argument goes to support the system proposed. Yet we are certain that it is unworkable; it will not do for the busy modern library. We are still convinced that books from all ages, but dealing with the same subject, should be found together, as far as is possible. Nor is it clear from the article whether books about a particular chronological period, but produced in a later one, are to break the seal of the parallel chronological expansions and obtain admission – as the scheme is described as 'non-expansive' they will probably not. If this is so, one of the basic rules of classification is broken; can we really justify, for example, the separation of modern critical works on the various periods of English Literature from the relevant original texts?

Yet the idea is both interesting and attractive; Lund and Taube make us aware of one of the deficiencies of any subject classification;

the fact that it is difficult to cater for different movements and periods in history really adequately and, above all, that it is difficult to arrange the knowledge relating to our own age – for every age is best assessed and classified in retrospect.

Dismissing the above as interesting but unworkable, we may decide that if the policy of gradual change in a classification will not do, then new schemes are needed. Certainly the CRG/BNB scheme is awaited with great interest. In contrast to its emphasis on retrieval, the last general system to come from the United States is for the shelves and suggests that there is probably as much pessimism as hope there with regard to the future of detailed shelf classification in general libraries. Rider's *International Classification* (1961) is really rather lacking in detail and adopts the principles favoured in the nineteenth century, in that it relies totally on the enumerative approach and concentrates on obtaining short class-marks at all costs. Of course, much earlier, in his biography of Melvil Dewey,[1] Rider had told us that 'many would-be experts in classification . . . have not realized that because a certain amount of classification is a good thing, an infinitely larger amount of it is not necessarily better. It should have been obvious that the more detailed a classification is made, the more quickly it tends to become obsolete; that the more complex it is made, the more its original easily-grasped simplicity becomes lost.' There is even a surprising note of pessimism in the introduction to Rider's scheme, where it is stressed that it is meant only for new general libraries; re-classification, Rider believed, is never justified unless the existing system proves completely inadequate. It would be interesting to think that IC will give a new lease of life to the older ideas, but it is scarcely possible to imagine much interest being aroused in new, enumerative, general systems. Rider's scheme is still reasonably up-to-date at present, but the lack of synthesis and of a revision policy will surely tell heavily against it in coming years. Yet it emphasizes the opinions of a large number of American librarians. These can be stated succinctly as postulating that broad classification is best for shelf order in general libraries, that call numbers should be shorter, and that synthetic systems have not yet fully proved their worth in any context.

Some of these ideas can be found in the many writings of a prominent American writer, Jesse H. Shera. Shera sees the future of the organization of knowledge, in large and specialized libraries at least, as lying with the employment of mechanical methods of

[1] ALA, 1944.

retrieval. Machine systems are indeed becoming more popular and he thinks we must accept them gladly, as of course we must, when they contribute speed and accuracy to our library work. With regard to classification in the traditional sense, Shera thinks that it has 'been convicted by the ample testimony of its own inadequacy'. One of its greatest faults, as he sees it, lies in the fact that any classification on the shelves can only present a linear or uni-dimensional picture of knowledge; a true view, of course, would be a multi-dimensional one. That is to say, assuming we have a hierarchical notation, the classes 731, 732, 733, 734 · · · 739 will all have the same relationship to the parent class, 730. But the shelf classification does not clearly show this family hierarchy at all; it presents the class in a line – 730, 731, 732, etc. Thus 739 is far removed from the parent class, but 731 is close to it. The linear pattern imposed (shades of McLuhan!) by the shelf arrangement has seriously distorted, it is contended, the true pattern of relation-ships which the classification has tried to offer. Again, we must concede the point. No one-dimensional arrangement – and this type of arrangement can hardly be avoided in libraries – can fully reveal the hierarchy of subjects as envisaged by the classification. But the objection is, to some degree, an academic one; bibliographical classifications have worked quite well in the past, despite this limitation.

Other matters which can be dubbed 'classificatory problems', have been dealt within reviewing the administrative implications of classification. The important matter of time and costs is one; another is the need for a detailed vocabulary, with the implication that notation may sometimes become too unwieldly as a result. This notational problem may be non-existent in a mechanized retrieval system, where logical structure rather than length is the essential; it may not matter too much either within the classified bibliography or for the arrangement of a well-guided classified catalogue. But for a sequence of books on the shelves and for a link between the cata-logue and the shelves an economical set of call-marks is highly desirable. This dilemma has driven some librarians to seek refuge in the simplicity of broad arrangement, but a more interesting and imaginative idea, although akin to broad classification, is the notion of *Reader interest order*. This originated in the United States, but has been used elsewhere[1] also – sometimes unconsciously – in many general libraries where a high proportion of the literature is

[1] The SESO adaptation of DC in Holland seems to aim at it.

recreational reading. It involves the arrangement of stock in popular categories based upon the observed interests of readers. These often cut across conventional subject groupings to produce useful sections such as 'Do it yourself books'.

Volumes in such groups are prominently displayed and well guided; in most cases, a book may be moved to another category if it seems to receive insufficient attention in the category in which it was originally placed. In some categories fiction and non-fiction could be blended. The whole idea may be regarded as a genuine attempt to provide a better service for readers in general, popular, libraries; it must be applied with care even here, for the relatively broad groupings which it favours may not correspond to the long-term interests of readers. Also, to move books about from one grouping to another may create serious location problems from time to time. In the larger library, and perhaps in any library providing a reference and information service, the idea does not appear to be very practicable; its existence, however, is a further indication that subject classification, as most of us know it, does have imperfections and that some librarians are prepared to explore alternative methods of displaying their stock to the general reader. It is possible that, if a strong challenger to the DC ever could emerge for use in the general library with a high percentage of popular or leisure literature, it would be based largely on 'reader interest'. The great difficulty would lie in ascertaining an 'interest based' order that was objective, reliable in a wide range of libraries, and relatively stable. Much more knowledge about popular reading needs and searching habits at the shelves would be needed before such a goal would be possible. If it ever is feasible, it might just be – for public libraries – that 'happening of massive proportions' to which Desmond Taylor once referred.[1]

A final problem concerns classification by discipline. This is undoubtedly an essential asset in most cases within the context of a shelf classification. It is right to differentiate between the moon in the context of astronomy and primitive or comparative religion. A problem arises, however, in dealing with interdisciplinary topics or with the admittedly very occasional, but not unheard of, example of a single document which deals with a subject in all or many of its possible contexts. (There is also the problem that disciplines tend to reflect inflexibly a view of knowledge which, in some cases, may be in process of being abandoned in the light of new discovery.) Brown,

[1] Taylor, D. *Is Dewey Dead?* Library Journal *91* (16), September 15, 1966.

despite inconsistencies and glaring faults, sometimes scores here; his reach, unfortunately, exceeded his grasp and it would, in any case, seem necessary for a shelf classification to concentrate on the many advantages of classification by discipline rather than on the few afforded by classifying 'by attraction' around themes such as water, the moon, gold, the Jews, and various artefacts or mental concepts which can fall into many contexts. BC now makes provision for the rare type of work which confounds this advice and Sarah Vann has suggested the possible use of two figures being used before the decimal in DC to represent new emerging disciplines and inter-disciplinary themes.

In the context of a computer-based retrieval system, however, there would be a considerable shift of emphasis as far as this classificatory theme is concerned. Machine-held files are concerned with the individual concepts as distinct and uniquely coded 'packages' and can throw off the idea of development from main classes down, by gradual stages, to specific ones. It is this latter approach which makes shelf classifications inevitably discipline orientated. In a computer-based retrieval system concepts are not rigidly subordinate to a chosen discipline and its citation order; various 'strings' of concepts can be established, with significant concepts taking the lead position in the string in turn.

There are members of our profession who think that indexing of various kinds, once the core of our examination syllabus, is rapidly declining in importance. Librarians, it is argued, need to be more concerned with meeting readers and getting books and various non-print materials to them; they must thus become more outward looking and socially aware. There is some truth in the argument and no one should dispute the positive side of it. But even in these days of centralization, computerization and MARC tapes, the investigation of classification is for many both rewarding as a discipline and a task of significance as a prelude to their professional years. Those who dispute its worth are (apart from the few who find difficulty in the study and react accordingly) usually people who, because they find no use for it in their current post, assume that it has no professional utility and is a costly and time-consuming luxury. Although a busy librarian can be excused for being engrossed with his own immediate problems and situation, one must plead for a vision wide enough to encompass all libraries and various strands of professional work and circumstances. Such a liberal and synoptic view is an irresistible corrective to the concept of classification as –

to use Raymond Moss's memorable although deplorable phrase – a bibliographical bingo. Most of us welcome the widening of our syllabus and the consequent shrinking of some of its traditional components, although the shrinkage is often not as drastic as some would claim. However, if we do not use our knowledge of technical processes extensively in one professional post we may need them in another, and we all must know enough about classification and catalogues to use them fully on our reader's behalf, to understand their achievements and limits, and indeed to be able to criticize them intelligently.

Some of the difficulties outlined here are intellectual ones; others, more mundane, may nevertheless be equally telling in practice. To sum up, the chief problems in classifying are the time, cost and shelf space consumed by the process; the fact that notation is sometimes long and complex when precise subject specification is achieved; the physical forms of new media and other factors which necessitate parallel orders; the inevitability of *some* 'scatter'; the difficulty of multi-topical items; conflicting needs in up-dating and revision; the linear nature of a classified order; and the fact that there can be weaknesses in classifying by discipline. Even as the points discussed are summarized, thoughts of other 'problems' arise, such as the task of replacing an outmoded but established classification, or the difficulty for an international scheme in giving a balanced view with regard to different cultures and systems. (Rider's IC scores well on this last point, for its late creation enabled it to heed this particular criticism). All this does not mean that the limitations of classification are innumerable or insuperable; it is simply that they have involved recapitulation over a very wide area, for they essentially affect and pervade the whole of our subject. Classification can and must be complemented and its defects minimized by the use of other tools and the impact of the various defects identified and listed here must be carefully weighed. Some defects spring, paradoxically, from the very advantages of classification; others are more serious in some situations than in others and certainly the development of facet analysis has taken some of the sting from some traditional objections to subject arrangement.

One is fully aware of the reality of what Sir Frederic Kenyon once called the *idola classis*, the danger that a librarian may become obsessed with this or any of the technical services in a way which is detrimental to other aspects of his work and which inhibits the development of a well-balanced, progressive library or information service. To accept this warning, as we must, is not to deny the value of those technical services. Classification, whether done in our own library or produced for us by a reputable bibliographical service, is much more than a desperate number calling and labelling and pigeon-holing of materials. It is an orderly and rational process which should be at the heart of the librarian's work and thinking. Imperfect in certain ways and impermanent in some details as our schemes may be, and inadequate as our classing occasionally is, the benefits which we have derived from classification outweigh the defects immeasurably. To enhance those benefits by the vigilant scrutiny and progressive improvement of classification systems should be an aim of those who work in or for libraries, because the good order and effective management which many of them present today is due, in no small measure, to classification.

Bibliography on Section Four

On the classified catalogue, there is:

Shera, J. H. and Egan, M. *The Classified Catalog.* American Library Association, 1956.

On the limitations of classification, readings include:

Maltby, A. *Classification – logic, limits, levels.* In Maltby, A. (editor), *Classification in the 1970s.* (Already cited).

Moss, R. *How do we classify?* Aslib Proceedings. February, 1962, pp. 33–42.

Kelley, G. O. *The Classification of Books: an inquiry into its usefulness to the reader.* H. W. Wilson, 1938.

Still helpful, especially chapter one and chapter four.

Shera, J. H. *Classification: current functions* ... In Shera, J. H. *Libraries and the organization of Knowledge.* Crosby Lockwood, 1965.

Lund, J. and Taube, M. *A Non-expansive Classification System.* Library Quarterly, July, 1937, pp. 373–94.

Rutzen, R. *A Classification for the Reader.* In Allerton Park Institute. *Role of classification in the modern American library*, 1960.

On re-classification, we have:

Perreault, J. M. (editor). *Reclassification: rationale and problems.* University of Maryland, 1968.

Papers on many aspects, with pleas for conversion to DC, LC and UDC by appropriate contributors.

There are many books and articles on the classification of special materials. They include:

Hobbs, J. L. *Local History and the Library.* 2nd edition, revised by G. A. Carter. Deutsch, 1973.

Whatmore, G. *Classification for News Libraries.* Aslib Proceedings, June, 1973, pp. 207–15.

Daily, J. E. *Organizing Non-print Materials.* Marcel Dekker, 1972.

Grove, P. S. and Clement, E. G. (editors). *Bibliographic Control of Non-print Media.* American Library Association, 1972.

Redfern, B. *Organizing Music in Libraries.* Bingley, 1966.

Classification for Information Indexing and Retrieval

Special Classifications and the use of Classificatory Principles in Index Vocabularies

Many of the problems, practices and theories outlined so far affect all libraries, but some of them chiefly concern general libraries. The emphasis now is upon indexing procedures in the special library and this is perhaps a logical sequel to the previous chapters, since the problems of organizing special collections is the general library's nearest equivalent to the indexing work of the special librarian-cum-information officer, while the limits of traditional general classifications are almost certainly felt most keenly in special librarianship. There are many types of special library, including those of learned and professional societies, industrial libraries, and the libraries which serve research organizations and government departments. Shelf arrangement is sometimes – although certainly not always – of little or no importance, since it is often the research report, the government paper, the periodical article, the standard or the patent that is required for the rapid location of information which is often highly precise and specialized. The three basic questions for organizing material, then, are: 'Does one classify in these circumstances?', 'Should all material be organized through classification?', and 'Which classification does one use?'

It seems almost axiomatic that a special library which does classify should have a special classification, that is, one with an appropriately restricted subject coverage. Although UDC is aimed particularly at the world of documentation, and LC and the new BC are quite detailed, there are factors which may militate against the use of any general system. General schemes sometimes, as Palmer once suggested, offer more than enough detail for most special libraries in nearly all subject fields, but lack the right amount of detail or the appropriate emphasis in the one field in which a library specializes. What some special librarians truly need is a system which provides a really detailed arrangement for their main area of interest and a broader classification for peripheral topics. General classifications often offer long call-numbers for specific topics and a theme of major interest might in, say DC, have a basic class-mark of six digits. Thus the adoption of a general scheme in a special library is almost always notationally undesirable; true, adaptations could be made to effect greater brevity, but most special librarians would argue that it is best to have a scheme which allocates virtually the whole of its notation to the area of activity with which their organization is principally concerned. Other reasons for rejecting the general systems include the absence of really thorough and speedy revision policies in schemes which cover all knowledge, lack of helpful order, and the fact that the users of a special library tend to look at many other branches of knowledge from the viewpoint of their own activity; thus, in an industrial library with 'the literature of paint manufacture' as its focal point, other subjects tend to be viewed with regard to their interest to the paint technologist and this under-standable bias distorts classification needs. Naturally, no general scheme can dare to be other than neutral in this respect.

There are, of course, some arguments in favour of a general system. There are the benefits of participation in centralized classification and the fuller use of MARC tapes, assuming the chosen scheme allows such participation. There is the benefit of having a system which caters not only for a library's core subject material but also for fringe disciplines and which is widely used, adequately financed and revised regularly – even if revision sometimes seems too slow. UDC, in particular, has a continuing vogue in many special libraries, although examples of the use of LC, DC and even BC can be found. The use of UDC for 'prenatal' classification in many technical periodicals and reports and – in Britain – its publication as a standard are two factors which tell heavily in its favour. UDC might well be the best choice for many special libraries and information bureaux, especially if they operate in fields where there is no appropriate special classification. Certainly any attempt at extensive adaptation of a general scheme is unlikely to be successful and the creation of a suitable special system from scratch might be considered a daunting task – although not an impossible one. The adoption of a general scheme, probably UDC, would thus seem to be a wise as well as a safe step. It has international backing and allows, through synthesis, the exact specification of most compound topics.

There are, of course, a number of special schemes and many of these, having been created within the last twenty years, are of the faceted variety. Good examples of schemes built on traditional lines are C. C. Barnard's *Classification for medical libraries*, originally devised for use at the London School of Hygiene, but also employed elsewhere, and the *Harvard Business Classification*. The former clearly shows the influence of Bliss and the latter that of Cutter through his nephew, William Parker Cutter. The building industry's sfB system which originated in Sweden is best thought of as one of the oldest examples of special faceted schemes. It is worthy of attention and study and can now be seen in the construction industry's revised form as CI sfB. Fully faceted systems also now exist for subject areas as diverse as soil science and library science; food technology and the performing arts; education and office management; baroque music and aeronautical engineering; or diamond technology and insurance. They all employ the idea of rigorously sorting basic concepts from the subject field into distinct, homogeneous categories and of providing for combination of the concepts according to a preferred and constant citation order. The idea of listing compound subjects, as such is repudiated. The schemes do not, however, slavishly follow a PMEST citation order; the order selected is carefully based on the needs of users and the nature of the subject field.

It would be superfluous to repeat the advantages already claimed for the faceted approach, but some writers – Douglas Foskett among them – have included in these claims the suggestion that the special library user should (and sometimes does) appreciate or accept such a scheme, since its construction is 'scientific' and reflects the world of reality with which scientists deal. It is probably safer to assess such schemes in more readily demonstrable pragmatic terms than these, but unfortunately most have not been widely applied; indeed some seem to have been drafted as a theoretical exercise rather than planned as a working tool. At the 1957 conference on Classification for Information Retrieval, Ranganathan claimed, in characteristic fashion, that 'enumerative classification is suitable for a finite and lethargic universe of knowledge, but the analytico-synthetic classification is needed for the turbulent universe of knowledge embodied in microdocuments'. Those who accept his words, would probably include some who advocate UDC as an international and soundly supported analytico-synthetic scheme which can help in preventing a specialist from taking too narrow and restricted a view by showing him the classificatory map for knowledge in its totality. It is impossible to be dogmatic and to lay down a firm choice, for the varieties of special library are many and there are more and more alternatives. (Indeed, there are more and more special classifications, including some such as the *Cheltenham Classification* for schools, which are special not in the sense of a restricted subject coverage, but rather in the sense that they are designed for only one type of library.) If, by special classifications, we usually mean those which confine themselves to a single subject or group of kindred subjects rather than covering knowledge in its totality, then some will definitely commend themselves in certain special library situations. In other cases, a general scheme – often UDC – is preferred and sometimes adaptation is the answer chosen, although the latter in a special library environment is almost always destined to prove an unhappy compromise.

If a suitable special scheme does not exist, it may, alas, be necessary to invent one, although this means extra work which the librarian/information officer is loath to do because of other pressing duties. A librarian wishing to make his own scheme on faceted principles must study and note the terms used in the subject field. These must then be arranged in categories, each category or facet consisting of a list of concepts produced by the application of a single characteristic. The concepts must be arranged in the most helpful order in an array within their category and the categories will be checked by a tentative application of the analysis carried out to a fairly small, but fully representative, collection of documents. If the vital categories appear to have been distinguished, the librarian must then check to see if each basic concept likely to arise has been listed in its appropriate category. The way is then clear for the allocation of notation to the various facets (it may well be advisable to draw upon the extra capacity which an alphabetical notation offers and to provide some means of revealing each change of facet and phase in the notation) and for an exploratory testing of the completed system. Only experience with the scheme can reveal whether the classificationist has succeeded in revealing all the relevant foci in each facet; it is, of course, possible to add some later, if need be. What is most essential is that the appropriate facets be clearly recognized and distinguished from the outset; it is also necessary that clear rules be made for the combination order of facets to keep the primary facets to the fore.

Of course, there are other solutions. Classification may be used for the book stock and other forms of indexing employed for the organization of non-book materials. Alternatively, the rejection of formal classification may be seriously contemplated. It is clearly in special libraries that it faces its greatest challenge, for one seeks precise specification without over-long class-marks and looks for a modern and frequently revised order. The problem of parallel arrangements is often experienced and the linearity of any scheme with a fixed citation order, however helpful that order may be, is often keenly felt. If these factors seem to militate against the use of a formal classification scheme, the answer may well lie in the use of post-co-ordinate indexing techniques. There are many post-co-ordinate systems, differing in various ways but with the same essential feature[1] – they practice concept co-ordination as a faceted classification does, but the concepts are kept separate in an A-Z sequence until the actual time of searching and therefore any concepts can be freely co-ordinated. We are thus emancipated from the irksome restrictions of a controlled but rigid and linear citation order. On the other hand, post-co-ordinate indexing is less sensitive in that, while it enables concepts to be brought together readily, it does not necessarily tell us how they are to be associated and we are back to the problem of linguistics and semantic control. Pre-co-ordination and the resulting citation order on the other hand, provide us with the sense in which the linkage is used. To say this is not to deny the great merits of post-co-ordinate indexing in many situations. Pre-co-ordination through an accepted classification has, as we have seen, its own problems. The conventional enumerative schemes are inappropriate for special library needs and even a fully faceted system retains the constraints of linear arrangement and a settled citation order, which may not be helpful on all occasions. Chain indexing may not atone for this in a special library situation. Classifying and indexing a technical report on 'the welding of sides of aluminium cans', for instance, may produce a citation order Cans–Aluminium–Sides–Welding which reflects a facet sequence Products–Materials–Parts–Operations. The index made by chain procedure would offer (notation is hierarchical, but imaginary):

Welding: Sides: Aluminium Cans	WXYZ
Sides: Aluminium Cans	WXY
Aluminium Cans	WX
Cans	W

This creates two basic problems. Firstly, some information is hidden. For example, the person wanting data on 'welding of cans' might need the technical report just mentioned, but may have to

[1] The basics of post-co-ordinate indexing are outlined in Chapter Six.

search extensively to find it, since 'welding' and 'cans' do not come together in the index. Secondly, even if a preferred order is established, some quite important themes may necessarily be scattered by the classification. A person wanting *much* or *all* information on 'welding' may need to look in many places in the index, as the operations facet is viewed as a minor one. The information can be found, but it is a tedious and time-consuming process. Thus, in some cases, a preferred order with chain indexing in support is vulnerable; one may then wish to turn to a fuller A–Z key, such as that offered by SLIC (Selective Listing in Combination) indexing, or resort to other techniques altogether. We need to remember constantly too, especially if we have a general library background, that within most specializing libraries the forms and types of information source are extremely diverse and classification, for the shelves at least, can be impracticable when most of the material is in the form of research reports or periodical articles. Of course, *some* material may be organized through classification and *other* material through post-co-ordinate indexing – although this does not appeal as the likely wise or economical method.

SLIC might come into its own in the situation just described. Without altering the reverse citation order used in indexing to make the index complement the classification, there are fifteen possible entries and SLIC reduces these to eight by eliminating those contained in a larger grouping:

FULL A–Z INDEXING (all possible special-to-general entries)	SLIC A–Z INDEXING	
Aluminium		
Aluminium Cans	Aluminium Cans	WX
Cans	Cans	W
Sides	Sides: Aluminium Cans	WXY
Sides: Aluminium	Sides: Cans	WY
Sides: Aluminium Cans	Welding: Aluminium Cans	WXZ
Sides: Cans	Welding: Cans	WZ
Welding	Welding: Sides: Alumium Cans	WXYZ
Welding: Aluminium	Welding: Sides: Cans	WYZ
Welding: Alumium Cans		
Welding: Cans		
Welding: Sides		
Welding: Sides: Aluminium		
Welding: Sides: Aluminium Cans		
Welding: Sides: Cans		

SLIC indexing as a key to a pre-co-ordinated information file might not be feasible in economic terms when five or more elements are involved. It does, however, remove some of the weaknesses of chain indexing and it must be remembered that the entries, once made, stand for all the documents on the subject concerned. When the index becomes established, therefore, the rate of growth might be a good deal less than the above example would suggest.

If post-co-ordinate indexing is chosen, it should not be because it is thought to involve a saving of subject analysis and 'input' time. Many special librarians may argue understandably that they want to spend the maximum amount of time meeting and serving their enquirers and a minimum on indexing the collections. There would seem to be little difference, however, with regard to intellectual input and certainly post-co-ordinate indexing, like the pre-co-ordination of concepts, has its own specialized technical jargon. A preference for post-co-ordination does not necessarily mean the complete rejection of classification. True, we shall not use an established and recognized classification scheme as such or employ notation, but we should remember Bliss's sound advice that classification essentially deals with concepts or their terms and that notation is subsidiary. One of the earliest of all the post-co-ordinate indexing systems, that of Dr Batten, relies heavily on classification type hierarchies and coding, while on the other hand the well-known 'Uniterm' system of Mortimer Taube may appear to be a negation of everything classificatory. Taube is often – and largely rightly – viewed as the true father of modern post-co-ordinate techniques and he was extremely reluctant to establish rules for control and consent to the idea of the systematic building up of appropriate thesauri, although he seems to have relented a little in this attitude in some of his later writings. The original concept of using only single words as units – 'Uniterms' proved however to be far from trouble-free. The great difficulty lies in the various associations which words may have and the ways in which they may be fused. This means, in practice, that the strict use of Uniterms has often to be abandoned in favour of phrases or unit concepts. Even the way in which concepts are bonded together can make a difference; 'the women of the Bible' is not the same as 'the biblical view of women', nor is 'the exports of cars from France to Britain' the same as 'the export of cars from Britain to France'. We have, of course, already come across this problem and discussed it in the context of Derek Austin's work, but the question of controlled citation or assembly of terms at the searching if not at the indexing stage is all important in retrieval theory and Uniterm does not seem to have the right answer. Batten perhaps clung too closely to the need for classification in the most basic and conventional sense of that word. Yet both he and Taube made immensely important contributions and helped to lay the foundations upon which others have since built.

Post-co-ordinate indexing systems usually lie somewhere in between the techniques of Taube and Batten; they use verbal concepts without hierarchical coding, but do employ various devices to control indexing vocabularies, demonstrate relationships, and often refuse to be limited to the 'natural language' of the document indexed. These control devices are often of a classificatory kind, although this is not always admitted or recognized. Control devices may be used in the index itself or in the thesaurus of terms which acts as a key to it. Whether they involve classification or not, their object is either to promote *precision* in the retrieval of documents in response to a subject request or to boost the total number of documents *recalled*. The terms recall and precision are important since they have much to do with our assessment of a system's performance. Recall can be measured in each instance by noting the number of documents which could be retrieved in response to a specific request and expressing the proportion of these yielded by an actual system as a percentage of this figure. Thus if there are ten relevant documents and only six are retrieved the *recall ratio* is a mere 60%. Recall is extremely important, but needs to be considered along with precision. The latter takes into account the unsought material recovered through the 'noise' or inefficiency of a system. Thus if ten documents are retrieved in relation to a specific request and only one is irrelevant (assuming we can define relevance satisfactorily) then we have a high precision ratio – 90%. Recall and precision are inter-related and both have been regarded as highly significant in testing. To some extent, of course, they pull in opposite directions; if we 'filter' the retrieval of documents to boost relevance, we have an adverse effect on recall. Likewise, a higher rate of recall is likely to produce more that is irrelevant. Some information workers think that the recall of unwanted material does not matter, provided the wanted material is recalled; they may sometimes have a point, but it is wasteful and time-consuming to retrieve masses of documents which must be examined individually and sifted for relevance.

Recall depends on many factors, including the depth and accuracy of indexing, but attempts to achieve greater precision involve the use of controls of various kinds and these often are distinctly classificatory in character. Although the testing of systems has shed doubt on their utility, they are still very widely employed in post-co-ordinate indexing. One such attempt is seen in the measure of simply inverting specific compound terms to facilitate collocation. We might note, for example, that at the library of British Insulated Callenders Cables Limited at Prescot, in the indexing of documents on *The computation of sag in steel-cored aluminium conductors on overhead lines* the headings selected are 'Sag', 'Conductors – steel cored aluminium' and 'Lines – overhead'. This is of considerable assistance in broadening searches and enabling, for example, requests for literature on conductors in general to be satisfied, in addition to the meeting of highly specific requests. In fact, many thesauri do use specific expressions, but this alphabetico-classed approach remains available, if required. The idea of *semantic factoring*, used at Western Reserve University, whereby vocabulary is restricted to a limited number of basic semantic units and concepts are assembled by the linking of these units, is also in effect a form of 'classification', albeit a somewhat subtle and complex one.

The usual forms of controls applied in the index itself, as opposed to the thesaurus are seen in the use of *role indicators* and *linking devices*. The former help to 'classify' a term by specifying the role or purpose for which it is used in each given context; the latter attempt to show that certain associations exist between some concepts used in indexing an item, but that others do not. In employing a term such as 'analysis' in an indexing vocabulary, some kind of role indicator would be wanted, for example, as this concept is used with rather different meanings in several scientific disciplines. Again, a term like 'twisting' can, as Johnson[1] points out, be a process or a fault depending on the context in which it is used. The need for a linking device might arise in an example such as 'Developments in motor fuels, oils and tyres; with special reference to the effect of self-inflating tyres upon the future pattern of breakdowns and road accidents' where, without some kind of control to show the inherent concept linkage, the document might be retrieved in a search for, say, 'the contribution of motor oils to breakdowns on the road.'

Linking devices are a common method of attempting to increase

[1] Johnson, A. *Co-ordinate indexing: a practical approach.* In Bakewell, K. G. B. (editor). *Classification for information retrieval.* Bingley, 1968, p. 82.

precision and are often thought of as a classificatory step on account of their 'associative' task. They may at times be helpful, although experience in the testing of systems to date suggests that their use may often be limited and that the effort of using links and roles on a large scale would yield a less than proportionate reward in terms of improved precision. This certainly seems to be the view of Lancaster and, of course, of Taube, who – although he accepted them in his later writings – argued that in preventing the false co-ordination of concepts, linking devices might at times impede the achievement of legitimate associations. In indexing a complex document it may sometimes be better to treat its two subjects separately (ie, by considering the document as two separate packages of information) rather than by the employment of linking aids. Even the British, despite their normal zest for things classificatory, have writers such as John Blagden and Michael Keen, who have grave doubts about links and roles. It seems likely, however, that there is scope for their selective use, especially when the indexing vocabulary is large. Here again, Lancaster is dubious about roles and points to the success of the mechanized MEDLARS system without them.

Control devices can also be used within a thesaurus; indeed, the very provision of such a tool for the selection of vocabulary implies the need for controls. If they are neglected, the task of converting the language in which the enquirer states his request into the vocabulary chosen by the indexer is definitely more difficult. The question of the size of vocabulary may be important – for many information officers consider that the larger an indexing vocabulary is the more scope there is for error in co-ordination. A well-planned thesaurus can help us to avoid redundant terms and cope with the problem of synonyms and near synonyms, although in some cases a comparatively large indexing vocabulary is still inevitable. The good thesaurus, like a good traditional classification, has itself an educative value in that it displays the structure of a subject field. It normally shows the scope of each term and the context in which it is to be used, while 'signposts' direct us to chosen terminology from rejected alternatives. Thus in the Engineers Joint Council original *Thesaurus of Engineering Terms* (1964) we have advice such as:

Build up	Employees
Use accumulation	Use personnel

and the scope of terms is shown by the aid of the abbreviation UF (used for) thus:

LIQUID METALS
  UF Molten metals

REACTIONS (NUCLEAR)
  UF Nuclear reactions
    Transmutation (nuclear)

This thesaurus adds explanatory or advice notes at times, for instance –

REDUCTION
(Use more specific term
if possible)

RESERVOIRS
(For water storage – not oil
or gas reservoirs)

Not all of this advice can be interpreted as disguised classification, but the thesaurus also refers to broader terms (BT), narrower terms (NT) and related and presumably co-equal terms (RT). Thus we find entries such as:

CRYSTALLOGRAPHY
  RT Bragg angle
    Crystal defects
    Isotropy
    Lattice parameters
    X-ray diffraction, etc.
    (16 other related
      terms are listed)

MOTOR GENERATORS
  NT Amplidynes
    Dynamotors

SILICON BRONZES
  BT Alloys
    Copper alloys
    Silicon alloys

Such structuring is of great assistance in enabling the searcher to move up and down hierarchies where necessary, although we must always remember that some terms can belong to several contexts and thus any one specific term may belong to more than one hierarchy. The example used is typical of the content of thesauri, but the second edition of the EJC thesaurus is called TEST (Thesaurus of Engineering and Scientific Terms) and Gilchrist[1] has drawn attention to the fact that its classificatory nature has actually been enlarged for – in addition to the indication of related terms of various kinds – there is a certain amount of discriminating pre-co-ordination. The aim of this is to boost precision further by linking some concepts in the thesaurus lest they be joined in the wrong way in a search. (Single words in an indexing vocabulary are always a liability if one is determined to avoid false associations in retrieval.) But then in the words of F. W. Lancaster[2] 'there is no

[1] Gilchrist, A. *The Thesaurus in Retrieval.* Aslib, 1971, pp. 43–44.
[2] *Information Retrieval Systems.* Wiley, 1968, p. 38.

magical distinction between pre-co-ordinate and post-co-ordinate systems. Most current manipulative systems are hybrids incorporating a certain amount of convenient pre-co-ordination.' Thus a term such as 'water' might legitimately be employed alone and has a clearly defined usage or meaning, but would also be needed, if confusion is to be avoided, pre-co-ordinated with other terms –

WATER – CEMENT RATIO
WATER – PUMPS
WATER RIGHTS
WATER WHEELS, etc.

To be obliged to co-ordinate 'water' and 'wheels' at the searching stage to get Water Wheels, for example, would create enormous headaches and chaos in an indexing vocabulary of any size. Some judiciously chosen pre-co-ordination in thesauri can thus be vindicated.

In many cases too the sub-division of terms, or their inversion for collocative purposes in an index is, as has been shown, a hidden kind of classification and this trend away from the purely specific alphabetical heading approach in favour of some systematic clustering is naturally carried over into the thesaurus. It is also becoming increasingly common to find thesauri and faceted classifications combined and more and more special schemes of classification are in future likely to attempt this role of the multi-purpose retrieval tool. The work by Croghan already cited is one such example, but much larger and better known is the *Thesaurofacet* which grew out of the English Electric Company's faceted classification for engineering and can be regarded as the fourth edition of the system. (To some the very name seems like a prehistoric monster, but it is scarcely that; there is certainly nothing prehistoric about it and it loses its terror for us upon examination.) It is, in fact, a most ingenious way of attempting to provide the full range of indexing services from the needs of shelf arrangement to those of computerized information retrieval. Associated chiefly with the name of Jean Aitchison, the work is a faceted classification with a fully structured thesaurus as index. It covers the whole of science and technology and has borrowed parts of the London Graduate School's faceted *Classification of Business Studies* for the relevant areas of management. (This borrowing habit seems sensible when excellent schedules already exist and has been carried out also in the new BC).

The *Thesaurofacet*, published in 1969, covers some themes in much more depth than others and in this it reflects, of course, the interests of its parent organization. In earlier editions, the idea of facet analysis with Ranganathan's categories had been applied to the whole field of engineering, but the *Thesaurofacet* recognizes conventional disciplines and then applies faceted classification within each. It is not bound by PMEST limitations.

In essence the idea is to offer a tool which can be used in post-co-ordinate or pre-co-ordinate indexing. But anyone searching under a broad subject would do well to obtain the notation from the alphabetical thesaurus, if necessary, and then to begin his search in the classification schedules, where he can find a helpful 'map' of his area hierarchically displayed. The person wanting a specific topic starts with the thesaurus and is helped by the customary pattern of showing relationships via the abbreviations BT, NT, and RT. The thesaurus and classification are complementary, however, and the thesaurus does *not* show many of the terms in the three categories because several of these are displayed by the hierarchy of the classification itself and need not be repeated. One must obviously, whatever method of application is favoured, use the two parts of this tool to see relationships between chosen indexing terms. If a specific term is selected, most related terms can be gained from the classification hierarchy. But those which do not belong to the single hierarchy in which the specific term has been placed can be collected via the thesaurus.

There are frequent links between classification and thesaurus too. For example, in the schedules we have:

KTB Electromechanical devices (see thesaurus).

Some use has been made of a sensible pre-co-ordination of certain concepts for the indexing language and there are also opportunities to 'build up' concepts by means of notational synthesis. Thus capacitors are at KK, Paper products are at VIE, and Paper capacitors is shown in the hierarchy at KK/VIE. The *Thesaurofacet* should, however, be examined at first hand to see these features and to note how the task of a subject search is assisted by the clear display of categories, hierarchies and modes of sub-division. This tool[1], with

---

[1] The London Education Classification has now been revised in thesaurofacet form also for use as the EUDISED thesauri for a council of Europe educational documentation programme.

its 16,000 index terms, is clearly most versatile, although one suspects it will be used more for post-co-ordinate indexing. The choice is that of the user, but even those who want post-co-ordination and prefer uncontrolled natural language indexing will, in Mrs Aitchison's phrase, find that the combined apparatus serves as a convenient 'memory-jogger'. There are some errors and imperfections which have been admitted, in a more generous fashion than is customary, by its editor-in-chief. The present writer, however, despite his expressed grave doubts about a single system being applicable for shelf arrangement and sophisticated retrieval, finds much to admire in it. It represents a colossal amount of effort and planning by its compilers and will undoubtedly have a seminal influence on indexing methods; indeed, while many thesauri use classification, several classifications now give thesauric type references and directions.

Classification has other miscellaneous uses in this sphere. A formal classification, faceted or otherwise (eg, LC, BC or UDC), can assist in the selection and building up of terms for a thesaurus and its hierarchies can assist in the making of references to broad terms, and narrower terms, although the related terms from other hierarchies must be sought and referred to also. Classificatory structuring within a conventional thesaurus (as opposed to the *Thesaurofacet*) is also a boon if generic as well as specific searches are sometimes to be carried out. It must be remembered, too, that thesauri encounter the language barrier and a notated classification schedule may at times be of use as a 'switching language' or international lexicon – witness the interest in the possible development of UDC in this way. How, then, do classification schemes (in the form of classified catalogues or information files) and post-co-ordinate indexes with control devices, compare with natural language A–Z indexing from the point of view of retrieval performance? All are obviously indexing vocabularies and the notation of a formal classification scheme should not hide this fact. Attempts to test systems are many and vary in their approach and methodology on the one hand, and the significance and value of their results on the other. They are now so well reported in the literature that little need be said by way of description of them, except to point out that the tests carried out in Britain, include, in addition to the well-known Cranfield projects, the ISILT programme at College of Librarianship Wales. Cranfield–I, the visual name for the first test to be set up by Aslib at the College of Aeronautics, was initiated in 1957 with the aim of testing UDC, a faceted aeronautics classification, Uniterm, and an alphabetical subject headings list. There were no significant differences in the results obtained and no one system could be deemed superior in the light of this experiment. Cranfield II work, which ran throughout most of the '60s, tested very many more index languages and arrived at the startling conclusion that index vocabularies based on natural language (the language of the documents indexed) might well give better results than a structured or controlled indexing language – that is, one that is classified or has classificatory features. The Information Science Indexing Languages TEST (ISILT) mentioned above arrived at the same conclusions after comparing (in the field of librarianship) a minimum-term vocabulary, a hierarchically structured list drawn from the faceted classification for library science of the CRG, an uncontrolled 'natural language' vocabulary and Farradane's system of relational analysis.

The above description of the tests and their conclusions is grossly simplified and ignores the number of documents indexed, the speed of the indexing, the nature of the testing, and the methods used to measure performance and draw comparisons. The test procedures are somewhat involved and the detailed findings demand careful first-hand study. We should certainly note the conclusions of the experiments in forming an opinion of the merits of rival retrieval systems. There is still a need for further testing and evaluation, however, and we should remember that the two terms are not exactly synonymous. At present, one of the chief judgements we can make is negative; it is, in the words of Cyril Cleverdon, who has directed the work at Cranfield, 'increasingly obvious that there is no single best way of designing and operating information retrieval systems'. Despite the comparatively unimpressive performance of classification schemes and control devices in tests carried out to date, they still have many supporters. Much in fact may depend on the size of vocabularies, the nature of a subject field and the need for generic as well as specific searching. In some 'hard' factual areas of technology, specific searches may always be the rule. But where they are not, or where terminology is more vague, certain control devices would seem almost a *sine qua non*, especially in larger vocabularies, despite the denials of some sceptics. The arguments in this chapter are all unashamedly in favour of classification methods or techniques akin to them in almost all situations. Perhaps this is not surprising in a text devoted to classification. But, in fact, the discussion in this chapter has tried to show that it is often difficult for us to evade rationalization of indexing vocabularies and thesauri through a certain amount of systematic grouping or control, especially as systems grow. Some systems which almost seem to have rejected classification principles do use a few of them unconsciously and perhaps those who would have us reject such principles altogether are too ready to equate the word 'classification' with the rigidity of enumerative notated systems in general libraries. Of course, not all control devices are truly classificatory and – of those that are – not all are necessary in every system. There remain some indexers who, Occam's razor in hand, see classification as an unjustified luxury within even large alphabetical indexing vocabularies. They would perhaps agree with the hero of a modern novel, Richard Frobisher, who objected, 'I dislike all this classification. I'd rather take my chance in a free-for-all.'[1] It need only be said that, without rational grouping, some pre-co-ordination and cross-references for hierarchical linkage in thesauri, and the use of precision-promoting devices in the index, retrieval *is* often much more subject to chance and a 'free for all' system is not a recipe which augurs well for efficiency or success. Gilchrist[2] sums up the true position succinctly when he says that 'successful schemes have been devised without conscious recourse to classification theory, but the fact is that classification, facet analysis, the formulation of hierarchies are all disciplines that can and should be used intelligently in the design of any type of indexing language.'

[1] Forster, Peter. *Self-Made Man.* Hutchinson, 1960, p. 214.
[2] Gilchrist, A. *Op. cit.*, p. 3.

CHAPTER TWENTY

Classification and the Computer

Many references to computerization have already been made, but in contemporary classification for information retrieval it deserves a short chapter in its own right. The eighteenth-century Italian Jesuit, Saverio Bettinelli, once predicted an age of 'bibliographic Malthusianism', when the birth-rate of newly recorded knowledge would exceed man's ability to store and exploit it; such a time – despite increasing specialization by experts in all fields – would surely be almost upon us, but for two factors. One is the active steps taken by librarians and information scientists, who know that indexing must not only show us what is available on our subject, but must also be sufficiently subtle to demonstrate what we can afford to ignore. The other factor is the boon of mechanization. To concentrate for a while upon the latter, it is clear that already digital computers in particular have demonstrated convincingly their ability to take over logical routine library 'housekeeping' operations and to relieve staff of repetitive drudgery.[1] They have also had a tremendous impact on library cataloguing, particularly in the way in which they have made what is perhaps a highly conservative profession think again about alternative physical forms of catalogue presentation.

In both these spheres they will continue to gain ground, but what are their specific purposes and achievements in relation to classification? One such achievement is that they can be of great assistance in speeding up the revision of conventional classification schemes. This has often been suggested for UDC in particular, the reason being that international consultation, although both democratic and diplomatic, tends to make revision by conventional methods very

---

[1] Those wanting a technical account, in not too technical language, of computer hardware and software might read: Artandi, S. *Introduction to Computers in Information Science.* (Chapter 3), Scarecrow Press, 1968.

slow. The UDC notation is largely hierarchical and despite some arbitrary (from a computer viewpoint, at least) indicator devices, UDC is, of the three widely applied existing general schemes, the one that is far and away best suited to computer manipulation. For revision purposes, this would involve the feeding of new data, in the form of corrections and additions, to an existing file, into the machine-held store. For quick up-dating of UDC schedules and index via relatively cheap and regular computer print-out, the case for COM (computer output on microfilm) instead of 'hard copy' is quite strong and this could be a method profitably employed in the longer-term future revision of several internationally used classifications.

The aid which the computer can give in the prompt revision of classification schedules is considerable, but there is no doubt that its greatest links with classification and allied processes lie in the sphere of ISAR (information storage and retrieval). Does the digital computer with its formidable hardware, including a huge memory store, its capability for carrying out quickly and reliably the operations for which it has been prepared, and its self-evident and impressive modernity, eliminate finesse by sheer power and therefore restrict the need for classificatory refinements in indexing by its great capacity, speed and manipulative ability? Or does it, on the contrary, fulfil rather than destroy the true objectives of control devices in indexing languages or the uncompromising insistence on exact and minute subject analysis which we find, for instance, in CC? Each of us may form his own judgement, at least at present; certainly some computer applications in information retrieval rely heavily on classification, conventional or otherwise, but others do not, and there are even works on the subject which omit the word classification from their contents and index.

Before glancing at several applications, the pros and cons of any employment of computers in information retrieval should be briefly considered. Advantages in computer use (apart from a possible one in the realm of 'status' or 'prestige') are few, yet extremely important. They are the ability of the computer to tackle enormous work loads which are beyond the limits of the human brain or manual storage systems, and its ability to merge new data quickly into an existing file or bank. To these we can add its utter logic and reliability in doing what it has been programmed to do, storage powers (very many thousands of index references can be led on a single reel of magnetic tape) and, of course, its speed.

Potential problems (if we ignore the possibility of 'breakdowns') may well include the costs of computer applications and the fact that computer time or storage space could have to be shared with other users in ways that might prove disadvantageous to the library and information service. Quite apart from the *opportunity* to use a computer for information retrieval is the question of scale of operations. An information store must be very large and in most circumstances involve many thousands of documents before its transfer to magnetic tapes or discs for computer records preparation of suitable 'software' in the form of a programme can be justified in terms of efficiency or economy. It is possible too that time may be lost in preparing information in a form suitable for computer searches or that retrieval principles may be blunted or compromised in order to conform to machine requirements. (There are those, it must be admitted, who think that if there is a clash between index principles and computer demands, it is the indexing input which should be modified and made more pliable.) Unless time-sharing facilities are available, the simultaneous access to the information store by a number of users may be impossible. In some computers, too, the application of the idea of 'fixed fields', whereby a certain maximum number of spaces is reserved for descriptors or class-marks, is a limitation, but this is highly unlikely to prove an enduring one in mechanized systems. The distinctive rules of computer filing may also give rise to some minor problems in retrieval.

To mention any or all of these things is not to deny the great value of computers, already well-proven and destined to increase, but to stress that a particular retrieval environment must be able to justify one and that the right kind of computer ought to be used. Digital computers are not all-wise machines either; they accept their electronic signals in inexorable fashion, but if given wrong, incomplete or ambiguous instructions in their programming 'theirs not to reason why' – or indeed to reason at all. A faulty programme or a silly question may well produce a silly answer – on a gigantic scale. Nor will computers carry out the intellectual work of classifying or indexing documents – they can 'index' in a sense, as we shall see, but they do not contribute the creative and original intellectual work of a skilled human indexer in subject analysis. In one of his several books, *On Retrieval System Theory*, B. C. Vickery has suggested that only a part of the operation of recalling items from a classified store can be handed over to a machine. The whole operation consists of –

(a) Naming the subject for which we are searching in the standard terms used by the index;

(b) locating the subject terms in the index;

(c) locating the documents to which the machine refers us;

(d) the study and integration of the retrieved documents.

Vickery suggests that, at present only step (b) may lend itself to mechanization and there is no assurance here that machine manipulation of data is superior to human searching. The machine can never tackle step (d). There is thus the warning that, while the computer can save much time and drudgery in large-scale operations, it is not the panacea for all our indexing problems and cannot in itself remove a need for control devices or structured thesauri. Vickery points out, too, that one may at times find that advantages claimed for mechanized retrieval systems are due to factors other than mechanization. Farradane too, writing in the *Sayers' Memorial Volume* warns us that 'many have been dazzled by the large memory capacity and fantastic speeds of the computer into thinking that new principles of organization of knowledge have been introduced; they have not. A third warning, if one is needed, comes from a later work by Henley[1] – 'the system is only as good as the indexing... employed.'

Thus, although some most important achievements can, have been, and will be made by mechanization, there are problems too and the need for skilled subject analysis is most unlikely to disappear. There remains then the perpetual and teasing issue of natural language versus classification or controlled language. A mechanized retrieval store is like a vast post-co-ordinate system; concepts are distinct and uncombined until the moment of searching. If we accept the need for *some* classificatory ideas in indexing languages in a manual system, we must surely do so in – presumably larger-scale – mechanized retrieval methods. This does not mean that a conventional enumerative system aimed at shelf arrangement of books can be suitable; to use such in a computer retrieval system is like 'building a locomotive to run with legs', to borrow R. A. Fairthorne's expressive phrase. A suitably complex and sensitive system, perhaps combining some of the advantages of pre- and post-co-ordination should now be within the grasp of our profession. Certainly the opportunities for classification are there. The computer has a

[1] Henley, J. P. *Computer Based Library and Information Systems*, 1970, p. 37.

'memory unit' which allows related ideas to be connected and promotes generic as well as specific searches. One should always take advantage of such a facility, even if it is thought that, in fact, many searches will be specific. The person who wants information on cultivating strawberries is likely to be interested in other similar fruits in the future and even now may find what he wants on the strawberry in a document on soft fruit in general; the person interested in some narcotics may well need information on others and so on – the principle of broadening or narrowing searches holds for the whole of knowledge and for mechanized as much as for manual information systems. 'So far as we know,' argues Borko, 'the human mind *associates ideas* rather than storing terms alphabetically by topic'[1] (his italics). We need to provide for this persistent need of association at all levels of organization and retrieval. To do so may require not only some linking devices and hierarchical structuring of vocabulary, but also a limited amount of intelligent pre-co-ordination of concepts. The latter helps to assure that concepts are joined in the correct way and that the right relationships between them are stressed. This is important, since a machine cannot recognize a false relationship.

Mechanized ISAR systems are legion and more continue to be produced although many are, in reality, but variations on an existing theme. Some, with their Boolean algebra, may daunt the non-mathematician. As these systems (and their acronyms) continue to grow, we must expect to find current information upon them not only in *American Documentation*, ASIS *Journal*, *Journal of Documentation*, *Program* and *Information Storage and Retrieval*, but also in technical periodicals such as *New Scientist*, *Metals Review*, and *Computer Journal*. Some of the most interesting, certainly from a classification viewpoint, are the systems which have used UDC. These are quite numerous now and they represent a wide geographical spread – several European countries and the United States being involved. The pioneer workers from the latter country, who include R. R. Freeman, Malcolm Rigby, Pauline Atherton and T. W. Caless, may be justly singled out, since, in a very real sense, they have been seeking to cultivate the plant of classification for mechanized retrieval in soil which is at times known to be somewhat stubborn. Their experiments on UDC file organization and search strategy have covered such technical fields as meteorology, metallurgy and nuclear science. This does not mean that developments

[1] Borko, H. *Automated Language Processing*. Wiley, 1967, p. 112.

elsewhere have been insignificant and in Germany, for instance, K. Schneider has experimented with UDC organized machine-produced indexing of the key word-out-of-context (KWOC) variety. Freeman and Atherton have expressed misgivings over certain UDC notational devices and have suggested that, until or unless changes are made, it may well be inferior to an indexing language specially made for machine processing. Yet they point out that UDC may score, despite acknowledged imperfections, because indexers are trained in its use, because it is employed in the international interchange of information data and because very large files already organized by it may now justify mechanization and a change of indexing system would scarcely be feasible. Rigby has also suggested that it would take at least a decade to develop a mechanized indexing system as 'universal' as the UDC.

There are, of course, many very different systems which involve mechanization. The huge medical literature retrieval programme MEDLARS, with its list of subject headings (MeSH) and the inevitable categorization and cross-referencing is one of the best-known and notable examples of a computerized information system. The work of Austin and others towards a new general classification also belongs here, since the picture which is slowly and yet steadily emerging from the research is of a vast notated meta-language designed for machine sorting and giving the advantages of free co-ordination of concepts while retaining the sensitivity of *a priori* citation through the use of operators based on a semantic analysis which seems common to many languages. The LC and BNB MARC projects are relevant here too; a machine readable catalogue with LC, DC plus perhaps UDC and other class-marks on which SDI profiles can be based, and which may be sensitive enough to 'filter' literature and thus tell the user what he can safely neglect, has every bit as much relevance for information retrieval as it has for cataloguing.

All of these are comparatively well documented, but there are many other important computer-based systems, some of which have received rather less attention in the literature. J. C. Gardin's Syntagmatic Organization Language (SYNTOL) is by no means an easy system to study, yet it warrants first-hand attention. The aim again is towards a meta-language which will combine the benefits of pre- and post-co-ordination. The paradigmatic and syntagmatic associations explored by Gardin are echoes of efforts made in other, sometimes purely manual, systems and it is interesting to see that its first applications have been largely in fields where terminology is notoriously vague. SYNTOL is designed for machine retrieval, although it relies on skilled human subject analysis and control devices at the input stage. Some manual indexing systems, as we have already seen, spurn control devices and these have their equivalents in a computer-based environment. Professor G. Salton's project, SMART, has, in addition to its own analysis and retrieval work, been able to act as an experimental tool to compare indexing through the scanning of natural language texts, abstracts of these texts, controlled language and the language of titles. Findings basically suggest that the selection of key-words from abstracts gives as good results as any other method, provided that synonyms are controlled. This leads one to wonder if the computer selection of keywords (based on the frequency with which a word appears in an abstract or paper) and perhaps measurement of the frequency of appropriate word associations can possibly provide us with the best possible kind of indexing language for large-scale projects?

Automatic Classification. Classification without classifiers seems a strange thought on first acquaintance, but it may – in certain contexts, be not only possible but of practical benefit. It is achieved by a consideration of the natural language from the text of each document and an examination of the frequency with which particular words are used. The computer can list words according to their frequency of occurrence and be programmed to select, as terms for an index, all words with a given minimum frequency. Some words may be of especial value because they appear in an author's summary or conclusions, in the opening sentences of paragraphs or in abstracts. This is an important factor in selection which can and must be acknowledged. If categories for the classification are pre-defined, it may be possible to use a small but representative sample of documents known to belong to a particular category, to make a statistical assessment of the frequency of the most-used terms in these and to determine from this to which category other documents belong – that is, new documents can be 'classed' by counting the frequency of the chosen terms within them. From these beginnings it has been found that in fact regular word associations may be much more telling than the mere frequent appearance of any single word.

Gerard Salton (director of the SMART project) and M. E. Lesk are two names that have been closely associated with this kind of work in the United States (but a perusal of periodical literature from the last decade will reveal others), while in Britain the investigations of Karen Sparck Jones and her associates at the Cambridge University Language Research Unit immediately spring to mind. The writings on the CLRU project span a number of years and now include a book as well as a continuing series of articles. In addition to the machine analysis of documents for the discovery of 'key words' for indexing purposes, this project, like similar ones elsewhere, has come up with the theory of clustering or 'clumps'. These are groups of words or of related concepts which are shown to occur regularly together. The total assembly of each clump may be a loose one, but each concept is related to at least one other. Examples of some terms linked as key words in a clump might be:

> Associative, Compound, Element, Magnetic, Memory, Recording, Storage

or

> Adjective, Ending, Grammar, Phrase, Style, Text, Tense, Thesaurus

and this form of machine-derived acknowledgement of associations which are statistically proven as recurring ones in sample documents is clearly and indisputably a newer form of classification. Clumps have been acknowledged for some time now, but other forms of relationship recognized at Cambridge for instance, are 'strings', 'stars' and 'cliques'. A string begins with a specific concept, this is found to be linked to another, this to another and so on. Stars involve the selection of an individual element and the mapping out of elements each of which is connected to the one originally selected. In a clique, each concept is related to each of the others. This can be shown, in diagramatic form, thus:

Strings (the most basic type of 'class')

Stars (these can grow very large)

Cliques

Clumps (the original grouping identified at Cambridge)

The statistical measurement of such associations by computer counting of word relationships is an eye-opener to most of us, but they are certainly classifications and are acknowledged as such. K. Sparck Jones and her co-authors deserve to be read, even by those who are solely concerned with conventional librarianship and are not mathematically inclined, for three reasons. Firstly, because it is impossible to summarize adequately their extensive and continuing investigations and their testing of new findings. Secondly, because they illustrate admirably the thesis that classification of some kind or other, do what we will, is ubiquitous in storage and retrieval methods. Last but not least, although their work may seem 'light years' away from that of some librarians, they have brought objective scientific method into an area in which librarians for some time have perhaps – let us admit it – relied too much upon opinion and intuition. We are assured that 'the differences between our term and classification performances are genuinely significant' and 'that automatic keyword classifications are worth constructing . . . on a very large scale'.[1]

Most of us will need to settle, however, for more mundane and traditional indexing than this, even in a highly technological age. *British Technology Index*, for instance, uses a computer for the 'housekeeping' aspects of its production, but prefers to leave even quasi-intellectual tasks in the hands of skilled human indexers. Robert Freeman has drawn attention to Cuadra's remark to the effect that these computer-generated classifications are as yet rarely relevant because of costs and the acceptance in libraries of established systems. Cuadra concludes that computer-derived categorization is really suitable at present for large-scale, minutely-indexed systems where conventional method is virtually non-existent or has broken down. On the Eastern side of the Atlantic, there remains Barnes's judgement of some years ago on *all* computer systems for retrieval[2] – 'the most promising applications . . . are in situations where the information threatens to outgrow existing filing methods and where the overheads of information input, computer programming, and computer operation can be spread over many enquiries'. It is possible that, in some instances, the spread mentioned could be achieved by some agreed form of sharing – several organizations in an area could participate in a retrieval system.

[1] Jones, K. Sparck. *Automatic Key-word Classification.* Butterworth, 1971, p. 240.
[2] Barnes, R. C. M. *The Present State of Information Retrieval by Computer*, vkaea 1964, p. 22.

Quite apart from all these information retrieval matters, there is other potential scope for computers in preparing for tomorrow's indexing. Schedules can be updated with their aid, as we have seen, or a particular procedure, say SLIC indexing, could be mechanized. The construction of large thesauri can be aided by the mathematical selection of key-words from the literature. The task of providing a comprehensive index to LC and of removing waste, inconsistency or ambiguity from its vast vocabularies also seems to suggest the use of mechanization. Perhaps the computer could also be used advantageously to compare the detail, specificity and coverage of various indexing languages. But when we think of computers and classification we tend naturally to consider retrieval systems first and foremost. Computer technology is still young and doubtless much more will be achieved both in the effective implementation of controlled index languages and in automatic indexing of texts. Computer output on microfilm coupled with peek-a-boo scanning facilities, for instance, is now being investigated by some. Meanwhile Farradane,[1] with customary perception, has pointed out that in many ways classificatory type of browsing has more in common with the simulating role of the analogue computer than with numerical calculations and wonders if the digital computer is really the right tool for the mechanized ISAR programmes of coming years.

This is a field in which innovation is exceeded only by speculation. What can be confidently said is that computer technology provides us with an opportunity to achieve the fulfilment and culmination of much of the classificatory theory from recent years. So much of Ranganathan's work for instance, as Bernard Palmer pointed out in his obituary notice on that great classificationist, seems on reflection to have been an unconscious anticipation of what future technology would make possible for classification. (In passing, are there not similarities between the theory of clumps and CC's seminal mnemonics?) Farradane's own work on relational analysis really suggests computer implementation and many of the modern retrieval systems in the United States are basically devised from the outset with computerization in mind. We cannot tell what the future holds; there are even those who predict that computers will eventually house the literature store itself rather than coded references to it and become libraries or vast information banks in their own right. Rather more feasible and realistic than this is the

[1] *The problems of input and their implications in mechanization.* Information Storage and Retrieval *4* (2), June, 1968, pp. 253–6.

suggestion of Freeman's that it may soon be possible to give each enquirer the impression that the store of information is classified according to his actual needs of the moment. All this is but interesting conjecture, yet there is every prospect that the future for classification will be just as interesting as its long history; indeed, the fully effective role of classificatory principles in large specialized information centres may be only just beginning.

Bibliography on Section Five

Some special schemes and thesauri should be examined. For other reading, some useful works include:

Lancaster, F. W. *Vocabulary Control for Information Retrieval*. Information Resources Press, 1972.
   Relevant, lucid and comprehensive.
Gilchrist, A. *The Thesaurus in Retrieval*. Aslib, 1971.
   Extremely useful. Sound and wide-ranging.
Bakewell, K. G. B. (editor). *Classification for Information Retrieval*. Bingley, 1968.
   Papers by A. Johnson and S. Highcock on alternatives to classification.
Sharp, J. R. *Some Fundamentals of Information Retrieval*. Deutsch, 1965.
Vickery, B. C. *On Retrieval System Theory*. 2nd edition, Butterworth, 1965.
Vickery, B. C. *Techniques of Information Retrieval*. Butterworth, 1970.
   The various books by this author give a continuing picture of the evolution of information handling. Two have been singled out here, but classification looms large in all of them.
   See also Vickery's justification of classification in Maltby, A. (editor). *Classification in the 1970s* (already cited).
Aitchison, J. and others. *Thesaurofacet*. English Electric Company, 1969.
   Well worthy of close scrutiny. Mrs Aitchison writes on it also in Journal of Documentation, September, 1970, pp. 197–203, and in Wellisch and Wilson (editors), *Subject retrieval in the seventies* (already cited).

Useful articles on classification (and its A–Z index) in a special library or retrieval context include:

Foskett, A. C. SLIC *Indexing*. Library World, July, 1968, pp. 17–19.
Holm, B. E. *Techniques and trends in effective utilization of Engineering information*. Aslib Proceedings, May, 1965, pp. 134–69.
   Very useful on 'links' and 'roles'.
Gilchrist, A. *Classification in the construction industry*. Journal of Documentation, December, 1972, pp. 296–321.
   A survey of problems and progress with a look at the interesting CI/SfB classification and a proposed meta-system.
McClelland, R. M. A. and Mapleson, W. W. *Construction and usage of classified schedules and generic features in co-ordinate indexing*. Aslib Proceedings, October, 1966, pp. 290–302.

A good 'state of the art' article with a bibliography is provided in:

Mills, J. *Progress in documentation: library classification*. Journal of Documentation, June, 1970, pp. 120–60.

On 'testing' there is:

Cleverdon, C. W. and Mills, J. *The testing of index language devices.* Aslib Proceedings, April, 1963, pp. 106–30.

Cleverdon, C. W. *The Cranfield tests on index language devices.* Aslib Proceedings, June, 1967, pp. 173–94.

Swanson, D. *The Evidence Underlying the Cranfield Results.* Library Quarterly, January, 1965, pp. 1–20.

Keen, E. M. and Digger, J. *Report of an Information Science Index Language Test.* College of Librarianship, Wales, 1972.

Keen, E. M. *The Aberystwyth Index Languages Test.* Journal of Documentation, March, 1973, pp. 1–35.
Note: Keen also criticizes classification for information retrieval, in the light of his findings, in his contribution to Maltby, A. (editor), *Classification in the 1970s.*

Many items already cited in this sectional bibliography apply to both manual and mechanized indexing. But specifically *on computers* a basic work is:

Artandi, S. *Introduction to Computers in Information Science.* Scarecrow Press, 1968.

For further information on mechanized indexing, especially on the role of classification, one might read:

Jones, K. Sparck. *Automatic Key-word Classification.* Butterworth, 1971. See also her several contributions to periodical literature.

Borko, H. *Automatic Language Processing.* Wiley, 1967.

Freeman, R. R. *Computers and Classification Systems.* Journal of Documentation, September, 1964, pp. 137–95.
Still valuable. See also his later summary in the book edited by Maltby, *op. cit.*

Farradane, J. E. L. *The Problems of Input and their Implications in Mechanization.* Information Storage and Retrieval, June, 1968, pp. 253–6.

Foskett, D. J. *Classification and Indexing in the Social Sciences.* Butterworth, 1963.
Chapters five and six are relevant and still most useful reading.

Wall, R. A. *Indexing Language Structure for Automated Retrieval.* Information Storage and Retrieval, November, 1973, pp. 607–17.

On SMART, there is:

Salton, G. (editor). SMART *Retrieval System.* Prentice-Hall, 1971. See also the various periodical articles, for instance:

Salton, G. *The Evaluation of Automatic Retrieval Procedures.* American Documentation, September, 1965, pp. 209–22.

A work which includes a contribution from Salton and also from many other authors, among them Vickery, K. Sparck Jones, Freeman and Atherton is:

Samuelson, K. (editor). *Mechanized Information Storage, Retrieval and Dissemination*. North-Holland Publishing Company, 1968.

On SYNTOL, the fullest statement is still that of:
Gardin, J. C. *Syntol*. Rutgers University, 1965.

Index

The index uses the same abbreviations for the main general classification schemes as have been employed in the text and is alphabetised on the 'all-through principle'. It excludes references to books and articles quoted in the sectional bibliographies.